THE POLITICAL ECONOMY
OF TRANSITIONS TO PEACE

The Security Continuum: Global Politics in the Modern Age

Series Editors: William W. Keller and Simon Reich

A series published in association with the Matthew B. Ridgway Center for International Security Studies and the Ford Institute for Human Security

THE POLITICAL ECONOMY
OF TRANSITIONS TO PEACE

A COMPARATIVE PERSPECTIVE

Galia Press-Barnathan

UNIVERSITY OF PITTSBURGH PRESS

Published by the University of Pittsburgh Press, Pittsburgh, Pa., 15260

Copyright © 2009, University of Pittsburgh Press

Manufactured in the United States of America

Printed on acid-free paper

10 9 8 7 6 5 4 3 2 1

Library of Congress Cataloging-in-Publication Data

Press-Barnathan, Galia, 1967–
  The political economy of transitions to peace : a comparative perspective /
Galia Press-Barnathan.
     p. cm. — (The security continuum)
  Includes bibliographical references and index.
  ISBN-13: 978-0-8229-4373-0 (cloth : alk. paper)
  ISBN-10: 0-8229-4373-5 (cloth : alk. paper)
  ISBN-13: 978-0-8229-6027-0 (pbk. : alk. paper)
  ISBN-10: 0-8229-6027-3 (pbk. : alk. paper)
  1. Peace-building. 2. Peaceful change (International relations) 3. Conflict
management. 4. Peace-building—Case studies. 5. Peaceful change (International
relations)—Case studies. 6. Conflict management—Case studies. I. Title.
  JZ5538.P76 2009
   327.1'72—dc22
                              2009000821

CONTENTS

PREFACE

My six-year-old son Ido is a very inquisitive boy. Recently, he became obsessed with studying the map of the world. Every morning he would wake me up with curious questions: "Are we 'in peace' with Egypt?" "Are we 'in peace' with France?" "Are we 'in peace' with Japan?" "Are we 'in peace' with Australia?" "Are we 'in peace' with Lebanon?" and so on.[1] After a week of early reveilles urging me to report Israel's "peace status" with various states around the world, I realized that in many cases I did not have an intelligent answer to offer. What does peace actually mean? Perhaps it was just the early hour of the morning, but I suspect that my confusion may have stemmed from the ambiguity of the concept itself. I also realized that probably only a six-year-old child in Israel could come up with questions like these, given his daily exposure to the issues of conflict, peace, and peacemaking.

These early-morning discussions are closely linked to this book. My inability to offer him clear answers was also one of the reasons that for a long time I chose to avoid writing about "peace." This is indeed a difficult topic to write about in a scientific manner. It is harder to define and operationalize peace than to define war, and such attempts are often associated with idealistic writing. Yet, as an Israeli citizen, a mother, and a scholar who has studied abroad, I have always been concerned with the wide gap between much of the peace literature discussing the European experience and the realities within which I live. I have been equally concerned, though, by the too prevalent belief in my region that "our" problems and conflicts are inherently unique and that therefore there is not much to gain from comparisons to the dynamics of conflict and of peacemaking elsewhere. These concerns, together with my underlying belief that we always stand to gain something from informed and systematic, though cautious and modest, cross-regional comparisons, drove me to embark on this project.

Many people assisted me along the way, and to them I owe my gratitude. On the financial front, a major boost for this project was the generous grant I received from the Israel Science Foundation (ISF). On the professional front, I would like to thank my invaluable research assistants Orit Bregman, Noa Dor, Lior Lehrs, Limor Lavi, Gallia Lindenstrauss, Mor Mitrani, and Rony Silfen. Thanks also go to my colleagues Yaacov Bar-Siman-Tov, Oren Barak, Dale Copeland, Ehud Harari, Korina Kagan, Alon Levkowitz, Steven Lobell, Benny

Miller, Norrin Ripsman, Avraham Sela, Etel Solingen, Alfred Tovias, and Tomer Brodie for their helpful comments. A special thanks for Ruth Lande for her help in my research in Egypt. I have also benefited greatly from lively discussions with the graduate students of the International Relations Department at the Hebrew University of Jerusalem and from comments I collected over the years from anonymous colleagues during American Political Science Association and International Studies Association meetings. I thank Peter Kracht from the University of Pittsburgh Press for his initial faith in the project and his kind support throughout. I would like to offer my deepest gratitude to Peter Katzenstein for taking the time to read and reflect upon most of this manuscript and for his kind encouragement. Finally, this book would not have been written and completed in this decade had it not been for the constant support, prodding, and faith of my colleague and friend Arie Kacowicz. This preface began with family and will end with it as well. My love and thanks to Rami, Amit, Ido, and Yael for their encouragement and patience throughout the long birth of this book.

THE POLITICAL ECONOMY
OF TRANSITIONS TO PEACE

BEYOND COMMERCIAL LIBERALISM

Conceptualizing the Political Economy of Transitions to Peace

SINCE THE END OF THE COLD WAR, there has been growing interest in the links between economics and security. The literature dealing with these links has focused on three issues: the links between economic interdependence and conflict, economic statecraft (most notably the use of economic sanctions), and the broadening of the concept of security to include economic and social factors.[1] Much of the debate about the power of economic interactions to advance peace is a reflection of traditional debates between the two main paradigms of international relations: realism and liberalism.

In recent years there has been a growing body of literature that developed the so-called commercial liberalism argument, according to which there is a positive link between trade (or economic interdependence) and peace. Most of this literature, however, does not focus on the promotion of peace but rather on the prevention of war and militarized conflict. This focus on preventing armed conflict leaves unexplored the positive side of the liberal argument, namely that economics can actually be used to promote peace. Furthermore, most of the literature assumes a preexisting level of interdependence and then goes on to examine whether this economic link does or does not have an impact on militarized conflicts. This assumption leaves out many cases of adversarial bilateral relations in which the transition to peace requires building a basic level of economic interdependence that did not necessarily exist before the conflict began. The current interdependence and peace literature does not have much advice to offer decision makers or scholars who try to manage, advance, or study such cases.

This situation is unfortunate since much of the third world would fall into the category of parties that lack even basic economic interdependence with their rivals. Consider, for example, the following questions: Can and should Israel actively promote economic engagement with the Palestinians or with its other Arab neighbors in order to promote the peace process? Will the grand U.S. scheme of creating a regional free trade area in the Middle East (MEFTA) actually help to promote regional peace? Do the European economic initiatives in the Middle East and North Africa offer a better path to peace? In the face of growing strategic competition between Japan and China in northeastern Asia, will Japan be successful in its ongoing efforts to ensure peaceful relations with China via economic diplomacy? Can economic tools be used to help India and Pakistan in their transition to peace? Can and should third parties such as the United States, the European Union, or international organizations invest in promoting economic cooperation among states in Africa in order to reduce the risk of more bloodshed between and within states in the region? If third parties are indeed to offer support for building regional economic cooperation, what form should it take? What are the obstacles? What is the impact of globalization on all these questions? These are but a few of the questions that decision makers must address in today's world. However, the theoretical literature of commercial liberalism has only limited answers to offer.

Unfortunately, the excessive focus on the realist versus liberal paradigmatic debate often leads us to ask the wrong questions. Focusing too much on whether it is politics driving economics or economics driving politics obscures the more complex interplay between economics and politics. As the empirical case studies demonstrate, there are two rationales operating in this process, sometimes simultaneously. The first is that economic considerations (e.g., globalization pressures or domestic economic crises) guide political decisions (e.g., the need to move toward peace with a former enemy). The second rationale is that political considerations (such as the desire to promote and stabilize peaceful relations with a former enemy) guide seemingly economic decisions and lead to the use of economic tools according to a political logic. There are thus two discrete aspects of the economics of peacemaking. The first aspect fits more comfortably with the standard arguments of commercial liberalism literature regarding the power of economic interaction to promote peace. The second aspect shows how economic tools can be used to help achieve peace, but this path is quite different from that charted by standard liberal arguments.

Furthermore, there is a need to distinguish between two stages in the transition to peace: first, the initial transition to a "cold peace," most often (though not always) symbolized by the decision to sign a peace (or friendship) treaty, and second, the process of normalizing relations (that is, the development of "warm" or stable peace). In each stage, economic factors play a different role, and these roles can be better understood by referring to three basic hypotheses. These hypotheses outline the role and influence of economic factors within each state's domestic politics (the balance between domestic winners and losers from the transition to peace), between the two states (the impact of economic power disparities between them), and in the economic actions of extraregional players. The three hypotheses are tested using a qualitative cross-regional comparison of transitions to peace in the Middle East, Asia, and Europe.

The State of the Art on Interdependence and Peace

The debate about the connection between trade and peace is an old one and already well documented.[2] It is also one of the basic debates between liberal and realist scholars.

The trade-peace link is at the heart of the commercial liberal argument and is associated with the work of Joseph Schumpeter but actually dates back to Immanuel Kant's *Perpetual Peace* and his argument about the "spirit of commerce." Liberals suggest a strong, positive link between the expansion of trade among states and peace, and they offer several causal arguments to substantiate their claims. One argument suggests that as states achieve high levels of trade interdependence, the cost associated with severing these ties in the event of a conflict becomes so high that rational decision makers will be extremely reluctant to choose violent means to resolve their differences. Such reluctance may also be strong if domestic special interest groups that benefit from foreign trade exert pressure on decision makers to avoid any interruption in business. Ruth Arad, Seev Hirsch, and Alfred Tovias develop the notion of "irrevocable interdependence" between states that would lead to the creation of a balance of prosperity —the positive and commercial equivalent of the balance of terror. When such a balance is achieved, they argue, the benefits of bilateral cooperation are enormous, the losses associated with discontinuing cooperation are unacceptable, and so peace is secured.[3]

A second argument for the link between trade and peace suggests that increased trade and interdependence between states reduce the value of the use of force and of conquering territory and instead create new, nonmilitary strategies for pursuing states' goals and advancing their international position.[4] This argument has recently been sharpened by a discussion of the ability of economic interdependence to provide new channels for signaling resolve in nonviolent ways.[5]

A third argument is based on the neofunctional logic of spillover. It suggests that cooperation in a certain issue area creates pressures to expand cooperation to adjacent issue areas. Cooperation then spills over to other issues and expands. This argument has been applied and demonstrated mostly with regard to cooperation within the economic sphere. The big question of whether spillover can occur between economic and either political or security-related issues has surprisingly not been rigorously tested on empirical cases.[6]

All of these explanations focus on the changing material incentives of rational decision makers and welfare-seeking citizens. They are deeply rooted in the rationalist perspective of international politics. Indeed, the bulk of the commercial liberalism literature is based upon these rationalist premises. A different version of the liberal argument, associated with the work of Karl Deutsch, is rooted in an ideational, more interpretive perspective. It focuses on the impact of trade and economic interdependence on people's perceptions of self and other. Commerce creates greater interaction among states and people. Interaction breeds familiarity and exchange of ideas. Familiarity leads to mutual appreciation, curbs national prejudices, and consequently reduces or eliminates warlike attitudes. Commerce thus civilizes and pacifies states and their citizens.[7]

Deutsch's early work on integration in Europe has been further developed and updated in more recent work by Emanuel Adler and Michael Barnett on the notion of "security communities." They focus on the sociological processes that gradually lead to the development of a community of states. Adler and Barnett point to the importance of various transactions (including economic transactions) as factors that contribute to the development of mutual trust and collective identity, which, in turn, are necessary conditions for the development of dependable expectations of peaceful change. Rooted in a social constructivist perspective, their argument suggests that a qualitative and quantitative growth of transactions reshapes collective experience and alters social facts.[8] However, beyond this observation, there is no significant discussion on the specific role of economic factors in the building of security communities. In fact, the literature on security communities does not intersect with the literature on the commercial liberal peace, as the former takes a clear constructivist path and the latter, a clear rationalist path. This book responds to the rationalist debate between proponents of commercial liberalism and proponents of the realist school. The hypotheses tested here address that basic debate and are therefore rooted within the rationalist perspective. However, in laying out each case I have tried to remain attentive to the ideational factors that either constrained or were influenced by economic interaction and changes in material incentives. In this sense, the book critically explores how far one can take the rationalist approach in explaining the impact of economics on peacemaking.

While there is little direct reference to the implications of commercial liberalism for the more specific case of former enemies making the transition to peace, it is possible to draw several conclusions regarding this issue. An argument grounded in the commercial liberalism view is likely to suggest that economic cooperation would be a good starting point for building ties, which may eventually promote cooperation on higher and broader political and security issues. Trade is likely to create a positive incentive for citizens on both sides to avoid lapsing back into conflict. It is likely to help create new and fruitful channels of communication between the two hostile societies, communication that will break through preexisting negative images and create new bonds of familiarity and friendship. Furthermore, as Schumpeter has argued, and as many liberals still believe, the encouragement of trade and international economic interactions can indirectly encourage a domestic shift to democracy, as citizens develop a rational, private material interest in openness and trade and gain political power that may undermine the central power of the state. If war and protracted conflicts are about passions, pride, and hate, then economic interaction can inject the necessary rational, individualistic, welfare-seeking approach needed to end such conflicts.[9]

Realist scholars, on the other hand, are skeptical about all of these arguments, suggesting either that trade has little or no impact on serious, high-politics issues or that trade in fact raises the potential for conflict. They argue that spillover cannot take place between "low-politics" economic issues and "high-politics" political and security issues. Liberals, argue the realists, have it backwards. Spillover may occur, they say, but it would flow from high-politics issues down to economic ones. As Geoffrey Blainey notes, the factors that liberals stress as causes of peace may in fact be the effects of it.[10]

The stronger realist argument suggests that there is indeed a link between interdependence and conflict, but it is a negative one. Liberals assume that interdependence is symmetrical or that asymmetries are not an important problem. Realists suggest that this is not the case. Given preexisting disparities in economic capabilities, different states will gain unevenly from foreign trade and other forms of economic interaction. Uneven gains, of course, become problematic in a realist world where states are concerned mainly with relative gains. If one state gains more economic benefits from trade, it can use these relative gains at some point against its partner. Enhanced economic capabilities can be translated into military capabilities. Furthermore, uneven interdependence can be used as an instrument of power for the purpose of increasing political leverage.[11] Since interdependence is, in fact, a form of dependence for the smaller state, it is likely to try to avoid it. Conversely, stronger states are likely to try to take political advantage of the leverage created through trade relations. Trade and interdependence, then, merely create an additional playing field for power politics, with both new issues to generate conflict and new tools of influence.

Consequently, realists are likely to see a very limited role for economic factors in transitions to peace. The realist premise, stressing the overwhelming impact of the anarchical environment on the likelihood of cooperation due to concerns over both cheating and relative gains, is accentuated when we are talking about relations between two states that were recent enemies. In such cases, it is quite clear that the concerns about relative gains will be greater. After all, one need not have much imagination to think about how new economic gains can be translated into military force or plain political leverage, given the memory of very recent conflict. We are likely to find little trust between former enemy states, and between two such societies there is likely to be very little familiarity or friendship. Realists would therefore argue that the road to conflict reduction or to peacemaking runs through the resolution of the major political and security obstacles. If economic cooperation is pursued, and even if it is successful on some issues, it is unlikely to have a significant effect on the status of the conflict as a whole. Thus, the functional notion of spillover cannot operate across the low-politics economic issues and high-politics security issues divide. This argument is quite intuitive if the major political issues between the states are indeed unresolved. However, it becomes more complex once a peace treaty is signed, meaning that most of the basic political issues, though not all of them, have been resolved. Consider, then what happens when a peace treaty has been signed but other political problems remain. Can economic interaction then play a role? Realists are silent on that question.

There are three main limitations to the existing literature on commercial liberalism: its heavy quantitative emphasis, its assumption of some preexisting economic interdependence between the parties, and its focus on explaining lack of conflict rather than the development and upgrading of peace.

The bulk of the research in this field is of large *n,* quantitative nature. However, it remains inconclusive. Scholars such as Solomon Polachek or Bruce Russett and John Oneal have found a negative correlation between trade and conflict. Others, most notably in the recent work by Katherine Barbieri, came to an opposite conclusion that in fact interdependent dyads are more likely to engage in militarized conflicts than those with less extensive ties.[12] In the past few years this literature has become increasingly complex and refined. However, to better understand the causal mechanisms through which increased trade relations may or may not influence the likelihood of violent conflict, it is also important to examine the trade and peace question through qualitative case studies.[13] The statistical nature of this research, while allowing various elaborate formal manipulations, limits its ability to truly unravel the causal mechanisms through which increased trade relations may or may not influence the likelihood of violent conflict.

Surprisingly, though, few scholars chose to focus more carefully on these causal mechanisms and examine them through in-depth case studies. Dale Copeland, for example, suggests that interdependence serves as a brake on aggression only as long as the state has expectations that trade will continue in the future.[14] Paul Papayoanou suggests that while trade relations may not prevent violent conflict, they do complicate the ability of state leaders to efficiently and quickly act against a potential aggressor with whom they have high interdependence.[15] Norrin Ripsman and Jean-Marc Blanchard offer an in-depth analysis of the impact of economic interdependence in the crisis of 1914 and during the Rhineland crisis of 1936. They make a point similar to the one offered here —that the debate on trade and war is carried out in an empirical vacuum. They offer a modified realist approach, concluding that during those crises, economic interdependence and sensitivity played no role in decision makers' deliberations.[16]

One of the rare examples of research examining the specific question of economic interaction and its impact on positive foreign policy change is an article by Papayoanou and Scott Kastner, who argue that cultivating economic ties with a nondemocratic great power can either help elicit cooperative foreign policy or lead to conflictual policies, depending on how much influence internationalist economic interests in the nondemocratic state have on policy formation compared to other domestic-oriented economic interests.[17] That article addresses the ongoing policy dilemma of whether to engage China economically, despite its rising strategic rivalry with the United States. It also demonstrates the question's relevance to relations between great powers. Finally, Ripsman examines in detail the case of Franco-German reconciliation after World War II, suggesting that realist factors are responsible for the transition to peace, while liberal factors, including economic interdependence, are responsible for the endurance of peace.[18]

What is common to all of these qualitative attempts to unravel the trade-peace link is their emphasis on the impact of foreign trade on the deliberations of various domestic actors. Beth Simmons best captured the importance of this factor by arguing that if we are to better understand the theory of commercial peace, we need to develop a theory of the state that would provide a plausible mechanism linking private trade to public conflict behavior. The domestic scene has recently gained importance in the quantitative literature, but in-depth case studies are better for shedding light on the politics underlying the trade and peace link. It is the politics that often gets lost in statistical analysis.[19]

Both the quantitative and the qualitative research described so far is insufficient if one wants to explain the impact of economic interaction on the transition to peace between two states. The question most of these works seek to answer is whether high levels of interdependence can, at times of crisis, constrain states from turning to violent means in order to resolve their differences. This is a sensible focus, since crises indeed offer the hardest test for liberal claims and are supposedly an easier case for realist claims. The problem, though, is that this focus limits the range of relevant cases to those states that already share a certain level of economic interdependence. Furthermore, by focusing on the impact of existing levels of interdependence, this literature neglects the dilemmas of leaders of former enemy states with no economic interdependence, where the goal is the very establishment of some level of economic interdependence to begin with. Such situations highlight the political nature of seemingly economic decisions.

Finally, while most scholars talk about the idea of "trade leading to peace," they all end up examining how foreign trade, or economic interdependence, limits violent conflicts. Again, this approach is not unreasonable. "Peace" is indeed an extremely difficult concept to define. Detecting and measuring the occurrence of violent conflicts is much easier, especially for the purpose of quantitative research. This bias may also be driven partly by the fact that the agenda of this debate is dominated by realist claims. Therefore, since realists focus on the phenomenon of violent conflict, the goal of liberal scholars as well is to establish that interdependence can indeed influence the likelihood of war or other militarized disputes.

However, as noted at the outset, this focus on interdependence and conflict leaves much of the liberal argument undeveloped. It focuses only on the negative side of the liberal thesis—that the more economic interdependence there is, the less likely it is that militarized disputes will occur. It completely ignores the positive, constructive side of the liberal thesis—that is, that economic interaction, trade, and interdependence can bring about peace or help upgrade peace. It is left unclear what this approach actually means, whether it actually works, and, if so, under what circumstances it works. This bias also created a wide gap between the classic liberal policy prescriptions calling for increased trade and economic interaction in order to "foster peace," the theoretical research that focuses only on the impact of preexisting interdependence on the likelihood of militarized conflicts, and the important policy dilemmas facing decision makers who want to develop economic interaction between former enemies as a means of pacifying their relations. This book takes a step toward filling this gap.

The Meaning of "Transition to Peace"

Peace is one of those murky concepts that everyone loves to talk about but few care to define. It is telling that within the subfield of peace studies there is still an ongoing debate about what peace really means.[20] The meaning of peace is not only an academic question but can also be a very political one when conflicting sides hold different perceptions of what peace should be. In fact, different expectations about peace may have a detrimental impact on the process of peace building. This situation becomes apparent in any discussion of the transition to peace in the Middle East.

Most scholars do agree that peace comes in different variations or different degrees. Several attempts have been made to distinguish among these variations. Kenneth Boulding distinguishes between unstable peace and stable peace, the latter defined as "a situation in which the probability of war is so small that it does not really enter into the calculations of any of the people involved."[21] Alexander George distinguishes between precarious peace (a conflictual situation in which peace means little more than the temporary absence of war), conditional peace (a less acute conflict relationship in which general deterrence plays the predominant and effective role in maintaining peace but parties do not rule out the use of force), and stable peace (a situation in which both states consider it unthinkable to use military force in any dispute involving them).[22] Arie Kacowicz distinguishes between negative peace (a mere absence of war in which peace is maintained by negative means such as threats or deterrence), stable peace (in which there is no expectation of violence and peace is maintained on a reciprocal and consensual basis), and a pluralistic security community (in which stable expectations of peaceful change are shared between the states that decide to abandon the policy option of war as a means of resolving conflicts between them, based upon their shared norms, values, and political institutions).[23] A somewhat different typology is offered by Benjamin Miller, who distinguishes between three types of peace. Cold peace, in his view, is characterized by the absence of war and of threats of force among the parties, with the main issues in conflict being mitigated but not fully resolved. With cold peace, there are intergovernmental channels of communication and strong limitations on transnational activities, significant revisionist groups exist, and the possibility of a return to war is present should international or domestic changes occur. His second category is normal peace, a situation in which the likelihood of war is lower than that in cold peace because most, if not all, of the underlying substantive issues have been resolved. With normal peace, relations between states have begun to move beyond pure intergovernmental relations but war has not been completely excised from regional politics. The last category is that of warm peace, a situation in which war is no longer an option for resolving disputes among the states and in which there are extensive transnational relations and a high degree of interdependence.[24]

Instead of talking about "peace," Adler and Barnett discuss the creation of a pluralistic security community, defined as a transnational region comprising sovereign states whose people maintain dependable expectations of peaceful change.[25] They also make a distinction between three stages in the development of such security communities. The first stage is a nascent phase in which governments begin to consider how they might coordinate their relations in order to increase their mutual security, lower transaction costs associated with their exchanges, and encourage further exchanges. This stage is characterized by various diplomatic, bilateral, and multilateral exchanges. The second stage is the ascendance of the security community, characterized by increasingly dense networks, new institutions and organizations, cognitive structures that promote "seeing" and acting together, and the deepening of mutual trust. The last stage is that of a mature security community in which regional actors share an identity and entertain dependable expectations of peaceful change.[26]

The most recent attempt to create a peace scale was made by James Klein, Gary Goertz, and Paul Diehl. They create a scale ranging from rivalry to negative peace and positive peace. Negative peace roughly parallels the notion of cold peace, whereas positive peace at its extreme parallels the notion of warm peace or a pluralistic security community. Their article clearly reflects the importance of understanding the degree of peace as a scale rather than as an absolute condition. Indeed, within their three categories they also offer different levels or degrees of either negative or positive peace. Thus, for example, within the range of positive peace there are situations of low-level positive peace, in which there is an expectation of peaceful resolution of conflicts but only a low level of institutionalization of relations or of functional integration. Their project, going beyond the well-developed quantitative rivalry literature, is an important contribution to building a more elaborate and refined data base of peaceful relations between states, an issue largely neglected by quantitative researchers.[27]

These different typologies highlight the complexity of the concept of peace. They also support my basic claim that, instead of discussing the general connection between trade and peace, it is important to distinguish analytically between different stages in the development of peace and their relationship to economic factors. However, none of these typologies provides a perfect fit for the discussion in this book, so I examine the impact of economic factors on two stages in the transition to peace. The role of economic incentives and considerations in the initial stage of the transition to peace is most often symbolized by the dramatic decision to sign a peace treaty that will officially end the conflict. This first stage in the transition can be identified with Miller's cold peace, Kacowicz's negative peace, or Klein et al.'s negative peace.

The second stage of the transition to peace encompasses the move to the different variations of stable peace described above as well as Miller's normal and warm categories of peace. My interest is in examining the process through which the initial cold peace is or is not being upgraded in the direction of a normal or stable peace. Kacowicz and Yaacov Bar-Siman-Tov themselves suggest that it is best to treat the notion of stable peace as an ongoing and dynamic process rather than as a single situation.[28] Adler and Barnett also stress that the development of dependable expectations of peaceful change should be seen as a process. To capture the dynamic nature of this stage, I describe the second stage in the transition as the stage of normalization. It is reminiscent of Kacowicz and Bar-Siman-Tov's description of the dual processes of stabilization and consolidation of stable peace. While stabilization is a process that is closely linked to the first stage of the transition and is aimed at managing this difficult feat, consolidation refers to the long-term process of reaching stable peace.[29] By looking at normalization, I can focus on the process of stabilizing and deepening relations rather than on identifying certain ideal types of "peace."

Methodologically, it is easier to identify the first stage in the transition, since it is marked by the public signing of an official peace agreement. The second stage is harder to operationalize. In order to identify the normalization process I look for different indicators, such as the expansion of economic cooperation in terms of scope of issues and actors involved; the development of interaction and interest in interaction on the official level only; an increase in diplomatic interaction and coordination; the development of interaction on the private level (trade, investment, tourism, etc.), among big businesses, and then among smaller business actors and consumers; the development of institutionalized links and especially the growth of institutionalized nongovernmental ties; and cognitive changes within both societies regarding the use of war and the dividends of peace. The last point touches upon another aspect of the transition to peace that is not being explored here: the process of reconciliation. Reconciliation refers to the social-psychological process of changing the motivations, goals, beliefs, attitudes, and emotions of the great majority of society members regarding the conflict. It is closely linked to the achievement of stable peace. Discussion of reconciliation is also related to the literature on the creation of security communities, particularly in the special case of relations between former enemies. However, exploring this aspect properly is beyond the scope of this project.[30]

I do not suggest that economic factors on their own can lead to a stable peace. The development of a stable peace requires various political, strategic, cultural, cognitive, and other conditions. Bar-Siman-Tov, for example, points to four conditions that are prerequisites for a stable peace: (1) mutual satisfaction with the peace agreement; (2) the development of supportive structural-institutional conditions, such as common political or normative characteristics, a high level of interaction and cooperation, and joint institutions and organizations; (3) strategic learning on the part of the leaders, followed by social learning by various elites and the public; and (4) reconciliation.[31] Clearly, there is more to peace than beneficial economic conditions. However, trying to discuss all of the factors that influence transitions to peace, across several cases, is likely to lead to a discussion that is too general to generate any new insights regarding the role of each factor. Therefore, this book is dedicated to an in-depth examination of the political dynamics of economic considerations in the process of transitions to peace. Exploring the political economy of transitions to peace is a worthwhile endeavor because economic considerations influence nearly all stages of the transition. If one looks at Bar-Siman-Tov's conditions for the development of stable peace, one can see how economic considerations affect each one of them. The degree of mutual satisfaction will be influenced by the perceived economic gains from peace and the way they are distributed. The development of economic ties between business groups on either of two previously warring sides can play a significant role in building the supportive institutional conditions. Similarly, economic pressures (e.g., the pressures of globalization) can play an important role in pushing leaders toward the crucial strategic learning that leads them to peace. As for reconciliation, the potential impact of economic interaction is more debatable. If one accepts Deutsch's communication thesis, as described above, then economic interaction can help promote reconciliation, if it is equitable and if it reaches broader segments of society and not only the elites.

Given those assumptions, the case studies presented here also demonstrate the limits of the influence of purely economic incentives. For example, very active trade did not lead to a warm peace between Japan and South Korea, and potential economic benefits (albeit not dramatic) were insufficient to push Egypt to greater economic cooperation with Israel. The underlying goal of this project is to focus on the economic dynamics surrounding the process of peacemaking, with the purpose of revealing their potential as well as their limits.

Breaking down the discussion of the dependent variable into the two stages of transition to peace is important because when assessing the impact of various economic incentives, there is a difference in the economic factors that can promote the first stage versus those that can enhance the second stage. In fact, the same factors that can contribute to the signing of a peace treaty may not help or may even slow down the second stage of normalization. This is another distinction that is lost in the standard trade-conflict literature. Also, in examining the role of economic factors in transitions to peace, it is important to note that I examine both policy formation at the national level and the strategic interaction between the two former enemies. What follows is an introduction to the three hypotheses regarding the impact of economic incentives on the two stages of transition to peace, which I explore throughout the book.

The Impact of the Domestic Balance
of Winners and Losers from Peace

A transition to peace between former enemies is bound to have some economic effects on both states. With the transition to peace, resources that were dedicated to the conflict can be redirected to other economic and social activities. The end of the conflict may also inspire other economic actors to invest in those countries, given that the risk of doing so is reduced. Furthermore, a transition to peace is usually accompanied by some level of economic cooperation between the parties, opening up new opportunities for trade and investment. The magnitude of such opportunities, however, varies from case to case. Since economic interactions have significant domestic distributional effects, it is important to examine who the domestic winners and losers are as a result of potential or actual economic cooperation with a former enemy.[32] The impact of economic factors on the transition to peace will differ depending on the economic costs and benefits, both for the state and for societal groups.

The discussion of who wins and who loses during transitions to peace is closely linked to the discussion of winners and losers during liberalization. It builds upon Solingen's coalitional argument, which identifies two types of domestic coalitions: internationalist and statist-nationalist coalitions. Internationalist (i.e., liberalizing) coalitions usually include the internationally competitive sectors. They are interested in freeing up resources to carry out reform at home, to weaken groups opposed to reform, and to secure access to foreign markets, capital, investment, and technology. Conversely, Solingen identifies as part of the "statist-nationalist-confessional" coalition groups such as import-competing firms, state-owned enterprises, segments of the military and security establishment, and various ethnic or religious groups. Solingen establishes the link between these groups' aversion to economic internationalization and their interest in the continuation of the conflictual situation. Continuation of the conflict either justifies their continued existence and power or supports their ideological or religious agenda. A transition to peace compels downsized military allocations, erodes statist privileges, and devalues nationalist and confessional mythmaking as a political currency.[33] While such groups are likely to exist in any state that has been inward-looking and protectionist for a long time, they are likely to be more entrenched in a state that has been involved in a protracted conflict.

Solingen's argument examines first the impact of globalization on the initial drive toward liberalization and then the impact of the rise of internationalist coalitions on broader patterns of regional conflict.[34] The argument in this book is more focused on the bilateral level and on the specific issue of the transition to peace. Despite her emphasis that these coalitions are not purely economic, Solingen's argument is still embedded in a strong economic logic (i.e., the pressures of economic globalization). My analysis examines not only situations in which economic pressures of various sorts influence the motivation to move to peace (as in Egypt and Jordan) but also situations in which there is a political motivation to move to peace (perhaps accompanied by economic motivations), thus leading political leaders to mobilize existing domestic coalitions to support the transition to peace (as in Israel and Germany).

A factor that is less prominent in the coalitional analysis is the independent role of the state. In an analysis of transitions to peace, however, the state needs to be accredited with a larger role. In postconflict situations, economic goals are likely to be perceived through ideological lenses shaped over years of conflict and therefore to acquire a strong symbolic meaning, something beyond just economic gains. For this reason, the making of foreign economic policy vis-à-vis a former enemy is likely to be interpreted in political rather than simply economic terms. Because foreign economic policy vis-à-vis a former enemy is likely to be considered a matter of high politics, we are likely to find that in transitions to peace after a long conflict, the state will play a central role. Also, because postconflict relations are likely to feature little or no preexisting economic interdependence, or at least a dramatic decline in the level of economic interaction due to the conflict, leaders have a serious political dilemma over whether to start developing such interdependence or not.

"State interests" may be considered from two perspectives. In the first perspective, the state is a unitary actor, and from this perspective one can examine what the state or, more accurately, the national economy stands to gain or lose from cooperation with the former enemy. What might be gained or lost can be predicted by examining the economic challenges facing the national economy and calculating the expected impact of a transition to peace on the overall health of the economy. The second perspective focuses on state leaders. Here, the analysis turns to what individual leaders stand to gain or lose from a transition to peace and ensuing economic cooperation.[35] I follow the common assumption in the literature that leaders first and foremost seek to remain in office. They will therefore be willing to make a dramatic and high-risk decision to move toward peace only when this strategy is perceived as necessary to ensure their political survival.

Understanding the process of making a transition to peace calls for an analysis of state interest, interests of key societal groups, and the interaction between them. The relative power of each of these actors is a function of both their expected gains and losses from the transition as well as the nature of the institutional arrangements within which they interact. A strong state, with autonomous institutional and bureaucratic capabilities, that faces a dire economic crisis will be both highly motivated and able to initiate the process of a transition to peace. The ability of different domestic groups to organize in support of or opposition to a transition to peace will depend on three factors: their cohesiveness and their ability to overcome collective action problems, as described by Mancur Olson; the magnitude of their expected gains or losses from the process, which will influence their motivation to mobilize and act; and finally, the nature of the institutional environment within which they operate and through which they can interact with the government.[36] Thus, in a strong state like Japan or Germany, for example, with a highly capable bureaucracy interacting with a business community that is well organized into peak associations, we find that close cooperation between government and business characterized the initial stages of the transition to peace with their neighbors.[37] This being said, the required coalitions and the dynamics between state and societal actors, which are most beneficial for a successful transition to peace, are different in the different stages of transition.

In order to create the necessary incentives to negotiate a peace treaty and establish cold peace, it is necessary to create what has been termed a "vested interest in peace" or VIP.[38] The first stage of the transition is likely to be centered in and dominated by the state regardless of whether the state is democratic or authoritarian. This consistency is due to both the highly political nature of such a transition, even if economically motivated, and the extreme uncertainty and potential risks associated with the early stages of transition, which are likely to deter private actors. Consequently, the transition requires a domestic coalition of winners comprising state actors and big businesses with ties to the government, which are likely to be the most powerful domestic economic actors. Such a coalition is most likely to lead successfully to a transition to peace when cooperation between the government and the business community is highly institutionalized, as it is in neocorporatist states. Such institutionalized cooperation will facilitate either the use of economic tools to promote peace or the influence of economic considerations on official policy making. Furthermore, such institutionalized cooperation will also promise a more enduring investment in the peace process. Conversely, if the business community cooperates with the government on an ad hoc basis, we are likely to find that coordination is less efficient and that the ability to use economics as a policy tool to promote peace and normalization is greatly impaired. Patricia Davis, for example, argues that Germany's successful use of economic tools (which she terms "the art of economic persuasion") to pacify its relations with Poland stems from the advantages of its institutional structure, characterized by a high-functioning autonomy, coordination and continuity within the bureaucratic process, and the significant degree of coordination between this bureaucracy and the parapublic institutions of organized capital.[39]

However, the development of a narrow yet politically powerful vested interest in peace is not sufficient to move significantly forward in the second stage, that of normalizing relations. We can find a move toward normalization stemming from either a government decision to expand economic cooperation to more fields or from big business's growing interest in expanding the relations. This move will be an important step, but such economic interaction will remain an elitist process. In the long run, in order to stabilize the peace and warm it up, it is important for broader segments of society to feel like winners. For that purpose, it is necessary to target the broader public—smaller producers, consumers, the "man on the street"—so as to develop a vested interest in peace at a broader societal level. Put differently, the average citizen needs to feel the economic dividend of peace if economic cooperation is to have a significant impact on the process of normalization.

Furthermore, if the ambitious goal of reconciliation is sought, then it is crucial that all group members in society share the economic benefits so that all will feel that peaceful relations are worthwhile.[40] If the peace dividends do not trickle down and remain instead at the level of the privileged elite, then societal opposition to peace will persist and remain a source of instability. Economic interaction across a broad range of society is also important because it permits a long-term process of social learning to take place. Adler and Barnett themselves point out that social learning may not be sufficient for the development of a security community unless this learning is connected to functional processes that are traceable to a general improvement in the state's overall condition.[41] While learning and trust building among political elites is extremely important, it is not enough. This is why analyzing the expected and actual distribution of domestic gains and losses from transitions to peace is so important. A broad-based vested interest in peace is not a sufficient condition for such social learning to take place, but I would argue it is a necessary one.

The ease with which normalization can proceed through economic means will depend partly on the objective economic conditions that create observable economic benefits for the broader public. It will also depend on an additional factor: the expectations of the broader public regarding future gains. These expectations will, in turn, be a function of past experiences of cooperation (or the lack of it), government rhetoric, and the nature of the institutional arrangements that guide state-society relations and the distribution of wealth in society. It is here that regime type may become more important. In an authoritarian regime, citizens are more likely to be skeptical that peace dividends will trickle down to them. Intuitively, expectations for sharing the peace dividend should be higher in a democratic regime, which is elected by the public and is accountable to the public. This, however, is not necessarily the case. A democratic state can still suffer from wide internal socioeconomic gaps, and citizens' expectations about reaping the peace dividend are based less on the democratic nature of their regime and more on the specific domestic economic policies used to distribute wealth (including the peace dividend) within society.

The Impact of Economic Power Disparities on the Role of Economics in the Transition to Peace

One of the main critiques of the liberal argument on interdependence and peace is that liberals assume that interactions are mutual and symmetrical or that asymmetry is not very important. However, in transitions to peace between two economically asymmetric states, the economic factor is likely to play a detrimental role, especially in the long run. Håvard Hegre establishes that trade reduces the incentives for conflict most clearly in cases of relatively symmetric dyads.[42] Elsewhere he demonstrates that the relationship between trade and conflict is contingent on the level of development.[43] While most of the quantitative literature on this issue tries to establish statistically whether there is a link between power asymmetry, trade, and conflict, I focus on the impact of economic power disparities on the deliberations and concerns of decision makers and other domestic groups within both states.

Wide economic power disparities have several implications for the transition process. One is that they create a different incentive structure for the two sides. For the more economically powerful state, expected economic benefits are likely to be limited since expansion of trade to the smaller state's market is not likely to add up to a large percentage of its gross domestic product (GDP) or total trade. At the same time, that power disparity also gives the powerful actor the opportunity to use economic statecraft and positive sanctions in order to help move the transition to peace forward. For the weaker party, this situation creates a dilemma. On the one hand, from an economist's perspective, gaining access to a large and prosperous market will bring absolute gains to the weaker party's own market and society. On the other hand, such gains from asymmetric trade may lead to several potentially serious political problems: the problem of coercive power, the problem of the influence effect, and the problem of agreeing on the meaning of mutual cooperation. Albert Hirschman argued in 1945 that asymmetrical trade relations accrue political benefits to the larger state, giving it coercive power vis-à-vis the weaker state, that is, using the much greater dependence of the smaller state on bilateral trade in order to coerce it to follow certain practices. This situation should be all the more disturbing for a small, economically weak state in creating relations with an economically strong former enemy, given the extreme sensitivity and lack of trust regarding the former enemy's future good intentions.[44]

Asymmetric trade also creates a second problem: it creates an influence effect that benefits the larger state. In asymmetric trade relations, the small state is likely to change its perceptions of its own interests and alter them to conform with those of the large state because trade relations are likely to lead to the creation of new interests and to the formation of political coalitions to advance them.[45] The influence effect is a much stronger and more effective instrument of power than mere coercive power. Consequently, for the economically more powerful state there is a strong incentive to develop economic relations and even to make short-term concessions in order to gain long-term access to and influence over the other state's market. By changing the former enemy's self-interest, it is possible to reduce dramatically the uncertainties and the risk of future defection. At the same time, however, the weaker state in the dyad will hesitate to develop economic relations with a stronger former enemy specifically because of the fear that such an influence effect will be created. This problem is likely to be more salient and politically sensitive in the special case of emerging economic relations between former enemies, where to begin with there is a high level of mistrust and concern over the stronger state's abuse of its relative economic power advantage.

In addition, broad power disparities and the uneven distribution of gains that result create a real difficulty in reaching a common definition of what mutual cooperation should mean, especially in postconflict situations in which there are major concerns about relative gains. One of the fundamental precondition for stable cooperation is a mutual agreement between the parties about what type of behavior qualifies as cooperation. But wide disparities open the way to disagreements about the appropriate concessions each side should make and about the meaning of "fair gains." For example, the weaker side may feel that it is gaining less from a trade agreement than its more advanced partner and therefore refuse to sign the agreement or expect the stronger state to make greater concessions in order to advance the relations.

Another potential problem stems from the finding of Oneal and Russett and others that the calculations of the lesser trade-dependent country in the dyad are what matters in predicting the restraining impact of trade. It follows from this observation that trade has the largest impact when it is important to both countries in the dyad. Consequently, in very asymmetric dyads, trade becomes less important relative to other considerations.[46] The relevance of this conclusion is diminished, however, once we consider the political logic of promoting trade within the dyad in order to promote peace, as discussed below. In that case, asymmetry may in fact offer a new policy tool for the stronger state.

Wide economic power asymmetries create a dialectic process of competing pressures: for the weaker party they create a temptation to gain aid and/or trade, tempered by the fear of becoming dependent and thus more vulnerable.[47] For the stronger party, they create an opportunity to make political use of its economic power to promote a transition to peace but with much more limited economic incentive. Conversely, when economic power disparities are narrower, concern regarding the development of dependence and vulnerability will be lower. Domestic societal actors in the weaker state will also entertain higher expectations of gain from the economic interaction. When power disparities are extremely wide, those actors are likely to believe that they cannot compete with their counterpart anyway, so any economic opening of their bilateral relations cannot bring them substantial benefits. At the same time, the narrower economic power disparities become, the less likely we are to find states engaging in classic economic statecraft vis-à-vis one another, because the cost of making economic concessions or gestures for political purposes becomes higher.

Broad power disparities create difficulties in both stages of the transition to peace. However, they may be more easily mitigated in the first stage and, at times, can also create initial incentives to sign a peace treaty linked to clear economic benefits. If the more powerful state is interested in using economic incentives in order to advance overall political relations and to encourage its former enemy to sign a peace treaty to end hostilities, it can use several strategies in order to ameliorate the negative impact of broad economic power disparities. First, it can offer an uneven bargain that will ameliorate the concerns of the weaker side. This is a good example of a situation in which the political rationale (pacifying relations) may be very different from the economic rationale (maximizing gains.) A second, related strategy is one of providing generous foreign aid to the weaker state, which will create the impression of compensating for the power disparities while at the same time encouraging the development of bilateral trade.[48] A third strategy is to focus on economic cooperation in issue areas in which the power disparities are less stark. For example, it may be easier to focus on infrastructure cooperation rather than on trade cooperation.[49] Finally, the negative impact of broad economic power disparities can be ameliorated or overcome through the involvement of third parties (individual states or multilateral institutions).

The negative impact of these disparities, however, is harder to mitigate at the second stage of the transition to peace. The dangers of creating an influence effect and coercive power are problems that become relevant after a longer period of interaction. They are therefore more likely to have a long-term negative effect on the period of normalization of relations, even if initial problems are overcome. Consequently, the weaker partner is likely to try to extract whatever short-term economic benefits it can by signing a peace treaty, but it will be much more reluctant to move on to a process of full economic normalization, which implies greater and freer economic interaction with its former enemy. This is likely to happen only when groups within the weaker state develop expectations that they can effectively compete (and therefore also benefit from trade) with groups from the other state. In the long run, if a warm stable peace is achieved, then power asymmetries as such are supposed to be less problematic because power considerations will be less dominant. Still, I would suggest that wide asymmetries will play a negative role in the transition, thus prolonging and entrenching old stereotypes and concerns.

There has been much debate within the quantitative literature on trade and conflict about how to measure power asymmetries and economic interdependence and dependence. Barbieri notes that in two decades of research, dependency scholars have come up with more than sixteen different operationalizations of trade dependence.[50] As Hegre argues, the easiest way to conceptualize power asymmetry between two states is to examine the differences in the size of the two countries' economies. Hegre also notes that asymmetries may be due to differences in the extent to which the two countries' markets or production are substitutable, either in partner or commodity concentration or in the extent to which the countries produce manufactured goods or primary commodities. He argues, though, that such asymmetries are positively correlated with size asymmetry.[51]

There are also different measures for dependence. Barbieri suggests that dependence can be thought of as either the relative importance of a particular trading relationship to that which exists with other partners or to the importance of that trading relationship to the overall economy. Consequently, she uses two types of measures: one is the ratio between the dyadic trade flow and the state's total trade (what she calls "partner dependence"), and the other is the ratio of dyadic trade flow and the state's GDP (an indicator for "economy dependence").[52]

These measures offer some useful guidelines for what is needed to determine the economic asymmetries between the states examined. However, it is important to bear in mind that they have a somewhat limited value when exploring relations between two former enemies. Whereas these measures seek to capture existing patterns of trade relations, the important factor in the cases examined here is the expectations regarding future trade patterns and their impact on interdependence. These expectations are based partly on economic research projecting trade potentials and trajectories and partly on noneconomic considerations, ideological biases, and political manipulation. It is therefore more important for the purposes of this study to understand the perceptions of the relevant actors regarding the disparities between them and regarding their implications, rather than to establish an exact economic measure of these disparities.[53] In each case, we need to examine how economic power disparities translate into actors' perceptions of potential future gains as well as their concern that various types of economic cooperation can potentially generate dangerous dependence.[54]

In making this judgment, actors apply a more complex analysis of dependence and interdependence. First, they dissect and differentiate economic dependence across different issues. Second, they take into account a wide range of economic activities: trade, joint ventures, cooperation on infrastructure projects, economic aid, and others. Whereas standard measures of dependence assess overall trade dependence, I suggest that when examining the interaction between two states in greater detail, it is useful to pay attention to variations in the level of potential dependence across different sectors and different economic activities. For example, while a free trade agreement may be rejected out of fear of dependence on a stronger partner, a controlled joint venture may be welcomed because it does not generate significant dependence.[55] This can lead to variation in the behavior of the weaker party across different types of economic activities. Furthermore, perceived dependence in one issue area can be balanced by a perceived dependence of the other state on another issue area, therefore mitigating concerns over the political misuse of economic relations in the future.[56]

The Impact of Third Party Involvement

The relevance of third party involvement in the transition to peace between former enemies is an obvious matter for most regional experts and scholars focusing on conflict resolution. However, most of the commercial liberalism literature has focused on what happens within the dyadic relations with the exception of the focus on the impact of third parties via alliances or preferential trade agreement membership.[57]

Especially in the case of transition away from conflict, a third party can also enhance the effectiveness of economic interaction as a tool of peacemaking by providing political and security conditions that help mitigate or neutralize concerns over relative gains stemming from the process of economic interaction. For example, a strong and reliable security guarantee can mitigate regional security dilemmas and, by doing so, neutralize at least one of the concerns surrounding economic cooperation with the former enemy. However, this in itself is not enough to encourage economic relations between the former enemies. Indeed, American pressure had little direct success in getting Japan's neighbors to trade with it, despite the U.S. military presence in Japan and the neutralization of the security threat Japan had previously posed. Similarly, an American military presence in Europe did play a crucial role in mitigating security concerns regarding Germany, but it had little direct impact on the nature of the evolving economic relations between Germany and France. These broader strategic conditions are considered in the detailed case studies offered in chapters 2 through 7, but the conceptual focus is more specifically on the economic involvement of third parties in the different stages of the transition.

A third party can influence the former rivals' economic interest in the transition to peace by providing incentives, trade-offs, and linkages. By offering economic or political benefits that are linked to the success of bilateral economic cooperation between the former enemies, a third party can help promote such cooperation. It can do that by changing the conditions described in the first two hypotheses: it can change the composition of the domestic constituencies that support economic cooperation with the former enemy by changing the magnitude of predicted gains and losses from such cooperation. This strategy follows a logic similar to that used by the stronger state in the dyad if it wishes to promote peace through the use of economic tools. If the third party is much more powerful than both actors (usually an extraregional great power), it can play an important role by practicing economic statecraft vis-à-vis both sides. The economic role of third parties has been discussed in the context of the literature on economic sanctions. David Cortright, for example, argues that most often the strongest incentive for actors to cooperate is access to improved economic and political relations with the major powers, especially the United States.[58] A third party can also mitigate the various problems associated with the asymmetrical nature of economic cooperation by providing side benefits such as selective market access or foreign aid.

One should also bear in mind the possibility of a negative impact of third parties, in case there is opposition to the process of peacemaking. Under such conditions, leaders will also have to calculate the treaty's costs, which would stem from negative third party reactions, such as economic or political sanctions. One final possibility to consider is that a third party may pose a mutual threat to the two former enemies and thus indirectly encourage direct cooperation between them. This would be another possible realist pathway for a third party indirect economic impact on a transition to peace. Here, however, I am interested only in the direct, active involvement of third parties.

Third party involvement can come in different forms. It can be initiated by one or both of the states involved in the transition to peace, or it can be initiated by the third party itself, seeking to advance its own interests. It can be directed specifically toward one of the parties or toward both parties, and it can also take place by nesting the economic cooperation of the two former enemies within a broader multilateral context. Under that scenario, the third party will not be an interested major power but rather a multilateral institution or international institution through which various interested states, or the organization itself, can operate to promote, stabilize, and lock in the bilateral transition to peace between the former enemies. The question of the impact of joint membership in institutions has been addressed in the commercial liberalism literature. For example, Edward Mansfield, Jon Pevehouse, and David Bearce demonstrate how participation in preferential trade agreements (PTAs) can reduce the likelihood of armed conflict because states will thus anticipate long-term economic gains within the arrangement. Such arrangements also provide a forum for bargaining and negotiations that can dampen disputes, and they can help to create focal points on which to coordinate behavior and avoid the breakdown of cooperation.[59] Bearce demonstrates how mutual membership in commercial institutions can lower the likelihood of militarized disputes between states, because such institutions increase the opportunity costs of war, allow the sharing of more private information between states, and serve as a forum in which leaders can meet, create trust, and reduce misperceptions.[60] By embedding the bilateral interaction in a broader multilateral framework, the two former enemies, as well as interested third parties, find it easier to use issue linkage in order to enhance the expected benefits from economic cooperation. Within such an institution, a weaker party can also find ways to mitigate the impact of the economic power disparities with its more powerful former enemy.

The exact nature of third party involvement, however, will have very different consequences for the two stages of the transition to peace. A third party can play an important role in leading to the decision to sign a peace treaty by promising to provide or by actually providing large indirect economic benefits linked to the signing of a peace treaty (e.g., provision of large sums of aid, tariff reduction, or economic agreements). It could be that the real economic motivation for advancing and maintaining peaceful relations with a former enemy lies not in the direct benefits to be gained from the new bilateral relations but rather in the indirect economic benefits from a third party that follow from such improved relations. This situation suggests that the development of economic cooperation can help stabilize the peace between former enemies by spilling over not into other bilateral issue areas but into relations with other politically and economically important third parties.

Under such conditions, the third party can play a significant role in the efforts leading to the signing of a peace treaty, but this preliminary role will not contribute much to the future normalization of relations and development of bilateral economic ties. In order to influence the process of normalization, a third party has to be able and willing to offer incentives to both sides to continue to interact economically. This can be done either by linking economic or political bonuses to the ongoing process of normalization (rather than to the signing of the treaty) or by actually investing in the development of bilateral ties between the two former enemies (e.g., providing financial aid or grants for joint ventures or regional cooperation projects). Such a strategy is likely to be complicated and costly and to require a long-term commitment and therefore be more difficult to apply.[61] Consequently, a more effective strategy for promoting economic normalization between the former enemies is likely to be the embedding of their bilateral economic (and possibly other) relations within a broader multilateral framework. Such an institutional context can offer a longer shadow of the future for both parties and provide a more stable basis for them to develop their relations than a reliance on a time-specific policy of a certain great power.

The three hypotheses I have introduced to describe the impact of economic incentives on the two stages of transition to peace can be summarized as follows:

1. If strong domestic players expect significant gains from economic cooperation, then economic cooperation can become an effective tool in promoting peace. Support for the transition to peace will be a function of the nature and magnitude of their potential gains from promoting cooperation. Alternatively, if economic cooperation entails high costs for central domestic players, then the attempt to promote such cooperation is unlikely to succeed or may cause greater instability in the relations.
2. Economic cooperation between former enemies will be more difficult to achieve and will have less of a chance to promote positive relations if the economic power disparities between the two states are very wide.
3. A third party can help promote the transition to peace between former enemies by providing direct economic benefits to one or both parties, but a third party can promote normalization only if it is able and willing to link direct bilateral cooperation between the former enemies to additional economic or political gains it can offer to one or both parties.

The hypotheses presented in this chapter are not competing with each other. The second and third hypotheses operate by influencing the balance between winners and losers from peace. Thus, for example, wide economic power disparities are likely to raise concerns among societal groups that fear losing their jobs or market share if economic cooperation is expanded. Similarly, what third parties in fact do is to offer such incentives so as to shift the domestic balance of winners and losers, expanding the winning circle or compensating losers.

The arguments regarding the different dynamics in the two stages of transition to peace are summarized in table 1.

Table 1. Summary of the hypotheses

Relevant factor	Impact on stage I (peace treaty)	Impact on stage II (normalization)
Domestic winners and losers	Strong interest of state actors or a coalition of state actors and powerful business groups is necessary and sufficient.	Expansion of vested interest in peace to broader segments of society (smaller producers, consumers) is necessary. Narrow state–big business coalition may eventually cause societal resentment.
Economic power disparities	Will cause concerns (fear of domination, influence effect and relative gains) for the weaker side but also can serve as an initial incentive to sign a treaty. Can be mitigated through uneven bargains, cooperation in issue areas where disparity is less stark, and third party compensation.	Main dangers associated with asymmetric trade become relevant in the long run; actual expansion of trade (normalization) can enhance strong party's coercive power and influence effect. Prospect likely to create opposition to normalization.
Third party involvement	Can provide substantial economic, political, or security side benefits that would increase the expected value of the peace treaty. Institutional nesting facilitates cooperation. Expected indirect benefits are sufficient to prompt signing of the treaty.	Indirect benefits from third party are insufficient to promote normalization. Normalization requires direct benefits within the dyad. Third party can help by promoting and rewarding such direct cooperation. Institutional nesting can facilitate cooperation.

Methodology and Case Selection

I use a structured, focused qualitative comparison to examine the three hypotheses introduced above.[62] There is a need to complement the large body of quantitative literature on commercial liberalism with more qualitative research. Only in-depth case studies can actually trace the dynamics of economics and politics in peacemaking. Using this method also enables me to focus analytically on the economic dynamics of peacemaking, while remaining sensitive to other strategic, political, cultural, or ideological factors that are an integral and often unique part of each case. Furthermore, this method allows me to identify, where possible, the impact of economic interaction on political and social processes and to pay attention to the role of interpretation in the process linking economic interaction, politics, and peacemaking.

I chose to examine in depth the political economy of the transitions to peace in six case studies. Two cases are located in the Middle East. One looks at the transition to peace between Egypt and Israel since 1979 and up to the very recent changes symbolized by the signing of the first major trade agreement between the two states (and the United States): the Qualifying Industrial Zone (QIZ) agreement, at the end of 2004. The second case examines the transition to peace between Jordan and Israel since 1994. The next two cases are located in Asia. One examines the transition to peace between Japan and South Korea after the end of World War II, including events leading to the 1965 normalization agreement and its aftermath. The second case examines the transition to peace between Japan and Southeast Asia, focusing on the experience of the Philippines and Indonesia and the developments leading to the peace and reparation agreements (1956 and 1958) and their aftermath. The last two cases bring us to Europe. One examines the classic case of the Franco-German transition to peace, focusing mainly on developments up to the 1960s (a point at which, I argue, normal peace already existed). The second case examines the transition to peace between Germany and Poland. It traces developments since the end of World War II, the breakthrough during the period of *Ostpolitik,* and the second breakthrough following the end of the cold war and German reunification.

The choice of both a cross-regional and an intraregional comparison was driven by several considerations. Most of the theories that have been developed regarding commercial liberalism were heavily influenced by the post–World War II Franco-German experience. It is important therefore to move away from this Eurocentric approach and examine the hypotheses on non-European regions. Also, the classic commercial liberal theory was developed with liberal democracies in mind. Once again, it is important to explore the argument in other institutional settings. The Middle Eastern and Asian cases I have chosen offer such variations.[63] For the same reason, I also chose to address the European cases last. They are thus analyzed in comparison to the other four cases and not vice versa. This way I hope to overcome the Eurocentric bias while being able to bring out similar logics and dynamics, as well as the unique aspects of the political economy of transitions to peace across all three regions analyzed.

While comparative studies of Asia and Europe (Japan and Germany) have already been made, most notably in the work of Peter Katzenstein, the Middle East–Asia cross-regional comparison is less familiar.[64] While much has been written about peace in the Middle East, most of the literature was produced by regional experts and retired practitioners, and relatively little work on the region has been conducted by international relations experts. As I have learned while conducting the research for this book, it is fascinating to examine the literature on the Middle East and the literature on East and Southeast Asia via a common conceptual framework. Such a comparison is not widely available, and despite its limitations, the reader should find extremely interesting insights and similarities in the economic dynamics of peacemaking in all three regions. One of the few existing cross-regional comparisons between the Middle East and Asia has been attempted by Ehud Harari, who, in a seminal paper, compared Japan's relations with East Asia and Israel's relations with Arab countries and found significant parallels in the context of trends toward peace, regionalism, and economic globalization. In that paper, he argued that the integration of major former enemies into their respective regions depends initially on the support of a world power, is enhanced by economic globalization, is related to their own contributions to regional integration, and requires the adoption of a low-posture "obliging" style of leadership. In his rich work, Harari examines various factors— economic, political, historical, and cultural.[65] In her book *Regional Orders at Century's Dawn*, Solingen offers a comparison of the regional dynamics of the Middle East and East Asia (the Korean peninsula) and demonstrates that it is possible to use a common analytical framework to examine cross-regional political dynamics. More recently, Solingen has pursued such comparisons in her book *Nuclear Logic*.[66]

Many regional experts suggest that the Middle East and Asia are simply not comparable, which is what would be called in methodological jargon the "unit homogeneity problem." The problem is that there are clear and significant differences in the nature of the conflict in each case, and in the historical and cultural circumstances.[67] I suggest, however, that by using a careful, rigorous, but empirically sound comparison, it is possible to delineate and fruitfully compare the three causal mechanisms advanced above. The different circumstances of each case will filter into these mechanisms and will be reflected, for example, in the nature of the specific domestic groups involved in the peacemaking process. The goal is not to explain how peace is achieved nor is it to examine the relative importance of economic factors as opposed to strategic or other factors in the process. Rather, it is to trace the distinct impact of economic incentives and the interaction of economic and political considerations on the transition process through careful process-tracing. These elements can clearly be traced under different political and historical contexts. Indeed, one of the goals of the book is to show that, regardless of the political context, there are common, basic causal mechanisms through which economic considerations influence the peacemaking process. By using a qualitative comparative method, I believe that this mission can be achieved without falling into the trap of monocausal explanations.

The six cases offer a variation on the dependent variable, that is, in the level of success in a transition to normal peace. Overall, the German case is often considered the hallmark of a successful use of economic tools to bring about normal peace. The Middle Eastern cases represent a limited level of success in using economic tools in a transition to peace. There is still only a cold peace between Israel and its neighbors Egypt and Jordan, and levels of economic interaction are still relatively low. Japan, in turn, offers an example of moderate to high success. It has managed to normalize its relations with its neighbors via sophisticated economic diplomacy. With South Korea, it managed to reach an impressive level of economic normalization, yet this success has not been translated into cultural or broader societal normalization.

By examining the interaction of three regional states (Israel, Japan, and Germany), each in two sets of dyads, I am able to increase my number of observations while controlling for the various background factors related specifically to Israel, Japan, or Germany. Instead of comparing only the different levels of success across regions, I am able to also examine the variation in levels of success within each region. I can then examine what changes in critical factors might explain the variation. To illustrate, in the two Middle Eastern cases the transition to peace between Israel and Jordan has been more successful than that between Israel and Egypt. That variation is best explained by the variation in the domestic balance of winners and losers in Egypt and Jordan (where only in the latter was there active support for economic cooperation with Israel by the state monarchy) and by the different role played by the key third party, the United States (which conditioned its economic incentives for Jordan and Israel upon building cooperation between them, via the Qualifying Industrial Zones or QIZs). Conversely, in a comparison between these cases and those involving Japan, the most prominent factor that explains the much greater success in Asia is the different nature of the domestic coalitions that supported the process (the strong state–big business coalition in Japan, Indonesia, and South Korea that supported economic cooperation). In the two Middle Eastern cases, the broad economic power disparities played a negative role. In Japan's relations with South Korea, the narrower power disparities (compared to the Israeli case) were more conducive to the transition, though they still created problems. Japan's relations with its Southeast Asian neighbors, in turn, offer an interesting deviating case of extremely wide economic power disparities that did not have negative effects in the long run. This case is extremely helpful in illuminating the importance of actors' perceptions of power disparities and of their implications. Finally, the German cases offer interesting variations on the power disparities factor. The interesting comparison here is between the dynamics of early postwar, economically ruined West Germany, as opposed to the prosperous and united Germany of 1990. France, while wary of Germany's power potential, initially perceived the economic power disparities with Germany to be low, a factor that mitigated initial concerns. The process of the transition to peace with Poland, in turn, did begin with West German Ostpolitik (its diplomatic turn to Eastern Europe) in the 1970s but became more intense after German reunification, when once again economic power disparities were wide. The two German cases also offer an interesting variation on the variable of third party economic involvement. In the Israeli cases, the economic benefits came from the United States. In the Japanese cases, despite some American attempts to promote economic cooperation, third party economic involvement played a limited role. In the German cases, we once again find the United States to be an important economic actor, but the crucial factor was the linking of the bilateral German-French or German-Polish relations to the broader multilateral institutional setting of the European Community (EC) and later the European Union (EU).

Despite the fact that three states (Israel, Japan, and Germany) each appear in two case studies, the analysis does not focus solely on them. Rather, each of the six cases examined offers a dyadic analysis of the domestic configurations, motivations, and policy-making process within both states involved in the transition. As discussed above, different strategic interactions in each dyad have led to different outcomes, also within the same region.[68]

Despite the varying levels of success in transitions to peace in the cases, this study also illustrates the similar problems and challenges that appeared in all of them. For example, in all of the cases, state-level decisions to move toward peace were related to economic considerations but met significant societal opposition. Also, in every case, economic power disparities created societal concerns over domination by the former enemy, which made broader normalization more complicated. An important finding, therefore, is that despite obvious historical and contextual differences, there are indeed many similarities in the logic of the political economy of transitions to peace in different cases across the globe.

SHIFTING PRIORITIES

Egypt and Israel's Attempts at Peacemaking

THE SIGNING OF A PEACE TREATY by Israeli prime minister Menachem Begin and Egyptian president Anwar Sadat on March 26, 1979, was truly a historic moment. After thirty years during which the Arab world refused to accept the legitimate right of the state of Israel to exist and after three bloody wars, Egypt was the first Arab state to acknowledge Israel and sign a peace treaty with it. On the one hand, this peace treaty managed to survive various challenges, from the murder of President Sadat, to the Israeli war in Lebanon, to the two *intifadas*. This durability is in itself an impressive achievement. On the other hand, despite initial expectations, the formal peace agreement never developed into a warm peace. After their peace treaty, Israel and Egypt signed normalization agreements, with negotiations on most of these agreements continuing until April 1982, the date of the completion of Israel's withdrawal from Sinai. These agreements, formulated by a joint committee of experts, presented in great detail the various political, economic, and cultural issues requiring normalization. However, after an initial short period of growing interaction, most of these elaborate plans for economic cooperation never materialized. The status of relations between the two states is still closer to the category of cold peace, as defined in chapter 1. The peace treaty was initiated by leaders and governments, with little involvement of the business sector, which was not a major domestic actor at the time in either state. The broader public remained largely unconvinced regarding the peace dividends, especially in light of many unfulfilled promises. Whereas Israel perceived normalization as the natural outgrowth of the peace treaty,

Egypt made a clear distinction between the two stages, holding the latter hostage to political developments on the Palestinian front.[1] In fact, some scholars argue that to begin with, President Sadat did not think about peace in terms of "normal" or "warm" peace at all but rather as an end to the war situation.[2]

The Israeli embassy in Cairo made many efforts to push forward the various economic aspects of the new relations, and the Israeli government earmarked a million dollars for promoting development cooperation with Egypt. But very early on it became apparent that the Egyptian regime was discouraging Egyptian business leaders from developing ties with Israel by instituting various regulations. Israel gradually stopped being invited to fairs, and trade of about $80 million in 1981 was reduced by 1990 to $12 million. By 2001, it was up again to around $67 million, and by the end of 2004, it had dropped to $44 million. The tourism sector also remained limited. In 1999, about 415,000 Israelis visited Egypt, mostly the resorts in Sinai, and that number dropped to only 130,000 in 2002. From Egypt, the number of tourists to Israel was minimal, reaching a record high of 28,000 in 1995 and dropping precipitously to 160 tourists in 2007.[3] Interestingly, the one economic issue on which cooperation was pursued successfully up to this day, regardless of political circumstances, is the sale of Egyptian oil to Israel, an arrangement that was part of the peace treaty. One should note, though, that the Egyptians have refused over the years to include oil revenues in their official trade balance with Israel.[4]

Any cultural normalization is seen in Egypt as hinging on a resolution of the Palestinian problem, and so, despite the existence of a detailed cultural agreement (attached to the peace treaty), there is hardly any Israeli cultural presence in Egypt or vice versa, with the exception of the Israeli Academic Center in Cairo, which operates on a very low profile. Furthermore, Egyptian artists and intellectuals, as well as the culture ministry (headed for twenty-one years by Faruq Husni), are actively working to prevent any such interaction and any Israeli penetration of this kind, not only in Egypt but also in the whole Arab world.[5]

Only in December 2004 did a breakthrough seem to take place, with the signing of the Qualifying Industrial Zone (QIZ) agreement between Israel, Egypt, and the United States. That agreement was made after nearly twenty years without progress, and since the end of 2004, several events have raised the possibility of a breakthrough in the movement toward economic normalization between Egypt and Israel. The U.S. Congress had initiated the QIZ idea in 1996, suggesting designated qualifying industrial zones between Israel and Egypt and between Israel and Jordan. The QIZs allow Egypt and Jordan to export products to the United States duty free if the products contain inputs from Israel. To gain this duty-free access, QIZ factories in the designated areas must add at least 35 percent to the value of the article. The Americans left it to the regional parties to negotiate the relative input of each party. While Israel had already signed a QIZ agreement with Jordan in 1996, the Egyptians consistently rejected the notion of the QIZ. This stance changed dramatically only in 2004. The United States initially designated three QIZs: in Greater Cairo, in Alexandria, and in Port Said. To qualify for duty-free entry to the American markets, goods have to include 11.7 percent value from Israel (as opposed to 8 percent in the QIZ with Jordan, calculated per quarter and not based on individual items, as in the Jordanian QIZ).[6] The bulk of exports under the QIZ are textiles, while both sides have announced their interest in expanding the use of the QIZ to other industrial sectors as well, such as ceramics, leather, luggage, shoes, processed food, and juice. To control the implementation of the treaty, a joint Israeli-Egyptian QIZ committee was formed (with an American observer) and is to meet every three months in Jerusalem and Cairo.[7] By the end of 2005, there were already eight industrial zones and 470 Egyptian companies registered in them, and under Egyptian pressure the Office of the United States Trade Representative (USTR) authorized two additional zones.[8] By 2006, Israeli exports to Egypt had jumped to a relative high of $126 million (compared to a meager $29 million in 2004).[9] This agreement created a window of opportunity for advancing normalization and warming up the peace. Practically speaking, that means expanding intergovernmental and private business relations, creating more institutional ties (e.g., the QIZ committee that was formed to follow the implementation of the agreement), more bureaucratic cooperation (between ministries of trade), and perhaps, in the long run, creating both an economic vested interest in peace and a spillover to noneconomic issues. For now, however, most participants are skeptical regarding the likelihood of such a scenario. This process remains very elitist (on the Egyptian side) and limited. The business people who are interested in working with Israel and promoting the QIZ are all part of a narrow sector of big business with close ties to the government.

This chapter's comparison across the time frame of 1979 to 2004, especially in light of the significant change in 2004, offers a good opportunity to examine the dynamics of the relevant causal mechanisms over time. The tentative changes offer an especially good opportunity to examine the impact of the nature of the domestic balance of winners and losers and the role of third parties.

The Economic Promise of Peace

If one wants to assess the economic value of peace, one has to make a distinction between the costs of the alternative route of continued conflict, the immediate benefits expected from peace, and the long-term benefits anticipated as a result of peace. Whereas the first two of these elements are crucial for understanding the initial transition to peace, the last is of greater significance for understanding the limited nature of normalization in subsequent years. Another basic distinction to bear in mind is the distinction between the expected and actual peace dividends for the state and its rulers, and for various societal actors within the state. In times of transition, expectations for gains are no less important than actual gains. In the longer run, discrepancies between initial expectations (realistic or not) and actual gains can be a source of problems.

In the aftermath of the October War in 1973, President Sadat perceived that the costs of conflict with Israel had become extremely high and unsustainable. After the end of that war, the Egyptian economy was in terrible shape. Awareness of the high economic price Egypt was paying for its continued conflict with Israel had already begun to develop in the aftermath of the 1967 war. On the eve of the 1973 war, President Sadat informed members of the Egyptian National Security Council, "We will not be able within two months to pay any of our debts, and we would not be able to buy an additional grain of wheat in 1974, that is, the people will have no bread."[10] After the 1973 war, Egypt found itself to be one of the Arab world's poorest states. Sadat began stressing in public the link between the continued conflict with Israel and Egypt's economic problems. His October Paper, published on April 18, 1974, presented economic development as the top national goal after the war and once again stressed the heavy economic burden of the conflict with Israel. Later on, Sadat often mentioned the 16 billion Egyptian pounds' worth of collateral damage that Egypt had suffered since 1967 due to its involvement in the "struggle for the Arabs." Such costs involved the loss of revenues from the closure of the Suez Canal, the loss of the oil fields in Sinai, and the cost of military procurement.[11]

The dire economic conditions created a real threat to the stability of Sadat's regime. Faced with external pressure from the International Monetary Fund (IMF), the regime decided to cut subsidies and increase prices on basic commodities. These decisions, in turn, led to the food riots of January 1977, in which seventy-nine people were killed and which made it clear that Sadat could not politically afford to cut subsidies on basic food items or basic services.[12] Clearly, Sadat himself came to the conclusion that both economic recovery and continuation of the conflict were impossible. He stated, "Egypt became a backward country because of the slogan 'war is supreme.' This is why I opted for peace."[13] The cost of continued conflict was paid by the regime and by the public, who actually bore the economic and physical hardships. It was the official rhetoric, though, that began making this link more explicit after 1973.

The immediate direct economic gains from the transition to peace between Egypt and Israel were limited. On the Egyptian side, the main economic benefit did not come directly from interaction with Israel but from the impact of the peace treaty on Egypt's political and economic relations with the United States. For this reason, the nature of the American involvement is critical. The expected gains from peace were directly linked to Sadat's domestic policy shift toward economic liberalization, known as the policy of *Infitah* (openness). A central component of this new policy was the attraction of foreign investment into Egypt. While in previous years Egypt had enjoyed generous aid from the oil-producing Arab states, it became clear that the main source of meaningful aid and investment was the United States.[14] Indeed, after the peace treaty was signed, Egypt enjoyed an annual grant of $2.3 billion from the United States, for both military and civilian purposes, and since 1978, there has been a surge in foreign investment as well as in revenues from tourism.[15] Beyond that, another significant immediate economic gain from the treaty was the return of the Sinai oil fields to Egyptian hands, fields that had been discovered and developed by the Israelis.[16]

On the Israeli side, the main incentive for going along with Sadat's peace initiative was political rather than economic. In fact, in the short term it was expected that Israel would pay an economic price for the peace treaty, resulting mainly from the return of the oil wells in Sinai and the need to redeploy troops.[17] This observation should be balanced with the fact that the economic costs of the conflict did appear to grow after 1973, finding expression in a significant decline in economic growth, decreased productivity, and an increasing burden of defense consumption (up from 21 percent in 1967–1972 to 28.9 percent between 1973 and 1979).[18] Michael Barnett describes the growing reluctance of Israeli society to carry the burden of high taxes after the 1973 war, forcing the government to increase its financial reliance upon the United States and to risk its financial autonomy.[19] The continued conflict thus did exert an economic cost that was growing. Unlike the Egyptian case, though, a sense of economic crisis was not a major factor in the Israeli decision to attend the peace talks at Camp David.[20] For this reason, the discussion regarding domestic winners and losers will focus on the Egyptian side.

Israel assigned major importance to the exploration and development of economic ties with Egypt, but for political rather than economic reasons. No one expected Egypt to become a major trading partner of Israel, but the basic understanding was that economic as well as other forms of interaction were crucial in order to give meaning and long-term credibility to the treaty. This Israeli understanding reflected the adoption of the basic commercial liberal argument —that once high levels of interdependence are achieved, the cost of resorting to violence will become too high, thus strengthening the peace and raising the cost of war. The notions of irrevocable interdependence and a vested interest in peace, introduced in chapter 1, were indeed developed by a group of Israeli academics.[21]

Consequently, in the years following the signing of the peace treaty, Israeli economists, political scientists, and politicians joined hands to explore various avenues for economic cooperation. Economic cooperation was considered very promising in agriculture, an area in which Israel had a lot to offer in terms of its advanced agro-technology for intensive cultivation of arid and semiarid lands. Great potential was foreseen for cooperation in the field of tourism, in the development of transportation infrastructure, and in the development of energy infrastructure such as a regional electricity grid and investment in new gas pipelines.[22] Economists suggested that the two countries could potentially derive many benefits from their geographic proximity, which offered cost advantages in transportation, marketing, communications, and servicing, especially for trade in goods that have high transfer costs. Experts also hoped to turn Egypt into a transit point for Israeli goods on their way to other Arab and Muslim states that did not have any relations with Israel.[23] However, few of these elaborate plans actually came into being.

Exploring in greater detail the domestic balance between the winners and losers from peace, or more correctly, who reaps the peace economic dividends, can help us understand why economic normalization did not develop between Egypt and Israel and why, only at the end of 2004, for the first time after more than twenty years, a sudden interest in such economic activity appeared.

Domestic Winners and Losers from the Transition to Peace

President Sadat initiated the peace treaty with Israel in light of the extreme economic circumstances threatening the stability of his regime. As noted before, the fact that the government (or ruler) had a lot to gain from ending the conflict was sufficient to push Sadat to sign a peace treaty with Israel. That the regime was a beneficiary of the peace is evident also from later statements by President Hosni Mubarak, who continued to stress the cost that years of war exerted on Egypt's poor infrastructure.[24] The regime, however, received its most significant economic gains from the act of signing the treaty. It did not perceive any significant economic gains from further normalization of relations with Israel. As explained in greater detail below, because the economic benefits for Egypt were not linked to direct economic interaction with Israel, economic normalization in itself did not offer any dramatic economic gain that could push the process forward. The Camp David accords comprised two parts, one addressing the bilateral relations between Egypt and Israel and the other addressing the issue of peace in the Middle East and the resolution of the Palestinian problem. With no dramatic economic gains to forgo by not normalizing relations with Israel, it was much easier (and domestically legitimate) for the Egyptian regime to link any economic normalization to its political demands on the Palestinian issue.

The Egyptian regime not only perceived that there would be no significant economic gains from normalization but also saw that such an action would be politically costly. As argued in chapter 1, actual normalization of relations could be achieved only if broader segments of society believed that they would benefit from the peace dividend. This was a problem in the Egyptian case because broad segments of society did not believe they were gaining anything and also opposed normalization for ideological and religious reasons. First, the peace dividend was closely linked to the liberalization policy of Infitah. As Etel Solingen argues, a liberalizing coalition also has more to gain from regional peace.[25] However, this coalition was rather limited. In an authoritarian state with enormous power vested in the presidency, the president's perception of gains from peace is sufficient to sign a treaty, but even in an authoritarian state, pursuing normalization is difficult without broader public cooperation.

Egypt's liberalization policy allowed new private sector interests to develop and some individuals to become millionaires. The pro-liberalization private sector did not play a significant role in the push for improved relations with Israel, however, because its main benefit stemmed from the inflow of foreign capital and new investment and trade opportunities with the United States and Europe. Certain businesses did see some economic gains from relations with Israel, but these were not significant. There were several exceptional Egyptian business leaders who did pursue opportunities of cooperation with Israeli firms beginning in the 1980s. Such cooperation was especially evident in the field of agro-technology, with Israeli technology being used to improve agricultural output in Egypt. Many Egyptians dealing with agro-technology understood the comparative advantage of Israel in the field of irrigation. However, they encountered a dual problem when trying to sell Israeli irrigation systems in Egypt: they had to convince people of the merits of using Western technology, as opposed to old-fashioned agricultural methods, and they had to convince people to buy such technology from Israel.[26]

This group of private businessmen who were interested in promoting cooperation with Israel was small. Furthermore, until the mid-1990s, the political clout of private business was limited. While Infitah enabled this sector to develop, at least initially it was efficiently co-opted by the government and thus did not serve as an independent source of influence on the government. Private capital in Egypt remains a relatively underdeveloped entity. Several business associations exist, but by law they have no political role.[27] This situation has changed in recent years, however. As will be seen in the Asian case studies (chapters 4 and 5), private business interests having commercial ties with former enemies, as well as influence on government, played a very important role in their economic diplomacy toward their former enemies. No such dynamic existed in this case.

The new business elite was not only politically weak and economically uninterested in relations with Israel but also numerically small. Only a limited number of persons among the wealthy class could profit immediately from the economic changes, the inflow of foreign investment, the development of ultramodern factories, and the massive imports. At the same time, most of the population did not experience any significant improvement. To the contrary, local industries had to compete with new imports, disparities between social classes grew, and unemployment was on the rise.[28]

The negative impact of the lack of significant economic benefits for the wider population was amplified by the fact that the regime had made many unrealistic promises regarding the economic relief that would come with peace. These promises created unrealistic expectations, which in turn led to greater public frustration.[29] This myth of an exaggerated peace dividend remains a serious danger today as well. Any quick survey of the Arab literature on the political economy of peace in the Middle East reveals many statements suggesting that when a "just and comprehensive peace" is achieved in the region, most of its economic malaise will disappear as well.

Rather than feeling they were reaping a peace dividend, most Egyptians were much more aware of the various costs of signing a separate peace treaty with

Israel. Beyond the general Arab embargo on Egypt following the treaty, there were also noneconomic costs. Politically, Egypt suffered with isolation from its fellow Arab states. Many Egyptians felt that the split in the Arab world was a heavy political and cultural price to pay.[30] Ideologically, many sectors in Egypt were not at all willing to accept the legitimacy of a Jewish state, and the Egyptian intellectual elite were among those who rejected normalization with Israel on ideological grounds. They had little interest in engaging the Israeli people, culture, or economy. Trade unions and professional unions were also consistently opposed to any interaction with Israel. Such opposition is usually explained by ideological factors, but it is also suggested that there was an economic concern over competition from Israel. Finally, Islamic fundamentalists, whose public support was growing, rejected both the regime's westernizing policies and its Israeli ties. It was the Egyptian intelligentsia and unions who actively led the cold peace and even tried to resurrect the official boycott against Israel on a popular level.[31]

Given the broad comparative perspective of this book, I cannot and do not wish to explore the roots of ideological and religious opposition to peace with Israel. Making peace with Israel challenged fundamental identity issues for most Egyptians and challenged the centrality of the pan-Arabist idea. Sadat's ability to make peace with Israel, as demonstrated before, was facilitated by the growing societal sense that the price of war was too high. However, the lack of a clear, significant economic dividend from direct interaction with Israel only enhanced preexisting opposition.[32] Opposition to economic or other normalization was thus overdetermined.

One could argue then that the burden of rising economic costs and the promise of future economic benefits opened a window of opportunity for an agent of change like Sadat to initiate his dramatic move toward Israel. The lack of substantial and easily observed economic benefits from the peace with Israel in practice did not create for social scientists the appropriate playing field to test the relative power of material economic versus ideational incentives. A potential clash between religious and ideological grounds for opposing cooperation with Israel and the economic logic supporting cooperation only emerged in recent years, against the backdrop of the QIZ.

One might certainly ask why it took eight years for the Egyptians to agree to the QIZ and what changed to finally induce them to sign the agreement. The QIZ agreement was signed eight months before Israel's withdrawal from Gaza, when the disengagement plan was already being discussed in Israel. Consequently, it seemed to many observers that the decision to sign the trade agreement was the result of improving political conditions. If, over the years, economic relations stalled due to official and public opposition to Israeli policies in the Occupied Territories, the apparent change in Israeli policy allowed some improvement in economic relations as well. This interpretation, however, is misleading. While the Israeli plan for withdrawal from Gaza may have provided convenient political timing for the signing of the QIZ, it was definitely not the trigger for the agreement. The Egyptian government signed the agreement because it perceived the possibility of a significant economic benefit and, even more so, because it had to avoid very serious economic losses. Public opinion in Egypt remained rather hostile to any normalization with Israel and opposed the QIZ. This is what makes the QIZ an especially interesting case for this study. If, as explained before, avoiding normalization earlier on was easy and overdetermined due to a lack of significant economic benefits for Egypt, now there was a clear tension between the public opposition on the one hand and the significant economic rationale in favor of an agreement. The economic logic was the clear winner.

The economic logic of the QIZ for Egypt is related directly to the viability of Egyptian exports to the United States. Egypt exports 42 percent of its textile and clothing output to the American market. Over the years, its exports were protected by a quota system that designated specific quotas for imports from different developing countries. However, in January 2005, the Agreement on Textiles and Clothing (ATC), part of the General Agreement on Tariffs and Trade (GATT), came into force. According to the agreement, by January 1, 2005, all quotas and quantitative restrictions on imports from developing countries to the United States were to be lifted. The practical meaning of this change was disastrous for the Egyptian textile industry. It meant that unlimited exports from China and India could enter the American market, providing competition that Egyptian producers had little chance to overcome. A study by the World Trade Organization (WTO) on the impact of the ATC showed that China and India would take more than 65 percent of the clothing exports to the United States, whereas all other exporters would lose market share.[33]

The Egyptian government and private sector preferred ensuring their access to the American market by signing a bilateral free trade agreement (FTA) with the United States, without involving Israel. Such negotiations had been going on for several years, but the Americans insisted on various significant domestic reforms in Egypt before it could be seriously considered as an FTA candidate. One step in that direction was the signing of the Trade and Investment Framework Agreement (TIFA) in July 1999, which was to encourage and facilitate private sector contacts between the states. However, much more remained to be done.

As the deadline of January 2005 drew near, it became clear that an FTA was no longer a viable solution to the imminent challenge of the ATC. This situation led to the beginning of more serious interest of the Egyptian private sector in the QIZ option. Leaders in big business, such as industrialist Galal Zorba, began exploring the QIZ option, informally, with Israeli officials, and began pressuring their own government as well. According to a senior Egyptian businessman, when a group of business leaders eventually met with President Mubarak and urged him to pursue the QIZ, they received his agreement within an hour. This businessman also suggested that, without such intense pressure from the private sector, it would have been very difficult for Mubarak to decide to sign the QIZ, given the considerable domestic political cost involved. The QIZ, which serves Egypt's national interest, was easier to justify in front of the public once demand for it came from below.[34] A senior advisor to the minister of foreign trade also suggested that the agreement was not signed a few years earlier largely because there was not enough pressure from below.[35]

The economic stakes in this case were very high. A report of the Egyptian Ministry of Foreign Trade and Industry (MFTI) predicted that 150,000 jobs were at stake, while the signing of the QIZ was expected to lead to the creation of 250,000 jobs.[36] It is difficult, however, to understand the impact of the Egyptian business community on foreign economic policy without referring to the significant ideological change that has occurred within the Egyptian government itself. Sadat's Infitah policy initiated a very preliminary process of economic liberalization, which was important in explaining the shift toward the United States and the signing of the peace treaty with Israel, as described previously. That process, however, was stalled. Only in the mid-1990s did a more intensive process of economic reform begin to take place in Egypt. In 1994, Egypt signed the GATT, and state subsidies were suspended except those for bread, edible oil, and sugar, as well as mineral oil and gas. Attempts to privatize huge public sector enterprises in different ways are being intensified, although the extent of the success of this effort is still under debate.[37]

Two developments have increased the political power of private business in Egypt. One was the strengthening of relations between the government and big business. Many senior officials in Egypt, within the government and the presidency, are themselves currently involved in significant business activity overseas.

A new generation of reformist and Western-oriented politicians is emerging in Egypt, led by the president's son, Gamal Mubarak. This new coalition is a classic example of Solingen's "liberalizing coalition." It has a clear understanding of the logic of globalization and the importance of Egypt's efforts to compete successfully under the pressures of globalization in order to ensure a better future for the country. It is telling that in an interview debating the QIZ, Sayed Abul-Omsan, head of the Foreign Trade Policies Division at MFTI, stressed, "Global trade knows no nationalities, no beliefs."[38] This reformist group, however, still has to contend with proponents of the old Nasserist school in the government and, no less important, within the bureaucracy.[39]

The growing involvement of the business sector in politics is also apparent when looking at the Egyptian parliament, where a significant increase in the number of business leaders was registered in the parliamentary term of 1995–2000.[40] This being said, one must still remember that overall private capital in Egypt is still underdeveloped and that business associations by law have no political role, and they do not have an institutionalized lobbying system.[41] The important interaction between big business and high-level government officials, therefore, is based more on personal connections and mutual interest and is opaque to the general public.[42] This group of reformers has a strong liberal economic worldview. In their perception, if people see a clear economic gain on the horizon, they would be willing to trade even with Israel. Opposition to relations with Israel, they argue, will always exist, but the economic outcomes can speak for themselves. If the trade relationship is successful, others will follow.[43]

Indeed, the QIZ agreement faced broad public opposition, before and after it was signed. A year and a half before the treaty was signed, many business leaders rejected the idea of a QIZ. The head of the Egyptian Commercial Service (ECS) said the QIZ was "politically unacceptable." Egyptian business, up to the last minute, was focused on the FTA solution.[44] The strongest opposition came from the various elements of the antinormalization coalition, who interpreted the trade agreement as a sign of normalization with Israel. In a typical statement, the deputy chairman of the Nasserist Party said that the agreement would give Israel a ripe opportunity to impose itself on the entire region. "Israel will no longer be isolated. It will gradually and smoothly infiltrate into Arab territories in a way that will make opposing [its presence] a very difficult task," he said.[45]

Part of the opposition stemmed from the fact that the agreement was negotiated in secret and was not brought up for discussion in the parliament. The agreement was seen as the Mubarak government trying to appease the administration of President George W. Bush and to divert it from pushing too hard for greater political reforms in Egypt. Opponents stressed the fact that being forced to cooperate economically with Israel was an insult.[46] While government officials were stressing that the agreement would benefit all levels of the Egyptian economy, the fact remains that it was perceived as part of an elitist process, serving narrow interests.

This view, of course, does not bode well for the process of normalization. In fact, government officials themselves have gone to great lengths to stress that the QIZ was only a trade agreement and not part of a broader process of "normalization." The official position is that the goal of the QIZ is to advance Egypt's national interest, not to warm relations with Israel. However, the concerns of the opposition stem from their understanding of the potential, even if inadvertent, impact of greater economic interaction with Israel. Ironically, they are in fact in agreement with the same people they oppose about the mechanism of peacemaking. When asked if Egyptians had an interest in normalization, senior Egyptian business leaders replied that there was no interest in "normalization" but that there was an economic interest, which, if encouraged, would eventually lead to broader normalization.[47] As liberals like Karl Deutsch argue, increased transactions can lead to greater trust building and familiarity, regardless of the trigger that led to them in the first place.

An overall assessment of the domestic balance within Egypt suggests that a strong coalition of big business and government had a clear and significant economic stake in signing the QIZ agreement. The broader public, however, remains unconvinced about the expected economic dividend and is still opposed to any other signs of normalization with Israel, whether economic, political, cultural, or other. This public opposition does create serious constraints on both the government and business leaders wishing to promote economic relations with Israel. Senior business leaders are reluctant to overpublicize their interaction with Israeli associates. A group of Egyptian business leaders who came to Israel to explore opportunities under the QIZ in September 2005 made it clear that they may pay a price when they return home. The head of the mission, who was planning to run for public office, suggested that his trip to Israel might cost him the elections.[48]

The government, while committing itself to the agreement, also feels more content letting private business follow it through. When he defended the agreement in front of his party in the parliament, President Mubarak argued that "signing the protocol was the demand of Egyptian businessmen . . . this is a matter first and foremost of the interest of citizens working in the factories, and therefore any debate about it is superfluous."[49] This being said, most of the proponents of the QIZ I have spoken to argued that in a state where the presidency has such overwhelming power, if there is official support from above for this process, it will end up changing public attitudes as well. The important fact to remember is that although public opposition was clearly foreseen, the Egyptian government still chose to sign the agreement. This shows that while the government and public opinion in Egypt mutually constrain one another, when national interests are at stake, the president will make decisions even in the face of strong domestic opposition.

The internal tension among Egyptians regarding this process of economic cooperation is apparent within society. It is perhaps most evident in the fact that while on the one hand there are demonstrations against and criticism of the very notion of cooperating with Israel via the QIZ, on the other hand there are similarly passionate demands to expand the scope of the QIZ to other areas in Egypt.[50] The Egyptian government was well aware of this tension and used it in its negotiations with the United States to expand the geographic scope of the agreement so as "to help them reduce the number of opponents to the treaty." Indeed, in his election campaign in September 2005, Mubarak pointedly noted his efforts to expand the number of Egyptian trade areas that could operate as QIZs.[51]

This problematic interaction between the Egyptian government and the broader public was also evident in the case of the agreement to supply Israel with natural gas, as mentioned earlier. In 2000, the Israeli government decided to allow the national electric company to negotiate with local and foreign suppliers of natural gas. One of the main contestants for this project was a private company called EMG, which was owned by both a senior Egyptian businessman, Hussein Salem, and a prominent Israeli, Yossi Mimen. Israel's agreement with EMG was for the company to supply natural gas to Israel for a period of up to twenty years, the total value of the purchases forecast to be about $3 billion. This agreement faced opposition in both Israel and Egypt.

In Israel, opposition reflected the classic realist concerns regarding the creation of a dangerous dependence on energy supply from a potentially unreliable or adversarial source. Opponents argued that it was doubtful that the Egyptian government would be willing to vouch for the continued supply of natural gas to Israel if political circumstances became difficult. Furthermore, should the supply of gas be disrupted, the damage to Israel would be very high because, unlike oil, gas cannot be stored in reserves.[52]

In stark contrast to the public debate in Israel regarding the gas deal with Egypt, Egyptian government officials consistently denied foreign reports that such a deal was being negotiated. The Egyptian public knew nothing about the negotiations with Israel, which had been going on for several years. The strategic decision to sell natural gas to Israel was made by President Mubarak, who appreciated the lucrative economic dividend that would result from such a deal. Egypt had significant natural gas reserves and wanted to find buyers. However, the only promising market in the region was that of Israel. Once again, economic logic triumphed. While the treaty was conveniently signed by the private gas company, Israel made an effort to upgrade this economic interaction by calling for an official state-level agreement in which the Egyptian government would ensure a continuous supply of gas. Eventually, the Egyptians agreed to sign a vague memorandum of understanding. When the agreement was finally signed, in July 2005, Israeli journalists attending the ceremony reported the great unease that surrounded the event on the Egyptian side.[53] This unease and complex maneuvering was already apparent in 2002, against the backdrop of the second intifada and severe criticism within Egypt of Israeli policy. President Mubarak announced that he would suspend all nondiplomatic relations with Israel. However, this announcement was not expected to hinder the completion of the gas deal with Israel. The government refused to sever all trade ties in practice because there was a real economic stake involved. This stood in sharp contrast to the public mood at the time. Chambers of commerce and trade organizations repeatedly issued statements of a boycott against Israel, but the government was unwilling to intervene. The head of the import sector at the Cairo Chamber of Commerce, Moustafa Zaki, concluded at the time, "It is up to the people. The government will not interfere. Consumers can refuse to purchase Israeli goods. That's the best we can hope for."[54]

As with the QIZ, one could choose to stress the promising fact that in the face of clear public opposition, the Egyptian government decided to sign and implement significant agreements of economic cooperation with Israel. However, if we are to project into the future of normalization, the broad public opposition, combined with the lack of significant public debate and interaction on this issue with the government, suggests that this economic tool is not likely to lead to the expansion of normalization at the societal level.

The Egyptian behavior regarding the QIZ and the gas deal suggests that even in an authoritarian regime, the government is not likely to push for an unpopular policy when no dramatic gains are expected to follow. In fact, many citizens feel that while they have little say on major political issues, they do have the power to actually bring about or withhold the implementation of economic normalization. This being said, the QIZ experience suggests that when significant gains, or more accurately, when significant losses are at stake, the regime pursued its economic logic while trying to mitigate the political problems that would result.

The major change in economic incentives occurred on the Egyptian side. On the Israeli side, however, the logic of signing the QIZ with Egypt was not primarily economic, since Israel already had an FTA with the United States. The initial economic rationale was only relevant to Israeli companies such as the large textile producer, Delta Galil Industries, which already had moved manufacturing to Jordan and to Egypt and whose products were thus unable to qualify under the Israeli-U.S. FTA. The logic of the treaty with Egypt was mostly political. In Israel, it was presented as a unique opportunity to push forward normalization. Ehud Olmert, minister of industry and trade at the time of the signing, argued that the QIZ was of historic importance, as it was in fact a political declaration of both states regarding their desire to improve relations and pour content into the peace agreement.[55]

Unlike the QIZ initiative with Jordan (discussed in chapter 3), the QIZ with Egypt was clearly a top-down, state-led initiative. In fact, Israeli industry was initially hostile to the idea, concerned that it would undermine their trade advantage with the United States via the U.S.-Israeli FTA. The Ministry of Industry and Trade had to work hard to persuade the Israeli textile industry that it actually stood to gain from this opportunity and would improve its competitive edge in the American market by reducing costs. Consequently, it gained the cooperation of local industrialists. Thus, the agreement gave, for example, a significant boost to one of the large textile companies in Israel, Polgat, which was experiencing serious problems before the QIZ signing.[56] The political nature of the agreement for the Israelis also found expression in the Israeli insistence early on to conduct the negotiations at the intergovernmental level, as opposed to the Egyptian preference to keep it at the industry level. The Egyptians grudgingly agreed but made every effort to keep this negotiating process at the lowest possible profile.[57]

Even though the Israelis' motive for pursuing the QIZ remained primarily political, once negotiations were under way, economic considerations kicked in. For Israeli industry, especially the textile industry, the QIZ offered an economic opportunity that had to be maximized. Representatives of Israeli industry vehemently opposed applying to the Egyptian QIZ the same rules applied in the Jordanian QIZ, namely, limiting the required share of Israeli input to 8 percent. Only after a stormy negotiation process did the two sides agree on an Israeli input of 11.7 percent. It is interesting that, during the negotiations, a central argument raised by the Egyptians was that if the Israelis wanted to promote peace, they should compromise and agree to a more limited input in the QIZ products. This political argument may have been used largely to promote Egyptian economic benefits from the agreement. Israeli producers, for their part, were thinking in economic terms. While recognizing the political importance of the QIZ, the Israeli side wanted to ensure economic benefits to Israeli industry.[58] This example highlights the complex interaction between political and economic motivations and how they can be manipulated.

The main problem in taking full advantage of this unique opportunity, however, stemmed from the gap between official statements, like the one by minister Olmert, cited above, and actual implementation. Both Egyptian and Israeli business leaders complained about the lack of coordination for and insufficient investment in this opportunity. To illustrate, only four months before the treaty was signed, the economic attaché position in the Israeli embassy in Cairo was eliminated. While stemming from bureaucratic struggles rather than strategic thinking, this move is one unfortunate example of how official agreements may fail to materialize due to poor implementation. Israeli business leaders complained about the Israeli bureaucracy's inability to coordinate and facilitate economic interaction. For example, one of the challenges of the QIZ was to find Israeli producers to supply the 11.7 percent Israeli content. The fact that different producers independently would approach the same Egyptian producer, with little governmental coordination, competing against each other, only made things worse.[59] Such bureaucratic mishandling is also a recurrent theme in the case of Jordan (chapter 3), and it can be sharply contrasted with the efficient government-business-bureaucracy cooperation that is described in the two German cases (chapters 6 and 7).

The Impact of Economic Power Disparities

The Egyptian public perception of limited economic gains from interaction with Israel was closely related to the broad economic power disparities between the two countries. In 1979, Egyptian GDP per capita was $1,052, compared to $6,434 in Israel. Egyptian overall GDP was only slightly higher than that of Israel, around $18 billion, despite the fact that the Egyptian population was more than ten times that of Israel.[60] These disparities grew over the years as the Egyptian government failed to advance significant reforms and especially since the early 1990s, when Israel was undergoing a dramatic process of economic liberalization and becoming a major high-tech power that was drawing increasing investment from the United States, Europe, and Asia. Just to illustrate, in 1990, the Israeli GDP had already surpassed that of Egypt ($52.5 billion compared to $43.1 billion), and by 2004, this gap had increased to $117.5 billion in Israel compared to $75 billion in Egypt and, in 2006, had shrunk a little, to $140 billion in Israel compared to $107 billion in Egypt.[61]

With regard to the nature of economic disparities, another interesting point should be mentioned. While in terms of economic development Israel has a significant advantage over the Egyptian economy, one cannot ignore the dramatic advantage of Egypt in terms of its domestic market size. Egyptian business leaders I have spoken to have time and again stressed this point. Israel, they stressed, had a much greater dependence on external markets due to its small domestic market.[62] The implications of this observation are interesting. When it comes to direct trade with Israel, Egyptians do not see any tremendous benefits for themselves due to the sheer size of their own market and large local industry. This industry may not have been competitive in the international arena, but it was sufficient to supply domestic needs. Egyptians, for their part, see economic interaction as much more lucrative for the Israelis. This perception made it easier to focus on and heighten concerns over the negative impact of interaction with Israel, should such interaction develop for other reasons. The implications of power disparities in the Jordanian case, explored in chapter 3, were different because Jordan did not have the luxury of a large domestic market and a vibrant domestic industry.

The broad disparities between the Egyptian and Israeli economies had a negative impact on the attempts to use economic interaction as a means of advancing normalization of relations between the two states. These disparities highlight the problem of the liberal argument linking trade and peace. The fact that the Israeli economy is much more advanced could serve as a good basis for trade, investment, and labor flows, as the various studies cited earlier show. Egypt could take advantage of Israeli know-how and technology, and Israel could take advantage of Egypt's low-cost and competent labor force, and both would benefit. This is the liberal economic logic. This logic was applied in several cases, such as the successful textile plant run by Delta-Egypt, an Israeli company that has been operating in Egypt since 1995, employing more than five thousand local workers and exporting high-quality, low-cost textiles to Europe. This enterprise, however, is still an exception.

Instead of prompting cooperation, the disparity in the Egyptian and Israeli economies created strong concerns in Egypt (and later, in other parts of the Arab world) about the dangerous impact of economic connections with Israel. Following the signing of the peace treaty, the opposition Socialist Labor Party called upon the Egyptian people "to be on full alert regarding the consequences of signing the treaty, so that Israel will not be able to take advantage of the trust of the Egyptian people and its love of peace in order to penetrate our markets and advance Israeli economic interests at the expense of our national economy."[63] The main path of economic complementarity, namely the use of Israeli technology and know-how, combined with the low-cost Egyptian labor force, was difficult to pursue because it was associated with notions of Israeli economic imperialism. There was concern that most linkages created between the Israeli economy and its Arab counterparts were likely to result in the creation of something akin to Immanuel Wallerstein's global system.[64]

The economic interaction between an economically advanced and a developing economy thus had a double negative impact. Practically speaking, the potential for significant economic complementarity was small. Israel's economy was geared toward the West rather than regional markets. The large Egyptian market was mostly too poor to absorb expensive Israeli goods and, at the same time, big enough to be able to satisfy its own needs via domestic production. In fact, some argue that the size and resources of Egypt and Israel render them natural rivals.[65]

The second impact of the economic gap between the two states was more perceptual and is closely linked to the economic ideology of each state. It is difficult to detach the liberal economic perspective of the Israeli government and business community that has emerged since the mid-1980s from the fact that the level of economic development in Israel made entering the global market a viable option. By contrast, in Egypt there was a close connection between the nature of the economy and the more realist, state-centered perspective.[66]

The application of this liberal perspective to Israel's role in the Middle East was most explicitly articulated by Shimon Peres in his book *The New Middle East* (1993). Once again, this approach cannot be detached from the fact that Israel perceived itself as economically much more advanced than its neighbors. In this vision, Israel was to play a central role in advancing the region. While not shared by all Israelis, this was the only explicit and public vision presented to the rest of the world and to the potential Arab partners. Critics of liberal economics often suggest that free trade is the policy of the strong. The economically more advanced actors are likely to gain more in the process of international economic liberalization. In a postconflict situation, this concern over relative gains is likely to be greater. Indeed, it is possible to find various studies making the point that Israel will reap a larger economic dividend from peace.[67]

The concern over the impact of these economic disparities first became clear in the aftermath of the Madrid conference of 1991, with the beginning of the multilateral economic cooperation process. The large and high-profile presence of many Israeli business leaders at the Casablanca conference in 1994 backfired and led to a very hostile response of Egyptians and others. The ambitious Israeli business initiatives were perceived as an Israeli attempt to take over Arab markets and establish Israeli hegemony. Egypt played an important role in discouraging other Arab states from developing economic ties with Israel.[68] The Egyptian opposition needs to be understood, however, in a broader context, in light of Egypt's own traditional aspirations for leadership of the Arab world. Egypt's position led to a greater sensitivity to the impact of the economic disparities with Israel than that expressed by Jordan, which had no such leadership ambitions.[69] Indeed, this sensitivity suggests that the impact of economic considerations should be understood in a broader framework than a purely rational economic cost-benefit analysis.

The fact that the economic power disparities were an obstacle to advancing relations was obvious to most Israeli economists and politicians. In light of sensitivity to the issue of dependency and "Israeli imperialism," the prominent Israeli peace economist Haim Ben-Shahar and his colleagues concluded that as long as peace remained fragile, it made sense to promote economic activities that tended to demonstrate their benefits and increase popular support. It would also be better to refrain from encouraging activities that might be profitable for a narrow sector of the population but that make peace less palatable to broader and politically influential strata of the population.[70] Following the liberal economic logic in this case would undermine rather than promote the transition to peace.

The QIZ agreement was structured in a way that mitigated several of the concerns stemming from the broad economic disparities between the two states. First of all, because this agreement focused on cooperation for the purpose of mutual export, any negative implications for the domestic market in Egypt were less significant. Furthermore, the fact that the size of the Israeli contribution to this project was set in advance (at 11.7 percent) also limited what some would view as the danger of Israeli products expanding disproportionately into Egypt. Economic cooperation agreements can thus be crafted in a manner that would limit the negative impact of power disparities.

The Impact of Third Party Involvement

The central economic peace dividend that led to Sadat's willingness to travel to Jerusalem and to the eventual signing of the peace treaty between Egypt and Israel came from a third party: the United States. The Special International Security Assistance Act of 1979 provided both Egypt and Israel with $7.5 billion in military and economic grants in 1979, at a ratio of 3:2, respectively. While this was a significant sum for Israel, it is important to remember that Israel had already become the largest recipient of U.S. foreign assistance by 1974. From 1971 to today, aid to Israel has averaged more than $2.6 billion per year, two-thirds of this total in military assistance.[71] American aid, however, was more dramatic for the Egyptian side. With the peace treaty, Egypt has become America's second largest aid recipient. While aid to Egypt had already begun in 1975, most of the subsequent aid, both military and economic, was largely a product of Sadat's trip to Jerusalem, and American administrations justified its continuation for years on these grounds. The aid was designed to give Egypt an incentive for making peace with Israel and to replace the substantial quantity of lost economic assistance from the Arab states of the Persian Gulf region, including Saudi Arabia.[72] The yearly package of about $2.3 billion was crucial in helping to ameliorate the problems of the Egyptian economy, the balance of payments crisis, and the surge in foreign debt at the time. The magnitude of the aid was itself large, equal to 10 percent of the Egyptian gross national product (GNP), paid on an annual basis.[73] That American aid served a very important symbolic political purpose is apparent in the fact that the sum Egypt received was beyond its economic capacity to absorb. In fact, development experts believe that had Egypt's economic assistance been based on economic need rather than on political objectives, Egypt would have received only $100 million to $200 million in U.S. assistance.[74]

While the United States did play a crucial economic and political role in bringing about the peace treaty, it failed to exert any meaningful impact on the process of normalization between the two states, at least until recently. Some attempts were made to induce direct cooperation between Egypt and Israel, but they were limited. Congress initially earmarked $5 million for direct trilateral (Israeli-Egyptian-American) cooperation. However, in practice, U.S. Agency for International Development money was not used for establishing tangible projects in the field. Money was given for so-called joint research projects. It was basically divided among the three partners for financing research in their respective universities. While the United States invested about $90 million in this program until 2001, it produced no concrete achievements.[75] Annual aid to Egypt was a reward for signing the peace treaty and a tool to entrench the peace, but it offered the Americans little leverage in terms of pressuring Egypt to interact more directly with Israel. Only in the late 1990s did the Americans change their strategy and begin to use their potentially enormous economic leverage to promote direct Egyptian-Israeli interaction.

One thing is clear. The QIZ dynamics would not have been put into motion at all without the American initiative or if the Americans had agreed earlier to sign a bilateral FTA with Egypt. As described previously, for the Egyptians, the QIZ was a second-best option after the FTA. The driving logic for them to eventually sign the QIZ was economic, not political. The American rationale, on the other hand, was political rather than economic. Economically, the United States had nothing to gain from promoting the QIZ. Egyptian exports to the United States amount to less than 1 percent of American imports. The QIZ initiative was crafted specifically to use economic tools and the attractiveness of the American market to promote peaceful relations between Israel, Jordan, and Egypt. Robert Zoellick, the former U.S. trade representative, explained the American rationale behind the QIZ: "It is a concrete, practical result of President Bush's plan to promote closer U.S. trade ties with the Middle East so as to strengthen development, openness, and peaceful economic links between Israel and its neighbors. These industrial zones will create a daily opportunity to build business and personal relationships among Egyptians, Israelis, and Americans."[76] It is also interesting to note that once the QIZ was in place, American companies also made a direct contribution to its operation by advising Egyptian manufacturers what components they should buy in Israel and at times by actually making the business connections between Egyptian and Israeli manufacturers.[77]

The QIZ initiative was part of a broader plan by the Bush administration to create the Middle East Free Trade Area (MEFTA). To advance this initiative, the United States has signed, beyond its 1985 FTA with Israel, additional FTAs with Morocco, Bahrain, and Jordan, as well as nine Trade and Investment Framework Agreements (TIFA) and two Bilateral Investment Treaties (BITs). The MEFTA initiative, in turn, is part of a broader Middle East initiative, which also includes the ambitious Middle East Partnership Initiative (MEPI), aimed at promoting economic, political/civil, and educational reforms in the region.[78]

In 1978–1979, the United States used its promise of economic aid to bring about the completion of the peace treaty between Israel and Egypt. It was not able to use its economic leverage later in pushing for greater direct interaction between the two countries. The QIZ initiative offers exactly that necessary mechanism to tie the benefits of the American market to direct, even if managed, Egyptian-Israeli cooperation. However, one should remember that if a regional FTA is envisioned to be in place by 2013, then the window of opportunity for the QIZ incentive to work is not very wide. Current assessments do not view the QIZ as a major success. On the one hand, the number of zones increased, more than six hundred companies qualified to participate in them, and QIZ-related exports initially seemed quite impressive (nearly $4 billion in exports and $49 million in imports for Israel in the first four quarters after the agreement came into force). On the other hand, this increase came against the backdrop of a sharp decline in trade in 2001. The project also did not generate the extent of foreign direct investment (FDI) expected by the Egyptian government ($1.65 billion in non-oil and gas FDI for 2005, while the government expected to attract $5 billion in investment via the QIZ). In addition, the treaty helped avoid major layoffs in the textile industry but hardly resolved Egypt's enormous challenge of creating at least 300,000 jobs per year to match its fast-growing workforce. The treaty helped the Egyptian textile industry buy time but did not redress the underlying causes of Egypt's uncompetitive industries. This form of managed-trade-for-peace can have only a limited impact due to economic realities. Due to the very different industrial character of the Egyptian and Israeli economies, the prospects of close cooperation, even with American encouragement, are limited.[79] Finally, recent requests by Egypt and Israel to further expand the number of QIZ areas in Egypt have met with little enthusiasm from the USTR. It was suggested that the American textile lobby is unhappy about further expansion of Egyptian textile exports to the American market.[80] Such domestic concerns, if they indeed exist, will also limit the ability of the United States to enhance the capacities of the QIZ.

THE HISTORY OF Egyptian-Israeli relations since Sadat's visit to Jerusalem suggests a dynamic interaction between political and economic logics. The relative importance of political and economic considerations has changed over time.

For example, the initial logic behind the peace treaty was economic for the Egyptian regime but political for the Israeli government. Once the treaty was signed, however, the political logic became dominant on the Egyptian side, with economic normalization directly linked to political progress on the Palestinian front. At the same time, on the Israeli side, greater attention was given to the economic component, since Israelis believed that only economic interaction could give substance and hence credibility in the long run to the treaty signed in 1979.

All things considered, over the years economic factors played a limited role in warming up the peace because of a lack of significant perceived economic gains for Egypt from economic interaction with Israel. Three significant changes created a new impetus to develop economic ties (albeit of a still very limited scope) with Israel in 2004: a significant economic benefit from coproducing with Israel goods for export to the United States; development of a close-knit government–big business coalition in Egypt, which has a strong interest in economic liberalization and global competition and is therefore more attentive to potential economic gains and losses; and an explicit commitment of the United States to play its economic cards (i.e., access to its market) in order to promote direct cooperation between Israel and Egypt.

Despite obvious difficulties, this agreement provides an important opportunity to warm up the peace. Some room for optimism is warranted. Immediately after the signing of the QIZ, a large number of Egyptian business leaders began exploring the agreement's economic potential. Egyptians now call for a larger number of QIZ areas, beyond those initially included. An interview with a senior manager of the Israeli-owned Delta-Egypt factory revealed the agreement's inadvertent impact on people when economic stakes are created. He argued that once a factory is built and jobs are created, ordinary people have a direct stake in the plant because it maintains their livelihood, and they thus have an indirect interest in promoting peace. Asked about the fortunes of the Delta-Egypt factory during the extremely difficult days of the second intifada, he recalled that while the factory walls were covered with pro-Palestinian and anti-Israeli slogans, the main concern of the workers and their families was not that they were working in an Israeli factory but that, due to Israeli security concerns, the factory would be shut down.[81] This is peacemaking at its best, without romantic slogans, but with real, direct economic impact on ordinary people.

THE LIMITS OF PEACEMAKING FROM ABOVE

Jordan and Israel's Stalled Peace Process

WHILE THE PEACE TREATY between Jordan and Israel was signed only in October 1994, fifteen years after the treaty between Egypt and Israel, many felt that it had greater potential for generating a "warm peace." Indeed, the history of relations between Jordan and Israel has included both enduring conflict and tacit strategic cooperation. Jordan fought against the new state of Israel in 1948 and again in 1967, consequently losing its control over the west bank of the Jordan River and over East Jerusalem. Since then, both countries have been part of a complex triangular relationship—Israeli, Jordanian, and Palestinian. Until 1988, Jordan continued to aspire to regain its control over the West Bank, but in that year it decided to terminate all of its administrative activity across the Jordan River. Since then, it has supported the creation of an independent Palestinian state. Over the years, there has been an ongoing dialogue between Jordanian and Israeli officials. At many points in time, both states believed they faced the threat of Palestinian nationalism.[1] However, tacit cooperation did not develop into an official public discussion of peace until 1994.

The economic dimension of the transition to peace between Jordan and Israel, unlike the case of Egypt, was clearly expressed and institutionalized within the peace treaty itself. Whereas in the treaty between Egypt and Israel strategic and security elements were dominant and the economic dimension received minor attention, the Jordanian-Israeli treaty explicitly referred to the desire to develop economic cooperation between the two states. The treaty was accompanied by a series of agreements regarding cooperation in various fields such as trade, transportation, energy, and joint development of the Red Sea cities of Eilat and Aqaba. A year after the peace treaty went into force, a trade and economic cooperation treaty was signed on October 25, 1995.[2] In December 2004, an upgraded trade agreement was signed, and it called for free trade between the two states on most goods by 2010.[3]

Given the history of Jordanian-Israeli relations and the strong commitment of the late King Hussein to the peace process, many observers were very optimistic about the treaty's prospects. Trade and tourism did grow between the two states, enhanced by the QIZ agreement signed in 1997 (discussed later in this chapter). This growth came to a halt with the outbreak of the second intifada, but even in the most politically difficult periods, economic interaction did not stop. Since the year 2000, the economic interaction has once again regained some positive dynamics. Trade has increased, new QIZ zones have been created, and the two states have negotiated a new and more comprehensive trade agreement to replace that of 1995. The data show that despite the political crises, trade expanded continuously. Israeli exports to Jordan climbed from $21 million in 1999 to $39 million in 2000, to $52 million in 2001, and up to $87 million in 2003. Imports from Jordan climbed from $20 million in 1999 to $37 million in 2000, to $42 million in 2001, and up to $45 million in 2003. By the end of 2007, Israeli exports were up to $250.7 million, an impressive increase. Jordanian imports, although still much lower, also increased, to $54.4 million.[4] At the same time, many of the projects envisioned early on did not materialize or got stalled along the way. Tourism to Jordan has also been relatively steady over the years, with approximately 150,000 visitors a year since the treaty was signed. While the numbers are higher than in the Egyptian case, here as well there is a dramatic gap between tourism from Israel to Jordan and vice versa. According to the Jordanian Ministry of Tourism and Antiquities, 276,069 Israeli tourists traveled to Jordan in 2007. However, only 3,724 Jordanians visited Israel in the same year.[5]

Thus, on the official level, results are mixed. Optimists could point to the continuation of cooperation despite many challenging experiences. Pessimists could point to the unfulfilled potential and the obvious negative impact of the ongoing conflict between Israel and the Palestinians. However, on the popular level, developments within Jordan have been very bleak and difficult for optimists to reinterpret. A public opinion poll in 1997 showed that 81 percent of Jordanians thought Israelis remained their enemies.[6] The antinormalization movement has become very wide and well institutionalized, leading to a situation in which the notion of "normalization" is anathema for most Jordanians. One can conclude that the Jordanian-Israeli peace is a cold peace. Most bilateral bones of contention were resolved and official intergovernmental interaction exists, along with some economic interaction, but the last remains very limited and is not spilling over to broader segments of society or to a wider variety of issue areas. Currently, the array of committees and subcommittees that were created to manage various aspects of bilateral cooperation are doing very little. Numerous interesting initiatives at the local level (e.g., people-to-people activities between Eilat and Aqaba) have been raised and then dropped.[7]

Many factors caused the disillusionment regarding real normalization and a warmer peace between the two states. On the political front, a rather standard list of events and developments is being routinely cited as poisoning the relations: the decision of former prime minister Benjamin Netanyahu's government to open a tunnel next to the foundations of the Jerusalem Haram a-Sharif, which led to violent protests, land confiscations in East Jerusalem, and the building of the new residential neighborhood of Har Homa in early 1997; the murder of seven Israeli schoolgirls by a Jordanian soldier shortly thereafter; the failed attempt by Israeli Mossad agents to assassinate Hamas leader Khalid Mashal in Amman; and the violent and bloody Israeli-Palestinian confrontations since the beginning of the second intifada (also known as the al-Aqsa intifada). Untangling the nature of peacemaking efforts between these two states shows that the economic rationale has been and still is of crucial importance for Jordan in its relations with Israel. This case, even more so than the Egyptian case, highlights the importance of distinguishing between official or cold peace and normalization.

The Economic Potential of Peace

Economic factors played an important role in the late King Hussein's decision to pursue a peace treaty with Israel. The potential economic benefits from peace are calculated based upon the existing costs of continued conflict and the potential benefits from transition to peace. On the eve of the peace treaty with Israel, Jordan was in a dire economic situation that threatened its political stability. To begin with, Jordan faces serious ongoing economic challenges given that its market is small, the country is poorly endowed with natural resources, and it is highly dependent on foreign aid. During the 1970s and the oil boom, Jordan's economy bloomed, with high levels of foreign aid from the Persian Gulf states and the remittances of Jordanians working there. By the 1980s, however, foreign aid had sharply declined and GNP per capita, incomes, and living standards had fallen drastically. By 1990, unemployment had reached 20 percent. The Gulf War of 1991 made things worse because Jordan was penalized by the oil-producing states for its support of Iraq. At the same time, the American-led embargo on Iraq also applied to Jordan, as Jordan was an important trading partner with Iraq.

Jordan found itself in the early 1990s in a serious recession and with a soaring external debt. Another economic pressure that likely contributed to the specific timing of the treaty stemmed from the Oslo Accords, a development in Israeli-Palestinian relations that caught the Jordanians by surprise. On September 13, 1993, Israel and the Palestine Liberation Organization (PLO) signed the joint Declaration of Principles in Oslo. Three weeks later, Prime Minister Yitzhak Rabin visited King Hussein, offering a peace treaty with Israel so as to allow Jordan to gain economic advantages in the West Bank before Israel and the PLO began implementing the Declaration of Principles. On April 29, 1994, Israel and the Palestinian Authority signed the Paris protocol, which codified the preexisting customs union between Israeli and Palestinian markets. While Jordan had a strong economic interest in expanding its preexisting economic ties with the West Bank, the feeling was that the Palestinian market was going to be linked mainly to the Israeli market and that the Jordanian market would consequently suffer big losses.[8]

Against this backdrop, King Hussein concluded that the only way for Jordan to regain its massive foreign aid, reduce its external debt, and develop its major resource (tourism) was by making a peace agreement with Israel.[9] The expected economic dividend was large, and its promise was mostly fulfilled. Since the beginning of the peace process, many governments, led by the United States, have canceled the Jordanian debt. At the beginning of 1995, the United States forgave $700 million of Jordan's debt. The peace process led to the rapid development and expansion of Jordan's tourism industry, which by 1995 was contributing more than 10 percent of Jordan's GDP. There was also growth in foreign investments in Jordan and a greater willingness of Western governments and international organizations to support Jordan's economic reforms and to finance new projects in various economic fields.[10] In 1994, on the eve of the peace treaty, FDI into Jordan amounted to $3 million. By 1997, this figure had jumped up to $361 million and had more than doubled, to $815 million, in 2000. By 2006, FDI had reached in excess of a staggering $3 billion.[11] The QIZ agreement signed in 1997 between Jordan, the United States, and Israel led to a sharp rise in exports to the United States. In 2000, Jordan signed a free trade agreement with the United States (its specific benefits are discussed later). On the Jordanian side, there was thus a clear and strong economic logic behind signing the peace treaty with Israel in 1994.

On the Israeli side, the outlook for economic gains was smaller. Potential Jordanian exports to Israel were seen as relatively minor. There are many Israeli products, such as processed food, electronics, chemicals, and industrial machinery, that can be exported to Jordan. However, the Jordanian market for these products remains small.[12] Beyond trade, Israeli and Jordanian academics and Israeli business leaders have pointed to several joint projects in the fields of infrastructure (water, transportation) and environment that have important potential. A proposal was developed to dig a canal that would link the Red Sea with the Dead Sea, a project that was to offer a solution to the water problems of Jordan, Israel, and the Palestinians. Plans were made to close the air terminal in Eilat, thus making available an important piece of land for the development of hotels, and to build a new terminal in the neighboring Jordanian city of Aqaba that would serve both countries. Plans were made for cooperation in the provision of electrical power, for major transportation projects, and for environmental cooperation in the delicate area of the Gulf of Aqaba. While many such plans for joint industrial projects exist on paper or have even been negotiated, little has happened on the ground.[13] In order to better understand, however, how this rather broad perspective of economic gains translated into the politics of peacemaking, one must carefully determine the domestic winners and losers in this process and their relative impact on policy making.

Domestic Winners and Losers in the Transition to Peace

On the Jordanian side, the main beneficiary from the peace treaty and the economic dividend that followed was the monarchy in general and the king specifically. It has been argued that at a very basic level the monarchy's policies are driven by its desire to maintain "budget security." The government is preoccupied with ensuring the financial flows necessary for its survival, which means using economic tools to maintain the political support of its two main support groups: the Transjordanians, who control the public sector in Jordan, and the Jordanian business community, which is mostly Palestinian.[14] The deteriorating economic conditions were beginning to threaten the regime's security, and riots in 1989 were an indicator of this growing risk. These riots followed the government's decision to raise prices, as part of Jordan's IMF recovery program.[15]

The expected peace dividends were closely related to the changing economic views of King Hussein and his brother, Crown Prince Hassan, who were beginning to appreciate the implications of globalization for Jordan, the need for economic liberalization, and, consequently, the need for foreign investment and aid from the United States. King Hussein was personally committed to the peace process and to normalizing relations with Israel, a commitment that went beyond the specific economic needs of Jordan. The central impact of the economic rationale, however, was more apparent under the leadership of his son, King Abdullah. Abdullah began his rule with a less sentimental approach than his father had toward peace with Israel. He focused on dealing with Jordan's economic problems first, rather than on relations with Israel. However, as a strong believer in liberal economics, King Abdullah came to realize by the second year of his rule that for economic reasons there had to be political stability, which would allow economic growth, the creation of new employers and jobs, and the expansion of foreign currency reserves. Abdullah had seen that an official, "cold" peace was simply not enough to draw foreign investors, entrepreneurs, and tourists. Getting them would require actual normalization of relations. He consequently decided to focus on building direct economic ties with Israel and lending his good offices for mediating between Israel and the Palestinians.[16]

The active support of the Jordanian royal house was enough to bring about the Washington Declaration of 1994 and then the peace treaty with Israel. It was also strong enough to protect the treaty from mounting opposition over time. However, it was clearly not enough to generate a significant process of normalization, which would increase interaction—economic, political, and cultural—between Israelis and Jordanians. In fact, despite many efforts to persuade people to believe otherwise, the overall perception was that the peace treaty was the peace of the king, serving only a small group of elites and not Jordanian society as a whole.

Societal opposition became wider and better organized over the years. One important factor leading to the expansion of opposition was the fact that people did not feel that they received a clear economic dividend from the peace. Although public officials tried to be careful in their promises regarding the economic benefits of peace, an expectation of a large peace dividend was fostered. The regime argued, for example, that the reduction of Jordan's huge $6.6 billion debt could be solved only through a pro-Israel U.S. Congress. While Congress did reduce Jordan's debt by almost $200 million, and Britain followed suit, the expectations of ordinary Jordanians were greatly inflated. The regime promised a sharp increase in foreign investments and in tourism. Consequently, 82 percent of the population thought in 1994 that the economic situation would improve as a result of the peace process. However, these expectations were not fulfilled. While the United States did give Jordan $1.65 billion in grants, loans, and loan guarantees between 1990 and 1997, Jordanian expectations and needs were still unmet. Tourism did not surge. An economic slowdown occurred in the second half of the 1990s, and to make things worse, a severe drought prevented Israel from fulfilling its commitment of transferring water to Jordan.[17] Against this disappointment, ideological and religious factors could play a greater role in enhancing opposition.

The peace with Israel created for the first time a convergence of interests between two very different opposition groups within Jordan that rejected the peace and any normalization. On the one hand was the Muslim Brotherhood, along with its political party, the Islamic Action Front (IAF). They opposed the very notion of the existence of Israel on Palestinian soil and stressed what they perceived to be the dark, "Jewish" side of the state of Israel. On the other hand were various pan-Arabist groups, which were always opponents of the monarchic regime in Jordan. They perceived peace with Israel to be a betrayal of the Arab cause. Both groups, who had never seen see eye to eye, now converged around the Palestinian cause and opposition to the peace with Israel.[18]

The most effective opposition group consisted of professional associations. By the mid-1990s, these associations were controlled by Islamists and were playing perhaps the most active role in opposing and preventing expansion of normalization. The power of these associations stemmed from legislation dating back to the 1950s, which stipulated membership as a condition for most professionals to work in their field. This meant that these associations had tremendous power over their members. Members depended upon these associations for their pensions, unemployment payments, health care, and so on. These associations began threatening to oust members who somehow participated in active normalization with Israel, and that threat was very effective, especially for engineers, doctors, dentists, and lawyers, who would be barred from practice if banned by their respective associations.[19]

The theoretical framework would suggest that the private business sector be viewed as a potential domestic actor that would push for greater normalization.

In Jordan, over the years, most private enterprises were relatively underdeveloped, small, and oriented toward local needs.[20] However, like Egypt in the 1990s, a new young business elite has been emerging in Jordan. The mostly Palestinian business community in Jordan has been the main benefactor of the IMF structural adjustment and the economic liberalization process. Export-oriented business leaders came to appreciate the huge potential benefits from cooperation with Israel, especially in the framework of the QIZ agreement, which allowed them to sell goods manufactured with an Israeli component, duty free, to the American market. Especially after the large market for exports to Iraq was closed, the possibility of cooperating with Israeli companies in textile production offered a new lifeline.

However, Jordanian entrepreneurs wishing to advance business with Israel faced many obstacles, which Markus Bouillon describes very effectively. Consequently, only a small, emerging young elite, with close social and kinship ties to the government and palace, could afford to enter into business partnerships with Israelis. Preexisting businesses, in particular the small and medium-sized enterprises, awaited the day they could return to the Iraqi market and in the meantime joined the growing antinormalization movement in large numbers. The elite young business leaders engaged in joint ventures or acted as consultants for foreign companies and gained a reputation for helping Jordan's overall economic development. This, in turn, helped them attain significant political influence.[21] This business elite continues to enjoy close cooperation with the government. Unlike other individuals who wish to interact with Israel, they are immune to the threats of the professional associations. They have their own lawyers (lawyers belonging to the association would not represent them), and they are protected by the state.[22] This business elite also needed the protection of the state from the pressures of the public sector (dominated by East Bank Jordanians, i.e., Transjordanians) to redistribute resources in their favor.[23]

The promotion of economic normalization with Israel is therefore in the hands of the royal house, which was relatively active in supporting such normalization, and a group of powerful business leaders. This in itself is sufficient to push forward QIZ-based cooperation. However, this coalition has dramatically failed to persuade broader segments of society to become engaged in the process. As such, the various positive mechanisms that economic interaction can offer for promoting peace have still not kicked in. The gap between official attitudes and popular opinion is wide. Unlike the Egyptian case, in which the government itself was interested in maintaining only a cold peace with Israel, the Jordanian royal house, at least until recently, has consistently supported warming up the peace. This support was not enough, however, to change public perceptions, and it in fact served only to enhance the tension between state and society. Many people in the street draw a distinction between "peace" (i.e., the diplomatic peace process that they could not control) and "normalization" (which is the process they believe they can resist at the individual and societal levels).[24] This empirical distinction serves to highlight the need for the conceptual distinction made here between the two stages of transition to peace.

The tensions between the monarchy-led peace process and societal opposition to normalization raise an interesting issue related to the democratic peace argument. One of the most common arguments about ensuring peaceful relations between states focuses on the nature of their regimes and suggests that democracies are more peaceful vis-à-vis one another. However, as Jack Snyder and Edward Mansfield have demonstrated, this argument may work for stable democracies, but the process of democratization in itself may actually increase the risk of violence.[25] The Jordanian case demonstrates another difficulty in the democratization process not previously discussed, namely, the tension between the promotion of democratization and the promotion of peace in postconflict situations. King Hussein started an ambitious process of political liberalization in Jordan after the food riots of 1989. He permitted parliamentary elections, the creation and functioning of political parties, and greater freedom of expression. However, once the king decided to pursue the peace process with Israel in a forceful manner, he had to contend with the strong opposition of the Islamic parties.[26] Their presence in the Jordanian parliament made things difficult. For example, when the government wanted to abolish laws that contradicted the peace treaty (e.g., the 1953 law banning trade with Israel), it had to deal with fierce opposition during public debate in the parliament.[27]

The need to contend with this growing opposition led to a gradual curtailment of many of the freedoms awarded during the liberalization process. The government changed the electoral system to a one person–one vote system, a change that greatly undermined the power of the Islamist groups in parliament. It adopted a harder line against the Islamic opposition and became less tolerant to opposition in general, including the various activities of the antinormalization movement (such as their publication of a "blacklist" of normalization supporters). While the government justified some of its actions by arguing that such activities of the antinormalization coalition were infringing on other people's rights, many observers came to conclude that the process of political liberalization developed in direct correlation to advancement in the peace process.[28]

On the issue of peace dividends, not only did many people not participate in any economic dividend but the antinormalization coalition sought to prove to the public that the retreat from democratization was another undesirable outcome of peace. It is therefore easy to observe the dilemma facing both decision makers and third parties involved in the process. On the one hand, it may be easier for an authoritarian regime to move to peace with a former enemy, should it have the incentives to do so. It does not have to deal with opposition, or it can deal with it forcefully and therefore face lesser domestic constraints in making such a dramatic foreign policy shift. On the other hand, however, without representative democracy, peace forced from above cannot easily trickle down and win the hearts of the people. Peace will belong to the elites, and it will be very difficult to develop real normalization that extends beyond high-level, big business economic normalization. (This problem will become relevant again in chapter 5, in the discussion of Japan's relations with the Republic of Korea.)

The reader may conclude that the main source of opposition to the peace treaty was religious and ideological rather than economic. As was the case with Egypt, I do not suggest that such factors were unimportant, for obviously they were. However, I contend that the lack of a clear economic dividend for broad segments of society made it easier for such opposition to bloom. Although the Islamic parties and the professional associations held extreme views regarding normalization with Israel, it is important to remember that, as Israel's first ambassador to Jordan, Shimon Shamir, argues, the majority of Jordanian society seems to favor a pragmatic approach.[29] One segment of the antinormalization group comprises pragmatic people, mostly from the middle class, who were suffering economically because of the Gulf War of 1991 and felt that it was worth trying the peace route to improve their conditions. As described previously, their unrealistic expectations for a quick and major economic improvement led to disenchantment, sending many of them into the antinormalization camp.[30] However, it is exactly this group that could swing back to the peace camp if it becomes apparent that significant economic benefits would result.

The most practical illustration of this argument is the testimony of Dov Lautman, the CEO of Delta-Galil, which was the first company to open a textile factory in Irbid, Jordan. That factory is now very successful and provides a livelihood for twenty-four hundred workers. Lautman describes the intimate interaction between the Israeli and Jordanian managers and how they managed to create a "win-win" situation in Irbid.[31] This type of experience is the reason why it is both inaccurate as well as harmful for decision makers and scholars alike to conclude too easily that religious and ideological considerations have a sweeping and unavoidable detrimental impact on relations between the states.

The interaction between material economic considerations and ideational ones is also aptly described by Marc Lynch, who examines Jordan's foreign policy, including its transition to peace with Israel, by focusing on the changing Jordanian identity. He does so by examining the public discourse in several public spheres. Lynch suggests that Jordan's decision to sign the peace treaty with Israel has to be understood within the context of the collapse of the Arabist public sphere during the Gulf War, the transformation of Jordanian preferences toward the West Bank after the severing of ties in 1988, and, consequently, the decision to emphasize state interests and reinterpret them so that anything that benefited Jordan was by definition good for Arab interests. These identity changes led to the signing of the peace treaty in 1994.[32] However, despite his constructivist, interpretive understanding of the changes in Jordanian foreign policy, Lynch still concludes that the competition between different interpretations of the meaning of peace with Israel for Jordan was largely influenced by material factors. "Popular opposition to the treaty," suggests Lynch, "was not foreordained, or inherent in the Palestinian origin of much of the population, Islamic beliefs, or Arab culture." It was the combination of Israeli behavior, the fact that the promised economic prosperity failed to materialize, and the growing political repression of political opposition that helped to persuade many Jordanians that the price of peace was much higher than any concrete benefits. Economic conditions fed the debates about the value of the new identity. Since the "peace camp" identity had partly been sold with the promise of regional economic prosperity, the failure of prosperity to materialize undermined more than just economic indicators.[33]

While the peace process became the center of a prolonged public debate in Jordan, in Israel there was an overwhelming consensus supporting both the treaty and the economic agreements associated with it. This consensus was based on both political and economic rationales, and the interaction between them is interesting. On the one hand, the central Israeli motivation was political—to strengthen and give meaning to the peace treaty with Jordan. In fact, Israel did not foresee the impressive success of the QIZ agreement and the dramatic expansion of Jordanian exports to the United States that followed it. However, once it moved on to negotiate with the Jordanians, Israeli negotiators often failed to perceive that this economic relationship was indeed different and that the approach to such negotiations should be different from any other bilateral economic negotiation. Israelis had very little economic information regarding the Jordanian economy and failed to understand that, beyond the problematic regional context, there was also at that time a large gap in the Jordanian understanding of the nature, dynamics, and potential of the global trading system. This created many misunderstandings and problems.[34]

As for the more specific economic interests involved, by the time the peace treaty with Jordan was signed, Israeli business leaders were openly and strongly supporting the peace process. This was not the case in 1978, when, on the eve of the peace treaty with Egypt, there were few signs of any active involvement of the Israeli business community.

Both the relative power of the business community and its new interest in promoting peace were the result of a significant process of economic liberalization that Israel had been undergoing since 1985. This process, which gradually opened up the Israeli economy to the global market and exposed Israeli businesses to the opportunities and threats of globalization, had two effects. It strengthened the political power of that part of the business community that succeeded in "going global," and it led many business leaders to conclude that economic growth depended not only on further economic liberalization but also on a resolution of the regional conflict.[35] As Dan Propper, CEO of Osem (a large Israeli food conglomerate) and president of the Manufacturers Association between 1993 and 1999, put it, "In a world where globalization is taking over, in a world of large economic blocs such as NAFTA, the EU, Mercosur, or Southeast Asia, there is no doubt that a country like Israel, developed as it is but with a population of only 6 million, has no place existing as an independent economic entity competing with world giants. Neither can Jordan or Egypt nor the rest of our neighbors, whose scope of economic activity combined is still smaller than Israel's GNP. Consequently, only the combined force of all these states can lead us to economic prosperity."[36]

Over the years, the business elite in Israel enjoyed close personal and professional ties with the political elite. With the election of Yitzhak Rabin's Labor government, the close ideological affinity of this business elite with Prime Minister Rabin created an even stronger link. The impact of these highly motivated business tycoons increased once the large business associations, namely the Manufacturers Association and the Federation of Israeli Chambers of Commerce, entered the picture. A division of labor emerged between the Rabin government and big business in which the government's peace initiatives created new opportunities for business people and the latter in turn took advantage of these opportunities and stimulated economic growth that was supposed to create the required public support for the peace process.[37] It is interesting that in Egypt President Mubarak also preferred to have the business community pressure him for action first, in order to legitimize the signing of the QIZ. A business interest is easier to sell to the public than an ideological or strategic shift.

A concrete and crucial example of the impact of private business is the initiation of the QIZ, which did not originate in the U.S. Congress but was initiated by Dov Lautman, CEO of Delta-Galil, the pioneer of textile production in Jordan. Lautman discovered that in moving production to Jordan, his products no longer met the rules-of-origin requirements in the U.S.-Israeli FTA, thus undermining the basic economic logic of moving production to Jordan (i.e., cost reduction). After raising awareness of this problem, the Israelis approached the Americans to try to find a solution.[38]

That being said, the impact of the business community on peacemaking, namely on promoting normalization, was still limited. When examining the role of private business in the economics of peacemaking with Jordan, one finds that a relatively small group of prominent business leaders is involved in the process. It is not a topic that is of interest to the whole private sector. With the few exceptions already mentioned, most beneficiaries of the QIZ agreement with Jordan are small companies belonging to traditional industries in decline. The QIZ offered an important boost for such small factories in the periphery, such as those producing zippers, thread, simple packaging, and the like. For such factories, the scope of trade with Jordan and later with Egypt, while still generally small, is very significant.[39] Such companies then benefited from the process, but given their nature, they were not the ones expected to push it forward at the political level. This positive impact of the QIZ on the periphery is not well publicized. Large segments of society, most notably those that are less privileged, believed that peace would largely benefit the elites. Some even suggested that while the elites were reaping the peace dividends, inequality, income disparity, unemployment, and poverty have grown.[40] This insight suggests that the problem of the trickling down peace dividends is not unique to nondemocratic regimes and is relevant also to a democracy with wide internal socioeconomic gaps.[41]

A second problem that limited the ability of business entrepreneurs to develop extensive cooperation schemes with the Jordanians appears to be much more mundane but not less important. The experience of the vast majority of Israeli entrepreneurs who attempted to promote business schemes with Jordan shows that although there was basic governmental support for such ties, these initiatives faced nearly insurmountable bureaucratic obstacles. Whereas on the Jordanian side, it was argued, the bureaucracy was efficient, on the Israeli side every step of a new project involved getting numerous permits, surviving bureaucratic politics, and dealing with the opposition of environmentalist groups. This process was very long and very often led to the abandonment of the project. To illustrate this problem, consider the following story. Gili Dekel, a wealthy and visionary Israeli businessman, proposed in 1995 the creation of an Israeli-Jordanian industrial park, to be called the "Jordan Gateway." Already aware of the difficulty of dealing with the Israeli bureaucracy, he decided to build the park on the Jordanian side of the border. While the Jordanian bureaucracy was very efficient in finalizing the initial steps needed to get the project going, the project got stuck in Israel in a maze of bureaucratic permits and regulations. Up to June 2003, even an agreement to settle the transit arrangements between the two sides of the border was not signed because the Defense Ministry could not reach agreement with the Airport Authority regarding armed security personnel at the crossing. Dekel concluded, and many agreed with him, that the state simply did not have the organizational capacity to deal with such major transnational cooperation projects. Shimon Peres also points to these bureaucratic difficulties as major stumbling blocks in building cooperation. There is no efficient institutional framework to coordinate such initiatives, to guide them from above, and to get private business involved in the various regional projects envisioned after the peace treaty.[42] This institutional problem comes into sharper focus when compared with the high level of institutional efficiency in the government–big business cooperation in both Japan and Germany after World War II.

The Impact of Economic Power Disparities

The economic power disparities between Israel and Jordan on the eve of the peace treaty and to this day remain very wide. In 1994, Jordan's GDP was less than 10 percent of the Israeli GDP (approximately $6 billion compared to $75 billion), and its per capita GDP stood at approximately $3,500, compared to almost $16,000 in Israel.[43] Whereas in the Egyptian case the disparities in economic development and per capita GDP were somewhat mitigated by the huge size of the Egyptian market, the Jordanian market was very small, only three-fourths the size of Israel's. While most of Israel's exports derive from industrial manufacturing, this sector contributed only 19 percent of Jordan's exports in 1994. Total Jordanian exports in 1997 were less than 10 percent of the amount of Israel's total exports.[44]

These wide economic disparities were fully acknowledged by negotiators on both sides. In the Washington Declaration, the two sides had already acknowledged that "imbalances and disparities are a root cause of extremism."[45] King Hussein and Prime Minister Rabin, as well as the negotiating teams, wanted to present the peace and the economic cooperation that was to follow as means of dramatically narrowing this gap between the two economies.

The negative impact of the disparities was undeniable. To begin with, the broad disparities and the dramatically different nature of the two economies limited the number of potential fields for cooperation. To this day, the fact that the QIZ-based cooperation is limited primarily to the textile industry is a central factor in its weak impact. Both sides sought to expand the QIZ to other sectors, such as furniture making, but that did not work due to the fact that this sector is not well developed in Israel. Even in the agricultural sector, Israel does not buy agricultural products from Jordan (nor Egypt) due to health concerns stemming from lack of appropriate health standards and control in Jordanian agriculture.[46]

Beyond that, the negative implications of the disparities were evident throughout the negotiations. In the negotiations leading to the trade and cooperation agreement of October 1995, the Jordanian representatives in the joint economic committee were very concerned about the negative implications of economic cooperation between the relatively large market of Israel and the small Jordanian market. Concern about the impact of the power disparities led the Jordanians to oppose the creation of a free trade area. Their unwillingness to commit to an FTA with Israel was partly related to the deep-seated fear of Israeli domination and concern regarding the ability of Jordanian domestic production to compete against Israel's technological edge.[47] An agreement on banking and investment also was not achieved due to the Jordanian concern that Israeli money would take over the Jordanian market.

The trade agreement that was reached was asymmetric. The Jordanians received better terms for selling in Israel than vice versa. The Israeli ambassador to Jordan at the time, Shimon Shamir, argued that Israel was willing to sign an asymmetric trade agreement in order to alleviate some of the Jordanian fears.[48]

On the Israeli side, the trade agreement was perceived to be an important economic tool to promote the political goal of advancing the process of normalization. When Israeli industrialists voiced concerns in front of Prime Minister Rabin about the danger of competition from cheap Jordanian labor, Rabin offered reassurances that the government would help them.[49]

Only in 2005 did Israel and Jordan renegotiate the asymmetric 1995 treaty and conclude a broader trade agreement, under which more than 60 percent of bilateral trade between the states would be duty free by 2010. The terms of this agreement are much more symmetric than those of the 1995 pact, under which about 10 percent of Israeli exports to Jordan enjoyed a limited 15 percent tariff benefit, whereas more than 50 percent of Jordanian exports to Israel enjoyed a full tariff exemption. It is interesting that in describing the background for this agreement, the Israeli Ministry of Industry, Trade, and Labor points to the increased capacity of both sides for economic cooperation vis-à-vis export markets. The main change has taken place in Jordan, which since 1995 has joined the World Trade Organization (WTO) and signed free trade agreements with the European Union and the United States.[50] In other words, the Jordanian economy grew stronger, and the ability of the Jordanian market to participate in the global economy has increased. As the Jordanians accumulated successful experiences with free trade, they gained knowledge they did not have in 1995. Their successes and growing comfort with the notion of free trade made it more acceptable to expand the preferential trade agreement with Israel in 2003.

Despite leaders' initial awareness of the problem of power disparities, those disparities still created problems that made it difficult to use economic tools to promote normalization. Public opinion in Jordan clearly was concerned about Israeli economic power. A public opinion poll conducted in 1995 revealed that most Jordanians thought Israel would benefit more from economic interaction; most respondents did not believe Jordan could compete with Israel in most economic areas. Of the Jordanians polled, 39 percent thought that Israel would provide little economic cooperation but considerable manipulation.[51] Given these public sentiments, it was easy for the antinormalization coalition to justify its opposition by arguing that normalization would not only allow Israel to swallow the weaker Arab economies in general but also to exploit the Jordanian system in particular and politically dominate the entire region.[52]

The broad economic disparities also made Jordanian business leaders more skeptical about the prospects of regional cooperation. One Jordanian said in 1994 that "Jordanians have this image of Jews as being master businessmen, and in the end they worry that they will just dominate."[53] At the same time, those wide disparities also meant that, for Israelis, there was a limited economic gain that was linked directly to the Jordanian market. Most Israeli business leaders focused their interests on overseas markets in Asia and Eastern Europe, not on the Middle East itself.[54]

As in the Egyptian case, the wide disparities raised concerns over Israeli "imperialism." Joint ventures in high tech, for example, which from an economic perspective would have made much more sense, became problematic because they would only reinforce Israel's image as a colonial economic power and deter its neighbors from cooperating. One concrete example of the negative impact of the power disparities on cooperation efforts is the failed attempt to establish an Israeli-Jordanian bromine plant on the eastern shore of the Dead Sea. The potential Israeli partner was the Dead Sea Bromine (DSB) company, which tried to negotiate a deal with the Arab Potash Corporation (APC). The bromine industry was characterized by a large technological gap between Israel and Jordan. Consequently, the Israelis assumed that since they were the world's leading producer of bromine products, the Jordanians should be grateful that Israel was willing to invest in their plant. They were overconfident and displayed a patronizing attitude toward their Jordanian counterparts. Eventually, the Jordanians ended up signing a deal with a major American competitor of DSB, thus establishing an independent bromine plant in Jordan that could become a serious competitor of the Israeli firm.[55] Several Israelis involved in the economic negotiations with the Jordanians also observed this patronizing approach and suggested that, due to the wide power disparities, Israelis could afford to be more generous toward their Jordanian neighbors. Moti Krystal, who followed the implementation of the peace treaty with Jordan, noted that Israeli negotiators often failed to realize the negative potential implication of the power disparities as well as the political significance of the negotiations. They did little to reassure the Jordanians and negotiated as if they were negotiating with a country like France.[56]

Thus, economic power disparities posed various problems and limited the ability of governments and private business to use economic interaction according to the liberal vision in order to advance normalization and warm the peace between Israel and Jordan. The disparities initially limited the potential benefits from direct interaction between the two markets, created anxieties on the Jordanian side that were effectively manipulated by the antinormalization movement, and created a problematic, patronizing attitude among some of the Israeli negotiators.

The one field in which power disparities were used as a force for advancing cooperation was that of development cooperation. In this area, the Israeli government, via the MASHAV Center for International Cooperation (part of the Foreign Ministry), is trying to offer Israeli technological know-how for the benefit of Jordanian projects. In 2000, Israel built and fully equipped a state-of-the-art intensive care unit in the Red Crescent Hospital in Amman, which serves the poorest population of the capital. The project included full training of all ICU staff in a series of on-site training courses. In cooperation with Jordan, MASHAV operates a demonstration farm in the Karak region for intensive sheep's milk production and processing, introducing to the country the advanced Awassi sheep, which can provide approximately four times the milk yields of indigenous sheep. The project involves more than four hundred animals, a milking parlor, and a state-of-the-art mini dairy for the production of yogurts and cheeses. In addition, the project's sheep have been used to upgrade local flocks through breeding activities. MASHAV also has a beekeeping demonstration and research project in Irbid. Israel sponsors an ongoing program of cross-border cooperation, training, and transfer of agricultural technology between Kibbutz Yotvata and farmers in the regions of Rahma and Umm-Mutlak.[57] It also sponsors numerous cooperative projects in pest control and environmental issues in areas close to the Israeli-Jordanian border. Such cooperation is less politically sensitive because it does not carry the potentially adverse implications of asymmetric trade interaction.

The Impact of Third Parties

While in comparison to Egypt, Jordan did have direct economic benefits to gain from trading with Israel, it is also clear that King Hussein's decision to conclude a peace treaty with Israel was closely linked to his interest in several economic benefits stemming from third parties, starting with the United States. In light of its dire economic conditions and the regime's policy of "budget security," described earlier, Jordan desperately needed to negotiate a substantial reduction in the size of its external debt. Scott Greenwood suggests that the king's support for the Madrid peace process was based on his hope of winning cancellation of Jordan's foreign debt.[58] The king was also interested in finding a stable source of financial aid, following the termination of aid previously received from the Gulf oil states, and in increasing foreign investments. All of these goals had little to do directly with Israel. Once the treaty was signed, the United States waived $700 million of Jordan's debt. Jordan received, as part of the treaty itself, an annual sum of $250 million in cash from the United States. In 2001, the official development assistance to Jordan amounted to a whopping $432 million, representing fully 5 percent of the kingdom's total GDP. Then, in May 2003, Jordan received a huge cash grant of $500 million from the United States as compensation for the losses incurred from the war in Iraq, bringing the total American aid to Jordan in 2003 up to $750 million. This massive amount of foreign aid enabled the Jordanian government to keep its expenditures at a normal level without increasing the budgetary deficit or the external debt.[59] Once Jordan signed the peace treaty with Israel, the United States basically assumed responsibility for the survival of the regime. This in itself was a very strong incentive to sign a peace treaty (i.e., to reach "cold peace") but not to go beyond that.

Whereas in the Egyptian case the United States lost its leverage for encouraging Egyptian-Israeli direct relations after the signing of the peace treaty and up to 2004, in the Jordanian case the Americans played a more constructive role in encouraging economic normalization from earlier on, by initiating the QIZ agreement. As described previously, the initiative for the QIZ actually came from the Israeli private sector. The U.S.-Israeli FTA created a disincentive for joint ventures with Jordanian companies, because products that were manufactured in Jordan did not qualify under the FTA's rules of origin. Consequently, Israelis and Jordanians approached the U.S. Congress with the request to recognize the rules of origin aggregation for products manufactured within a restricted designated zone. However, it is quite clear that the central actor here was the United States. In November 1996, Congress agreed, and in November 1997, Israel, Jordan, and the United States signed the QIZ agreement at Doha, Qatar. The first area to be designated as a QIZ was the Al-Hassan industrial zone in Irbid, where several Israeli-Jordanian joint ventures already existed. Since then, the USTR has approved thirteen industrial parks in Jordan as QIZs. Of these, three are publicly owned and ten are privately owned. Seven are active, three are not active yet, and two are in the process of becoming active.[60]

Under the QIZ, in order to qualify for tariff-free entry to the U.S. market, Israel and Jordan had to bear at least 35 percent of the production costs and each party had to contribute separately at least 11.7 percent of the direct production costs. In June 1998, the Jordanians requested a reduction in the minimal amount of production required in Israel. Despite strong opposition from the Israeli Manufacturers Association, the Israeli government agreed to make this concession and lowered the minimal production input to 8 percent (7 percent for high-tech products).[61] The political logic of fostering cooperation overcame the economic logic of maximizing short-term economic gains.

The American rationale behind the QIZ was also political, not economic: the goal of helping to promote the peace process within the Middle East. This was the first in a more elaborate series of steps aimed at using economic tools to promote regional peace. The QIZ was a managed trade strategy that was to change the domestic cost-benefit calculation in Jordan regarding the value of economic cooperation with Israel in order to pave the Jordanian route to the lucrative American market. Furthermore, unlike a free trade agreement, the QIZ agreement could neutralize the negative impact of the wide economic power disparities between Israel and Jordan. Jordanians need not have been concerned with Israeli products flooding their markets because, to begin with, they committed only to a set and relatively small percentage of imports from Israel. Finally, in political terms, such a trilateral arrangement was convenient for the Jordanians because it allowed them to minimize the significance of the Israelis' part in the deal. In fact, in the early stages of the QIZ activity, Jordan tried to keep the Israeli side out of the picture, not even inviting the Israelis to the QIZ initiation ceremony. This changed somewhat only after Israel put pressure on them, via the United States, and made it clear that active trilateral cooperation was necessary for the success of the project.[62]

The QIZ has generated significant benefits for the Jordanian economy, in terms of both an increase in foreign investment and exports to the United States. In 1998, exports to the United States totaled 6 million Jordanian dinars (JOD). In 1999, they reached 9 million JOD, but by 2000, they had jumped to 45 million JOD and by 2001 they had reached a record of 164 million JOD, representing an increase of 264 percent from the previous year. In 2001, exports to the United States represented approximately 12 percent of total Jordanian exports. In terms of employment, according to the QIZ Unit in Jordan's Ministry of Industry and Trade, total employment in the QIZ projects in 2001 amounted to approximately twenty-two thousand Jordanians and about five thousand non-Jordanian workers. Unskilled members of the workforce benefit from QIZ companies, which are willing to train people and enhance their skills.[63] In 2004, Jordanian exports to the United States reached $1.1 billion.[64]

In terms of Jordan's own success in expanding exports to the United States, the contribution of the QIZ was crucial. It is extremely difficult even for QIZ opponents to argue with the dramatic numbers. In terms of actually promoting interaction with Israel, however, the picture is a mixed one. Despite the problems, Israeli exports to Jordan increased, to more than $70 million, out of which $57 million are direct inputs to the QIZ, all in a period that was not politically ideal.[65] Furthermore, cooperation via the QIZ arrangement served as an important step in facilitating the signing of the revised trade agreement between Israel and Jordan in 2005. By 2006, Israel's exports to Jordan had reached a peak of $136 million, a dramatic increase. Improvements in QIZ management in early 2007 were expected to raise exports even higher, as the estimated figure for 2007 stood at $190 million.[66]

Given the overwhelming opposition to normalization with Israel, the direct benefits for Jordan from the QIZ were a crucial factor in the regime's ability to legitimize its policy. On a much more concrete level, when one examines the specific experiences of Israeli companies operating in Jordan, one finds that even a single successful venture can make a difference in people's perceptions. For example, as noted previously, most of the early joint ventures took place in the Irbid QIZ. Irbid, however, is heavily populated with supporters of the Muslim Brotherhood. The QIZ thus generated loud opposition. The most vocal protest was against the Century Wear factory, which cooperated with Delta, the Israeli company. At one point, the Muslim leader in Irbid discovered that his own niece was working in the factory. In response to his demands that she quit her job, the plant's manager invited her family to visit the factory and inspect the working conditions. After the visit, the niece received permission to return to her job.[67] Clearly, this story is a nice anecdote rather than a representative case of Jordanian-Israeli interaction. However, it does show very well how cooperation on the ground can actually make a difference.

This being said, the contribution of the QIZ to the normalization of Jordanian-Israeli relations was still limited. Some observers are more critical of the value of the QIZ arrangement for Jordan and for building peace with Israel. Critics note that, in fact, the largest percentage of firms operating within the QIZ areas are neither Jordanian nor Israeli but Asian companies. Furthermore, because new Jordanian legislation allowed foreign companies to employ up to 50 percent foreign labor in their operations, there are many more foreign workers. This in turn has a double adverse effect. It limited the expansion of employment opportunities for Jordanian workers (employment opportunities being the peace dividend). Also, in practice, the day-to-day interaction under the QIZ arrangement is between Israeli and Asian suppliers, rather than with Jordanians. This obviously undermines the practical capacity of the arrangement to foster greater understanding and reconciliation via interaction between the two peoples. It is interesting that, during the QIZ negotiations, it was Israel that insisted that the assessment of Jordanian-Israeli economic cooperation within the QIZ be based on an output test rather than the customary criterion of shared capital investment in standard joint ventures, for the very reason that it wanted to make sure that real Israeli-Jordanian cooperation would take place. While the output test was adopted, the unpredicted entry of the Asian producers into the QIZ seriously undermined the achievement of that goal.[68]

QIZ clothing manufacturers find it difficult to meet the 11.7 percent domestic content requirement since much of the cloth is imported and wages are so low. At the same time, they also struggle to ensure the 7 percent Israeli contribution, which is usually very minor and entails labels, zippers, and packaging.[69] The type of economic cooperation between Jordanians and Israelis generated by the QIZ areas is therefore rather low key and requires a relatively low level of commitment, which in turn undermines the long-term effects of such cooperation. The fact that the public, skeptical to begin with, does not perceive dramatic economic gains from the QIZ also limits its ability to further the process of normalization.

The role of the United States has taken an interesting shift since 2000, with the signing of the U.S.-Jordan free trade agreement. This FTA was related to the success of the QIZ experience. It was also very clearly motivated by political rather than economic concerns, being part of the American administration's commitment to supporting the Jordanian regime and its efforts toward economic reform. While the FTA was very significant economically for Jordan, it meant very little for the United States in terms of trade. The FTA had been under negotiation for quite some time. While the agreement was signed by King Abdullah and President Bill Clinton in October 2000, its ratification was delayed by bipartisan political debates in the U.S. Senate surrounding the clauses dealing with labor practices and environmental issues. What finally led to ratification was Jordan's immediate support for the United States in its war on terror, in the aftermath of the terrorist attacks on September 11, 2001. Intense pressure from the White House then convinced the agreement's chief opponent, Senator Phil Gramm (R-TX), to drop his opposition. He conceded that while he thought that it was a bad treaty economically, "we need to reaffirm our relationship with Jordan, a critical country in a very important part of the world when we are at this very moment beginning to look toward a war with terrorism."[70]

The U.S.-Jordan FTA raises interesting questions regarding the nature of third parties' economic involvement in promoting peace. On the one hand, this treaty is clearly related to the broader American strategy of promoting regional peace in the Middle East and rewarding loyal allies like Jordan. On the other hand, the logic of the FTA clearly undermines the logic of the QIZ. The FTA removed the provision requiring that at least 7 to 8 percent of the final product exported to the United States consist of Israeli components. After the outbreak of the second intifada in 2000, this elimination of the need for an Israeli connection to Jordan's U.S. exports was very popular in Jordan. The QIZ will remain an attractive option for the Jordanians only until 2012, when the implementation of the FTA is to be completed. The reader may recall that the Egyptian government and Egyptian exporters have rejected a QIZ with Israel for several years, in the hope of circumventing interaction with Israel through a bilateral FTA with the United States. Only after the Americans refused and the quota system on textiles was coming to an end were the Egyptians forced to accept the second-best (QIZ) option. Comparison of the American behavior in the two cases suggests that they are aware of the potential political leverage that can be gained via the QIZ for promoting interaction between Israel and its former enemies but that at the same time they also know the limits of such attempts to link trade to peace building. The QIZ strategy creates an artificial, politically generated economic benefit to trade with Israel. As such, it will always be limited in its capacity to generate the type of cooperation dynamics envisaged by proponents of the commercial liberal argument. Consequently, when economic conditions are good, as they were in Jordan by 2000, the United States is willing to promote its peace strategy via direct benefits to one regional state.[71]

The United States, however, was not unaware of the implications of the FTA for Israeli-Jordanian economic cooperation. The Israelis, concerned over the implications of the FTA for the QIZ, pushed hard for the insertion of a cumulation clause in the U.S.-Jordanian FTA. The Jordanians, for their part, and especially for political reasons, opposed tying their FTA to Israel in any way. Eventually, Jordan agreed to insert a clause suggesting that in the future cumulation "with a third party" could be considered upon request. Indeed, as the FTA application is drawing near, Israeli and Jordanian trade officials are working on a joint mission to push for rules-of-origin cumulation in the United States. It is important to note that there is a fundamental economic logic for such a move, given the fact that the small Jordanian market is likely to face difficulties in utilizing the FTA with the United States since it will have no foreign inputs.[72] It is still too soon to assess the impact of the FTA on the future of Jordanian-Israeli economic relations. While on the one hand the volume of trade is likely to decrease, any trade that remains or that will be generated will be voluntary, economically based, and thus potentially more viable in the long run.

THE TRANSITION TO PEACE between Jordan and Israel began on a more optimistic note than that between Egypt and Israel. Whereas in the latter case the Egyptian government did not want to pursue any normalization, in this case King Hussein did have a strong commitment to foster a "warm peace" and promote normalization. However, this normalization process remains very limited. It is a case that demonstrates the importance of distinguishing between the two stages of transition to peace and of analyzing the conditions leading to each. The Jordanian case, more so than the Egyptian one, shows the limited capability of the state to force normalization upon its citizens. It also reveals the tension between a process of peacemaking from above and the process of democratization, raising questions regarding the blind application of democratic peace theory to transitions to peace. While the regime was a clear winner in the transition to peace, broader segments of society did not feel they had reaped the peace dividend. Lack of such concrete economic benefits, in turn, made it easier for religious and ideological antinormalization sentiments to prevail.

The broad economic disparities played a negative role in this case as well. They minimized from the outset the economic potential of bilateral cooperation between the two states. They created concerns within Jordan about Israeli economic imperialism, which were used by the antinormalization coalition. While many on the Israeli side appreciated these problems and even tried to deal with them (e.g., by making the 1995 asymmetric trade agreement), others failed to demonstrate the appropriate sensitivity and developed a counterproductive, arrogant approach to their Jordanian counterparts.

When comparing the time span of the Jordanian and Egyptian treaties, it is clear that the United States played a much more constructive role in the former case, by creating incentives for the parties to deal directly with one another. The Jordanian experience, however, also highlights the limits of this strategy.

The Jordanian case is unique because the ongoing Israeli conflict with the Palestinians is also a domestic Jordanian issue, given the vast Palestinian population. Consequently, this is a case in which the political circumstances of the conflict are clearly of tremendous significance. Even so, this chapter has shown that at least for the first stage of transition to peace, purely economic consider-ations played a much more important role. In order to preserve the economi-cally beneficial peace, the regime was willing to halt its political liberalization and face fierce opposition. As for the second stage of normalization, if one ac-cepts Shimon Shamir's observation that the majority of Jordanians are in fact pragmatic, then the lack of a clear peace dividend for the broader population was an important factor in facilitating the takeover of the antinormalization coalition. Since that is a counterfactual statement, the point is empirically hard to prove.

POSTWAR RELATIONS IN SOUTHEAST ASIA

Japan, the Philippines, and Indonesia

IN A MARKED CONTRAST to the two Middle Eastern cases presented in chapters 2 and 3, the transition to peace between Japan and the countries of Southeast Asia has been primarily a success story. Many international relations scholars tend to talk about Southeast Asia as a whole, especially since the successful development of the Association of Southeast Asian Nations (ASEAN). This chapter looks at Japan's "return" to Southeast Asia in the aftermath of World War II by examining its experience with Indonesia and the Philippines. Looking at the bilateral rather than regional level is important, especially for understanding the dynamics of the transition to peace in its early stages. The experience of these two states has many characteristics that reflect the common Southeast Asian experience with Japan. At the same time, some differences between the two states' experiences provide more nuanced insights.

The outcome of the transition to peace in the Southeast Asian case has been a much greater level of normalization than in the Middle Eastern cases. However, the following discussion reveals that, in the early stages of the transition to peace between Japan, the Philippines, and Indonesia, there were problems regarding the use of economic tools in the transition, and they were markedly similar to those that appeared in the Middle East. One should bear in mind that the time frame of the Southeast Asian cases is much broader than that of the two Middle Eastern cases. In order to make the best of the comparison, most of the chapter focuses on the earlier years of the transition to peace, from the reparations negotiations to the anti-Japanese riots in 1974. This period is not often addressed in most current discussions of Japan-Southeast Asian relations, and yet it is the one that can tell us most about the role of economic tools in the transition to peace. It is in this period as well that one can find similarities to some of the Middle Eastern dynamics.

From Conflict to Peace

Within less than a year following its successful surprise attack on Pearl Harbor, Japan completed its conquest of Southeast Asia. It occupied the Philippines and Indonesia from 1942 to 1945. Especially in Indonesia, the Japanese were initially welcomed as liberators who were freeing the people from Dutch colonialism. However, it did not take long for people to realize that a fellow Asian state now oppressed them. In the occupied areas, the Japanese army ruled using harsh measures. Despite official rhetoric on the liberation of Asia, the Japanese treated the Southeast Asians poorly in general, disregarded their cultures, and focused on extracting resources and using local labor to advance their war efforts. This humiliating treatment, as well as what was perceived to be an overbearing attitude and rudeness of the Japanese soldiers, created deep hatred toward Japan. In Indonesia, the Japanese turned out to be more repressive than the Dutch. In the Philippines, beyond being a repressive force, the Japanese brought severe material destruction. At the same time, in most areas there was local leadership that cooperated with the Japanese. The Philippines, for example, received formal independence from Japan in 1943, and a puppet state was formed that signed an alliance with Japan and declared war on the United States and Britain. In Indonesia as well, the Japanese were preparing to give the Indonesians self-rule and for that purpose co-opted many national leaders, including the first president of postwar independent Indonesia, Sukarno.[1]

Following the surrender of Japan and the period of American occupation, Japan regained its independence in the Treaty of San Francisco, signed in 1951. The new states of the Philippines and Indonesia refused to sign the peace treaty until they negotiated and signed reparations agreements with Japan. This did not happen until 1956 for the Philippines and 1958 for Indonesia. The Philippines settled for about 10 percent of their original claim. They were to receive $500 million over twenty years in reparations goods, $30 million in technical services, including ship salvage, and $20 million in cash for Filipino war widows and orphans. In addition, the Japanese government agreed to facilitate $250 million worth of private, long-term, low-interest commercial loans in terms to be negotiated later. The Indonesians received $223 million over twelve years, plus $400 million in private loans and investments, and earlier debts to Japan were canceled. Both countries, however, made a clear distinction between the reparations and the resumption of normal trade and other economic ties.[2]

Until 1964, Japan's interaction with these and other Southeast Asian countries revolved around the reparations negotiations and the implementation of those agreements, with a single-track focus on economic diplomacy. From 1965 until the mid-1970s, Japan began to play a more active role in regional economic development schemes, putting more emphasis on regional development and not just its own economic profits. Following the wave of violent anti-Japanese demonstrations in Southeast Asia in 1974, Japan's prime minister, Fukuda Takeo, announced in 1977 the Fukuda Doctrine, which aimed at transcending the economic dimension of Japan's regional interactions and investing more in what he called "heart-to-heart diplomacy." The Fukuda Doctrine also stressed Japan's greater interest in cooperating with ASEAN.[3] The riots in 1974 served as an important indicator of the limits of a purely economic strategy and of Japan's attempt to separate politics and economics (known as the principle of *seikei bunri*).

It is important to note that the expansion of Japanese cooperation also involved greater societal cooperation initiatives. Thus, for example, it was ASEAN along with Japanese academics and private sector business leaders who pushed forward the establishment of the Pacific Economic Cooperation Council (PECC) in 1980. That council was expanded, and in 1989, it became the Asia-Pacific Economic Cooperation forum.[4] After the end of the cold war, relations between Japan and ASEAN countries strengthened, with Japan playing both an economic as well as a more active political role in regional politics. Today, Japan is a major trading partner of both Indonesia and the Philippines as well as their largest source of investment. Japan was the market for 20 percent of exports and 18 percent of imports for the Philippines in 2004. Indonesian trade with Japan accounted for 19.06 percent of exports and 13.07 percent of imports in 2004. At the same time, the asymmetry in the relations is still very clear, with the Philippines accounting for only 2 percent of Japanese exports and 2 percent of Japanese imports. Similarly, with Indonesia, Japan's trade accounts for only 1.6 percent of exports and 4.11 percent of imports in 2004. Indonesia is, however, Japan's largest supplier of liquefied natural gas.[5]

Economic cooperation between Japan and Indonesia has been significantly upgraded with the signing of the Economic Partnership Agreement in August

2007 (taking effect in July 2008). According to this free trade agreement, 96 percent of Japanese exports to Indonesia will be tariff free and 93 percent of Indonesian exports will be tariff free in value terms. An energy security pact was also signed between the two states. Finally, Japan, in a significant move, allowed Indonesian nurses and personal care attendants to come to work in Japan.[6] Japanese FDI in Indonesia has also grown dramatically, from $511 million in 2002 to more than $1 billion in 2005.[7] The Philippines signed its first-ever bilateral trade agreement (JPEPA) with Japan in September 2006, an agreement that would liberalize trade and also allow the entry of a limited number of Filipino nurses and caregivers to work in Japan. This treaty, however, has encountered opposition in the Filipino Senate and, two years later, was yet to be ratified.[8]

The normalization of relations has gone beyond trade and direct investment. Various nongovernmental organizations link the societies of these states, and there is movement of people and ideas. Japanese popular culture, for example, has spread to Southeast Asia. Japanese comics, music, and star-search TV programs are extremely popular throughout the region.[9] This type of cultural penetration is exactly the nightmare scenario for many Arab intellectuals and Islamist groups in Egypt and Jordan who fear that exposure of their markets to Israeli goods would lead to such an outcome.

While these relations are not free of friction, most of the recent problems stem from the north-south context of the relationship, not from memories of the past conflict. History has receded as a determining factor in defining the ASEAN states' perceptions of Japan. Present conflicts, therefore, could be described as part of a "normal" relationship between states. They no longer relate (for the most part) to the fact that the two states were former enemies. This was perhaps most evident in the lack of significant opposition or concern on the part of Southeast Asian states regarding Japan's passage of the International Peace Cooperation Law in 1992, which led to the eventual dispatch of Japan's Self-Defense Force (SDF) to Cambodia, and the passage of the anti-terrorism law in 2002, which led to the dispatch of SDF troops to the Indian Ocean in support of the American fight against terrorism.[10] A public opinion poll on Japan conducted in February and March 2008 in six ASEAN countries (including the Philippines and Indonesia) reflects the positive view of Japan prevalent within these societies. More than 90 percent of the respondents viewed Japan as "friendly" or "somewhat friendly," more than 90 percent considered Japan as "trustworthy" or "trustworthy with some reservations," 92 percent gave a positive answer that the economic and technological cooperation of the Japanese government had been helpful, and 93 percent welcomed Japanese business in their countries. In both Indonesia and the Philippines, Japan ranked in first place as an important partner for ASEAN countries. Although the poll was commissioned by the Japanese Ministry of Foreign Affairs, the results overall are very impressive.[11]

The process through which Japan succeeded in normalizing its relations with the countries it previously conquered was heavily dominated by economic diplomacy. Consequently, it is an illuminating case because it enables us to examine how far a pure economic strategy can go in promoting peace building.

The Economic Potential of Peaceful Relations

After losing its former colonial territories of China, Manchuria, and Korea, Japan found closer economic relations with Southeast Asia indispensable for its economic recovery and for fostering its heavy industries. The combination of Japan's extremely poor natural resource endowment with its ambitious goals of industrial recovery and catching up with the advanced Western states made it imperative to secure access to far more energy and raw materials than it possessed. This became more clearly apparent after the end of the Korean War. During the war, the Japanese economy began to recover with the high volume of American purchases. Once the war was over, the economic importance of Southeast Asia grew as it became clear to the Japanese that the United States would forbid it to pursue the option of resuming trade with mainland China.[12]

In terms of trade, poverty-stricken Southeast Asia was not seen at the time as a lucrative market. As Prime Minister Yoshida Shigeru noted, Japan wanted to trade "with rich men, not beggars."[13] However, compared with Japan and its lack of resources, the otherwise poor and economically backward Southeast Asian states enjoyed a relative abundance of such necessary resources. Indonesia was the richest source of raw materials in the region, mainly oil, but also timber and nickel. It could not, however, extract these resources on its own due to a lack of capital and technical experience. By the early 1980s, Indonesia had become the most important supplier of liquefied natural gas to Japan. This remains true to this day, despite the fact that Indonesia has become an energy importer.[14] The Philippines did not have oil but was rich with minerals and forest resources. Gold, copper, iron, chromites, manganese, and coal were the main minerals.[15]

For countries like the Philippines and Indonesia, which had to build a modern economy almost from scratch by developing basic economic infrastructure and finding markets for the export and import of necessary goods, economic cooperation with Japan was very lucrative. The Philippines, for example, found itself in a desperate situation after World War II. Not a single coconut oil mill was operable, most sugar mills were destroyed, highways were severely damaged, and 80 percent of the capital city, Manila, was destroyed.[16] Under such conditions, the new leaders were eager to gain whatever economic help they could. The most immediate contribution of Japan came in the form of reparations. Only later on did leaders in the Philippines begin to identify the value of trade with Japan and of foreign direct investments from Japan. These, together with official aid, played an important role in financing the industrialization of both the Philippines and Indonesia.[17]

While in some places reparations money was squandered on unnecessary or economically unwise projects, in other places, including the Philippines, the Japanese reparations projects played a crucial role in speeding up industrialization.[18] Over the years, Japanese reparations payments, loans, and official development assistance (ODA) in Indonesia helped build 31 percent of all electric power facilities, 14 percent of railways, 50 percent of microwave communications facilities, 76 percent of Jakarta's electric power lines, and 46 percent of its water supply facilities. In the Philippines, the funds from Japan accounted for 6 percent of electric power plants, 8 percent of national highways, 8.2 percent of water supply facilities for rural populations, and 70 percent of Manila's flood control operations.[19] This discussion suggests an important difference between these cases and the cases of Israel and Egypt and Israel and Jordan. Whereas in those latter cases the main peace dividend stemmed from the parties' relations with the United States, rather than from direct economic interaction with one another, in the Southeast Asian cases there was a clear and significant mutual economic peace dividend.

The Domestic Balance of Winners and Losers

The most striking observation in this case of transition to peace after World War II is the close and active cooperation between the government and big business. The economic potential of signing a peace treaty and developing normal commercial ties was clear to the governments of Japan, the Philippines, and Indonesia, as well as to the big businesses in these countries, and they all forcefully pushed forward both the reparations negotiations and the expansion of economic activities. At the same time, however, there was strong opposition at the broader societal level to doing any business with Japan. This in turn led to clashes, which eventually led to the imposition of martial law in Indonesia.

Postwar Japan was characterized by a tight alliance between the conservative government and big business.[20] Early postwar American reforms tried to break down the large economic conglomerates known as the *zaibatsu,* which played an active role in the prewar expansionist drive. These reforms, however, were halted in light of the growing communist threat in Asia and the decision to strengthen Japan as a bulwark against communism. Consequently, most of the old trading houses remained intact. Many of their leaders had close personal connections with leading politicians in Japan as well as solid ties with politicians and business leaders in Southeast Asia, whom they had met during the short period of Japanese colonial control.[21]

Leaders of big business in Japan were eager to enter Southeast Asia and were therefore eager for reparations payments to begin as soon as possible. They played a leading role in the shaping of the reparations policy and played an active role as well in the negotiations, both as representatives of the government and unofficially as representatives of corporations. They regarded the $800 million reparations settlement with the Philippines as "seeds from which a great harvest can be expected in a few years." The industries that benefited most from the reparations were shipbuilding, automobile manufacturing, electric machinery, steel, construction, and engineering consulting. The great attractiveness of the reparations agreements stemmed from their special nature. These were not simply cash flows to the victimized countries. Rather, once a sum was agreed on, specific development projects were suggested by the recipient state, which contracted directly with a Japanese company to perform the job. The Japanese government, in turn, paid the Japanese company with the reparations money. This created a good opportunity for Japanese companies to penetrate Southeast Asian markets without any worry about not being paid.[22]

Big trading companies such as Mitsui and Mitsubishi (which were active before the war) were soon very active in the Philippines. For example, a company called Marubeni-Iida was a postwar mutation of the old DaidōTrading Company, which had abaca plantations on Mindanao before the war. By 1961, the same company was handling about 15 percent of the Japan-Philippines trade.

Similarly, in Indonesia, Japanese business interests, in close coordination with the ruling Liberal Democratic Party (LDP) and the Tokyo bureaucracy, pushed ahead their personal connections and cultivated President Sukarno.[23] Japanese business leaders were quite articulate regarding the logic of reparations. This logic was presented in 1953 by Hara Yasusaburọ then president of Nippon Kayaku: "By offering goods in the course of paying reparations in the form of production-related services, we can inform Southeast Asian countries of how Japanese industries stand now, nurture bilateral and economically binding relationships of friendship with them, and start building in each of them a permanent market for Japanese products."[24]

This business interest perfectly coincided with official government policy in Japan. The official postwar Japanese strategy, known as the Yoshida Doctrine, emphasized the primacy of the goal of achieving rapid economic growth and economic security. For achieving that purpose, Japan was to avoid involvement in international political-strategic issues and closely cooperate with the United States, relying on the latter's security umbrella. This focus on economic growth had not only an economic rationale but also a domestic political one. In light of the severe ideological tensions within Japan during that time, the best way to maintain domestic stability was to avoid those political issues and focus on expanding the economic pie, to satisfy everyone.[25]

Government officials were well aware of the difficulty of entering Southeast Asian markets because of the strong anti-Japanese sentiments in the region. This awareness is reflected in the words of the chief of the Reparations Office in the Ministry of International Trade and Industry (MITI) Enterprise Bureau in 1957: "The newly emerging countries of Southeast Asia are extremely attractive virgin lands offering much promise to those interested in economic cooperation. Raging over these virgin lands at present, however, are stormy winds of xenophobic nationalism and apprehension about a Japanese invasion. *Can there be a better way for business to ride safely into the storm than to justify their advance there in the name of reparation payments?*" [emphasis added].[26] The reparations, therefore, were not perceived as a burden but as an investment.

This mutual interest of the government and big business was transformed into tight cooperation. Policy was formed by a triangle of strong economic bureaucracies, big business, and politicians. This alliance was highly institutionalized, which was also the case with regard to the economic efforts to establish a new presence in Southeast Asia. Thus, for example, Prime Minister Yoshida established the Asian Economic Forum within the Ministry of Foreign Affairs

(MOFA), in which private sector representatives also participated, and this group assumed responsibility for matters of economic cooperation with Southeast Asia. In 1954, the Asian Society (a foundation incorporating several preexisting organizations) was established to serve as the actual conduit of economic cooperation funds.[27] Japan developed what David Arase calls "business diplomacy." An institutionalized network for information exchange and policy coordination between private sector actors and the government was developed.[28] The reader may recall that one of the problems raised by Israeli business leaders who tried promoting business opportunities with Egypt and Jordan was the array of difficulties posed by the Israeli bureaucracy and by the lack of central planning and coordination. In the Japanese case, the institutional arrangements linking the economic bureaucracy and business were very efficient.

In Southeast Asia, business leaders also eagerly wanted to begin or resume economic ties with Japanese firms. Indeed, as early as 1954 (before the reparations agreement was even signed), Japanese business leaders had begun to try to form new relations or renew old ones with those families in the Philippine elite who controlled mining, timber, and certain other industries.[29] The development of postwar economic cooperation followed a similar pattern in both the Philippines and Indonesia, with the establishment of close ties between political leaders and powerful businessmen in both countries. Many of these connections in fact predated the war.[30] Indonesia's first president, Sukarno, actually became president with the help of the Japanese military administration, with which he collaborated. His successor, Suharto, was trained by the Japanese military.

Southeast Asian leaders, for their part, both in Indonesia and the Philippines, also perceived renewed economic ties with Japan as an imperative for economic development and, as such, crucial for the survival of their regimes. In the aftermath of the war, the new regimes of the new states faced tremendous challenges. They had to remove and rebuild what the war had devastated and lead their countries on the road to industrialization and economic growth. Any economic help, from Japan or elsewhere, was therefore crucial for their future.

The intensification of economic activity and cooperation with Japan, however, occurred only later, when Ferdinand Marcos came to power in the Philippines (1966) and tried to introduce foreign capital into his country and when Suharto consolidated his regime's control in Indonesia (1967) with his New Order program.[31] For both Marcos and Suharto and for the changing Japanese governments, economic growth was seen as a high policy priority. Suharto's New Order and Marcos's New Society policies were both rooted in the promise of economic progress. Because the elites upon which these governments were based were unwilling and unable to undertake serious redistribution programs to alleviate poverty, the only way to achieve that was to keep expanding the pie.[32]

In Sukarno's Indonesia, economic policies were hostage to his radical leftist ideology. Suharto, on the other hand, was highly influenced by a group of Indonesian economists with Western neoclassical economic training, and he made a conscious decision to pursue economic liberalization. The legitimacy of Suharto's position and the justification for the authoritarian practices of his regime rested upon the regime's ideology of development and the promise of providing a steady improvement in the standard of living for Indonesians. We should remember, though, that Suharto's main interest was to maintain power and accumulate wealth. He was convinced that by pursuing economic liberalization he could both promote his patrimonial domestic politics and allow economic capitalist development.[33] This shift to a liberalizing coalition, in Etel Solingen's terms, clearly increased the potential for economic normalization with Japan beyond the first step of reparations. It significantly increased interest in having Japanese investments pay for rapid industrialization.

Most of the business transactions that took place during that period were corrupt and based on personal ties among elites.[34] This is not surprising when one considers the nature of the regimes in the Philippines and Indonesia. In the Philippines, the period up to 1972 was characterized by a shaky democracy, dominated by the traditional oligarchy, and characterized by a high level of corruption. The economic interaction with Japan and the gains from it were monopolized by a handful of high government officials, the business partners of Japanese companies, and the few business leaders who had been able to secure contracts for some Japanese-funded projects. A narrow group therefore actually reaped the economic peace dividend.[35] After President Ferdinand Marcos came to power, he built a domestic power base among the military officers, civilian technocrats, and a fraction of the elite known as the president's "cronies." In 1972, Marcos declared martial law. Under his rule, the traditional oligarchy of the export-oriented agricultural producers (agro-exporters) narrowed to a smaller subset of the politically well-connected elite whom he favored.[36]

In Indonesia, corruption was even worse than in the Philippines. Beyond the close link between government agencies and the private sector, in Indonesia the army was heavily involved in economic affairs, especially after martial law was declared in 1957 and the military took over the previously Dutch-owned enterprises and used them to maintain its own budget. Under the New Order system, it was important to keep the military officers satisfied with the status quo, so their economic involvement kept growing.[37] On the Japanese side, the alliance of the LDP as governing party, big business, and the economic bureaucracies could operate rather easily, without much societal involvement, because the Japanese people were not that interested in Southeast Asia. Public polls showed that people were very ignorant about even the names of the countries in the region.[38] The fact that all three regimes shared a similar economic ideology was also helpful in promoting efficient cooperation. This is in contrast to the cases in chapters 2 and 3. The different economic ideologies held by Israeli and Egyptian elites further undermined the likelihood of forming mutual understanding on economic cooperation and created unnecessary misunderstandings.

Alongside the eagerness of Southeast Asian governments and big business to cooperate with Japan, there was very strong and widespread popular opposition to any such move. In the Philippines, most Filipinos viewed Japan with intense repugnance. Filipino nationalism was validated in their struggle against the Japanese, not in fighting the return of Western colonialism after the war ended. They had already been promised independence by the Americans before the war started; an agreement signed in 1934 promised independence in 1946. Thus, in 1941, the Japanese were not seen as liberators.[39] Filipino politicians wanted to reap political profits from the popular hatred toward Japan and consequently posed many difficulties for the government, forcing it to take a tougher line vis-à-vis Japan.

The government faced strong opposition in the senate, which consistently attacked its "soft" attitude toward Japan. This in turn prolonged the negotiations for the reparations agreement until 1956, when the agreement and peace treaty were finally signed. An earlier agreement had already been reached in 1954 but was not signed due to strong domestic criticism in the Philippines. However, it should be noted that while official negotiations were taking place, private firms were already working out joint ventures.[40] This is a striking contrast to the Middle Eastern cases, in which private business in Egypt and Jordan was less enthusiastic and clearly did not want to move forward before it received official government blessing. The situation in postwar Asia shows that a powerful and highly motivated private sector can push forward the process of peace and economic normalization, even in the face of societal opposition, as long as it is well connected to the state.

In Indonesia, there were more mixed feelings about the Japanese. They were remembered as those who delivered Indonesia from the Dutch colonial rule, but at the same time they were also remembered for their harsh military occupation. Sukarno, for his part, did not have a problem with exploiting the Japanese reparations even as his virulent nationalism fed on anti-Japanese feelings among the people.[41] Especially among students there was great antagonism toward Japan. This animosity developed as a result of Japan's wartime policy of forcing Indonesian students to learn Japanese as well as its harsh and autocratic administration of the schools.[42] This hostility and ambivalence had an impact on the country's ability to move from the peace treaty toward greater normalization of relations.

Indonesian students' resentment toward Japan, together with resentment toward their own government, led to demonstrations in the streets in 1974. Demonstrators demanded that the president's private assistants (known as *aspri*) be dismissed. They claimed that this powerful group of people was actually a pro-Japanese lobby that received large commissions for "selling the country to the Japanese."[43] While corrupt officials were making money, this intense interaction with powerful Japan was undermining Indonesia's independence.

The Impact on the Two Stages of Transition to Peace

In the Southeast Asian cases, the signing of a peace treaty was conditioned upon the prior signing of the reparations treaty. Direct economic interaction, therefore, was built into the peace treaty (i.e., into the first stage of the overall peace process). However, we find in both the Philippines and Indonesia that a clear distinction was made between economic interactions with the Japanese that are related to receiving reparations and "normal" economic interaction in the form of regular trade ties (i.e., the transition to the second stage of peace). In the same way that Egypt made a distinction between the formal peace treaty and actual normalization of relations, the Southeast Asian governments accepted the cold peace and wrestled with economic normalization, which faced strong opposition.

The Philippines signed the reparations and peace agreements with Japan in 1956. However, the Filipinos were careful to separate from the reparations issue from that of resuming normal trade and other economic ties. A formally designated Treaty of Friendship, Commerce, and Navigation that was to open the way for normal commercial relations was signed four years later, in December 1960. The treaty became a political issue that fueled nationalistic feelings in Manila. The Philippine senate strongly criticized the treaty, pointing to its too-generous approach to Japanese who might travel to or live in the Philippines. The senate actually passed several laws in order to remedy the perceived weaknesses of the treaty. Japanese businesses resumed quasi-normal relationships in the absence of specific legal prohibitions, but they lacked the legal sanctions that a treaty would allow them to invoke.[44]

Over the years, popular hatred of the Japanese, although waning, was used at times for political purposes.[45] (The issue of political mobilization of such public sentiments is extremely relevant in the Middle Eastern cases discussed in chapters 2 and 3 as well as in chapter 5, on relations between Japan and the Republic of Korea.) One of the questions for which there is no clear-cut answer involves whether the government is constrained by popular public opinion or, instead, shapes public opinion. (Most Egyptian business leaders I have spoken to suggested that the government could manipulate public opinion.) In the case of the Philippines, the government's persistence in interacting with Japan did eventually lead to a change in societal perceptions.

In Indonesia as well, while a reparations and peace treaty was signed in 1958, no friendship-commerce-navigation treaty was signed, and so branch offices of Japanese companies were not legally authorized to operate there. The Japanese attempted to satisfy Indonesian economic nationalism by using production-sharing schemes, especially in oil, timber, and nickel production, that were devised jointly by the two governments.[46] However, during the decade following the peace treaties, public opinion was suspicious of Japan, and the Japanese were well aware of it.

Japanese who visited the region concluded that the best thing to do was to maintain a relatively low profile in order to minimize concerns about Japanese aggression.[47] Prime Minister Kishi Nobusuke (between 1957 and 1960) tried to promote relations with Southeast Asia in a series of fifteen visits to the region. He proposed various plans for Japanese-inspired regional cooperation, such as the creation of an "Asian Fund." These overtures, however, were premature and were met with a hostile reaction. Newspapers in the Philippines and Indonesia threatened that Kishi's visit could herald the "revival of the Greater East Asia Co-prosperity Sphere." Kishi himself, however, chose to downplay the regional hostility and focus on the more positive feedback he received during his regional tours.[48] These failed attempts to play a more active regional role are reminiscent of Israel's failed attempt to raise its regional economic profile in the Casablanca economic summit, which followed the Madrid peace conference in 1991. In that case as well, Israeli enthusiasm to get involved in various regional development projects was interpreted as an Israeli imperialist scheme.

Japan's underestimation of the depth of anti-Japanese feelings in the region was exposed in 1974, when violent anti-Japanese riots erupted during the visit of Prime Minister Tanaka Kakuei to the region. The anger expressed in the riots had been building for quite some time. In November 1972, the Indonesian government decided to support a ten-day boycott of Japanese goods led by student organizers, and sporadic violence erupted. By June 1973, there were huge demonstrations. Days before Tanaka arrived in Jakarta, in January 1974, students were burning him in effigy. When he arrived, thousands of students were marching down the streets, burning Japanese cars, and shouting anti-Japanese slogans. Tanaka had to be airlifted from the palace when he departed. The only reason that similar riots did not erupt in the Philippines was that martial law had already been declared there.[49]

The demonstrations in Indonesia reflected the growing popular resentment toward Japan and its perceived economic aggression. However, they were also intimately linked to a strong resentment toward the regime itself, with its corrupt and problematic development strategies. People resented the dubious alliances between Japanese conglomerates and local big business leaders linked to the president. The riots were thus, in part, a social reaction to the growing oligopolistic control of the Indonesian economy under Suharto.[50] This combination of anti-Japanese sentiment with domestic criticism and lack of trust in the ruling government is reminiscent of the sentiments expressed in the public opposition to peace with Israel in Jordan, as well as in Egypt. Economic peace dividends that remain elitist not only do not promote further normalization but are also a source of public discontent. When citizens do not believe that they will benefit from the economic dividends, it is much easier for them to combine this frustration with the preexisting hostility toward their former enemy, which is now doing business with their corrupt government.

For the Japanese, the 1974 riots symbolized the limits of a purely economic strategy in Asia. They realized that most Southeast Asians had a very negative image of Japan as an "economic animal" that pursued a policy solely for the advancement of its own economic well-being. The events led to a reconsideration of Japanese Southeast Asian policy, which in turn found expression in a speech delivered in August 1977 by Prime Minister Fukuda. The thrust of that speech was consequently known as the Fukuda Doctrine and consisted of three principles: that Japan would deliberately reject a military role, would do its best to consolidate relationships of mutual confidence and trust based on "heart-to-heart" understanding, and would be an equal partner of ASEAN while aiming to foster mutual understanding with the nations of Indochina.[51]

With the new approach, Japan put more emphasis on developing cultural interaction with Southeast Asian nations and increased the number of prime ministers' visits to the region and regular meetings with foreign ministers. The business community made efforts to reduce frictions with the regional countries, and the Keidanren (the Japan Federation of Economic Organizations) set up guidelines for the behavior of Japanese multinational corporations. In the specific context of Indonesia, the Japanese made efforts to lower their profile and managed to camouflage their degree of economic involvement by handling it in a very sensitive manner.[52]

The anti-Japanese riots in Jakarta took place sixteen years after the peace treaty had been signed and after Indonesia was already a senior trading partner of Japan. This situation reveals the limits of economic diplomacy in promoting warm peace and the normalization of relations between states, especially former enemies. The ability of Japan to detach economics from politics, along the lines of the Yoshida Doctrine, was very successful initially in developing economic ties with the countries of Southeast Asia. This focus on economics was attractive to all the parties involved, and the separation was perhaps most clearly exemplified in Japan's continuous economic relations with Sukarno's Indonesia, even at the height of his revolutionary, anti-Western foreign policy.

However, maintaining this complete separation was impossible over the long run for two reasons. First, Japan's separation strategy was only possible in the first place because of the unique strategic circumstances during the early post–World War II period. By the mid-1970s, with the fall of Saigon and the declining importance of the United States in the region, Japan was facing mounting pressures to play a regional political role as well, thus compromising the convenient separation.[53] The second reason for Japan's inability to maintain the separation and successfully build on this economics-only track stems from the negative implications over time of asymmetric economic interaction between Japan and the Southeast Asian states, that is, the impact of economic power disparities.

While Japan made a conscious decision to separate the economic and political aspects of peacemaking and to formulate policy based on economic logic, Israeli politicians and economists consciously put up front the political logic of peace and were highly aware of the need to foster economic cooperation according to a political logic (i.e., forgo some economic gains to promote peace). Despite the success of the Japanese strategy in the first stage and in the early part of the second stage of the transition to peace, the same problems that Israelis predicted would emerge in an economically driven economic interaction with their weaker former enemies also emerged in Japanese relations with Indonesia, only later. These problems have much to do with the power disparities between the countries.

The Impact of Economic Power Disparities

The economic power disparities between Japan and the Southeast Asian countries after World War II were huge. Japan was the only industrialized country in the wider region, whereas other countries, including the Philippines and Indonesia, were still agrarian societies taking their first steps toward industrialization. Comparative data for the 1960s are difficult to find, but in 1960, Japan's GDP was approximately $45 billion, compared to the Philippines' GDP of close to $6 billion. By 1974, the GDP of the Philippines had risen dramatically, to close to $14 billion, but Japan's GDP had reached more than $461 billion, still a huge gap. Indonesian GDP in 1974 was $27 billion (1960 data were not available).[54] Even as late as the 1980s, when Southeast Asian states were making sound progress in economic development, these disparities remained huge. In 1984, the Japanese economy was nearly six times larger than that of all ASEAN members combined. Its GNP was $1.25 trillion compared to $85.4 billion in Indonesia and $35 billion in the Philippines, and Japan's per capita GNP was $10,390 compared to $169 in Indonesia and $56.80 in the Philippines.[55]

This wide disparity played an important positive role in achieving the first stage of peacemaking. As described previously, the extremely difficult economic conditions in both the Philippines and Indonesia made it economically imperative for them to make peace with Japan, despite the various concerns and despite existing hostilities. The fact that signing a peace treaty was conditioned upon the signing of a reparations agreement made that point very clear. Most early joint ventures were indeed related to the extraction of raw materials that the Philippines and Indonesia had in abundance but could not extract on their own. It was an attractive deal: desperately needed know-how in exchange for desperately needed resources.

However, the wide economic disparity also had a negative impact on the attempts to move the peacemaking on to the second stage. It was this disparity that was behind the strong opposition to the signing of the friendship and commerce treaty between the Philippines and Japan in 1960. The reparations agreements indeed created economic cooperation with Japan, but it was a very specific, managed type of cooperation. The notion of allowing normal trade relations with Japan stirred strong fears of an invasion of Japanese capital into the Philippines and overwhelming economic penetration. Obviously, there was no way for the Filipino people to respond in kind with any "counterinvasion" of Japan.[56]

In Indonesia as well there was a fear of Japanese economic dominance. This fear was intensified by the combined circumstances of Japan's past role as an aggressive military power, its postwar role as a dominant economic power, and Indonesia's own economic weakness. It is telling that only a month before the anti-Japanese riots of January 1974, in the first Indonesian-Japanese conference, Indonesian participants voiced dissatisfaction with the asymmetric economic relations between the two countries. Mohammad Sadli, one of Indonesia's most senior technocrats and an architect of the New Order economic policy, pointed out that while Japan was the number-one market for Indonesian exports and an important source of its imports, Indonesia was only a small trading partner for Japan. He stressed that Indonesians "worry about size and power relationship[s], first of all in economic terms but also about the probability that economic power will spill over in the political and other spheres."[57]

The wide and asymmetric economic disparities generated much ill feeling toward Japan, some of which was no longer related to the war experience but rather to its postwar economic might. As noted previously, there was a clear interest in getting Japanese aid and FDI, but the attitude toward that aid was mixed. Aid and FDI were seen on the one hand as a development tool for Southeast Asian states, but at the same time they were also perceived as a Japanese tool for maintaining a colonial relationship and creating dependence. These perceptions put the Japanese in a "Catch-22" situation, in which the more aid and investment they gave, the more they would be criticized for creating dependency, whereas the less aid and investment they give, the more they would be criticized for selfishness.[58]

One of the arguments presented at the beginning of this study suggested that, in a transition to peace, it is more difficult to use economic cooperation to promote peace because broad economic power disparities raise various sensitivities that make it difficult to follow a pure economic logic. The best example of this difficulty is the development of joint ventures in which one party provides the labor and the other has the know-how. While economically sensible, this arrangement is likely to create a problem in postconflict situations. (These concerns were quite prominent in the Middle Eastern cases examined in chapters 2 and 3.) If that is indeed the case, then why, despite the huge economic power disparities, was there still great willingness on the part of the Philippines and Indonesia to cooperate with Japan in numerous joint ventures?

Part of the answer lies in the causal mechanism through which power disparities cause problems. Wide power disparities are likely to create concern over asymmetrical dependence on the stronger party. Such dependence, in turn, can provide the stronger party with new means to influence its weaker partner, as Albert Hirschman describes. In this case, the huge gap between the size of the respective economies was mitigated by Japan's extreme lack of natural resources. On trade issues, the overall value of Japan's exports to ASEAN countries was indeed low compared to its total export trade, and therefore Japan was a relatively important market for ASEAN but not vice versa. This was not the picture, however, when it came to crucial natural resources. Japan was the most resource-poor country among the industrialized nations and was highly dependent on imports of various key raw materials, especially from Asia, for its export-oriented industries.[59]

Despite the negative public sentiments, this Japanese resource dependence ameliorated some of the concerns about Japan's ability and motivation to utilize its asymmetric relations for political or other influence purposes. For example, a former Indonesian ambassador to Japan, in discussing the potential threats to his country from Japan and China, argued that Japan's dependence on imports would act as a brake to its political aggressiveness. He contrasted this fact with China's much smaller dependence on imports, which made that country potentially more dangerous. Many in Southeast Asia share this interpretation.[60] To rephrase this in conceptual terms, the concern that power disparities will turn into an influence effect à la Hirschman is a function of both the perceived dependence formed (the dissociation costs) and the perceived motivation of the other side to abuse this dependence. Given Japan's own dependence on Southeast Asian resources, this motivation was perceived to be low.

When referring to the perceived motivation to abuse dependence, one cannot ignore the regional political realities at the time. In the Japanese–Southeast Asian interaction of the 1950s, there were no more thorny political issues to be dealt with. The only major issue was the question of Japan's rearming itself, to which Southeast Asians strongly objected. In those years, however, rearming was not a real issue, because Japan was restricted by its American-made peace constitution and by its security alliance with the United States, which involved the physical presence of American troops on Japanese soil. In turn, Japan's conscious decision to focus its foreign policy only on economic growth was enabled by this situation. In the Middle Eastern cases, on the other hand, while bilateral peace treaties were signed, they remained inextricably linked to the ongoing Israeli-Palestinian conflict. Consequently, sensitivities to influence effects created by asymmetric economic deals were much higher. It follows that the more conflictual issues are resolved between the parties, the less concern there will be about cooperating economically with a former enemy in an asymmetrical economic context.

As years passed, the Southeast Asian economies developed and strengthened. The economic power disparities with Japan became less extreme than they were in the 1950s, but Southeast Asian economies still remained a stage behind Japan. The narrowing of the economic gap stemmed not only from developments on the national level but also from the creation of the Association of Southeast Asian Nations in 1967. Over time, ASEAN established a reputation as a successful regional organization and Japan began to find itself dealing more often not with individual Southeast Asian states but rather with a coalition of states via ASEAN. Operating as a group provided the Southeast Asian states with a much-improved bargaining position vis-à-vis Japan, especially after the revitalization of ASEAN at its Bali summit in 1976. As the ASEAN region became more attractive to Western investors as well, more and more Western companies were interested in doing business in Southeast Asia and were competing with Japanese firms. This, in turn, helped to reduce concerns that the asymmetrical nature of the economic interaction might be abused by Japan.

This leverage also increased due to the fact that, in the 1970s, Japan had already begun to pursue a political role in the region as well, in the context of the events in Vietnam. Southeast Asian states, via ASEAN, now demanded greater economic concessions from Japan, an increase in its imports of Southeast Asian goods, the adoption of a preferential tariff and trade regime for ASEAN exports to Japan, and more.[61] In other words, they were demanding that Japan make an effort to narrow the asymmetrical nature of their economic relations. (At a much earlier stage, Israel chose to sign an asymmetric trade agreement with Jordan that clearly privileged the Jordanians in order to mitigate their concerns regarding the large power disparities. In that case, however, Israeli policy was driven by a political logic utilizing economic tools.) Japan's logic was exclusively economic until the 1970s, when the political dimension finally kicked in.

After the mid-1970s, Japan realized the value of interacting with the states of Southeast Asia via regional multilateral forums like ASEAN because it was politically easier to deal with these states via their regional organization. This was especially true if Japan wanted to adopt a more active political role. So beginning in 1976, Japan changed its rather negative approach to ASEAN and started nurturing a political and economic dialogue with the organization.

Economic conflicts and complaints about Japan's lack of policy initiative following the Asian financial crisis in 1997 are still a source of tension in relations between ASEAN nations and Japan. However, those conflicts were of the "normal" type that occur between advanced and less advanced countries. ASEAN-Japan tensions today are more characteristic of the classic problems of north-south relations rather than reflecting the previous adversarial relations and the burden of history. As such, they already fall beyond the scope of this book. As the next chapter shows, this is not the case for Japanese relations with South Korea.[62]

One interesting insight can be derived from the experience of Japan with ASEAN. If indeed the development of ASEAN gave Southeast Asian states greater self-confidence in dealing with Japan and forced Japan to interact with ASEAN on a more equal basis, one might wonder if the strengthening of inter-Arab regional economic cooperation (as a rough parallel to ASEAN) would allow the narrowing of the economic gap with Israel and consequently more normal trading relations with it. More often than not, the notion of promoting inter-Arab cooperation is intuitively perceived as an anti-Israeli move. This may not be the case. This scenario, however, does not seem likely in the foreseeable future.

The Impact of Third Party Involvement

It is nearly impossible to discuss Japanese–Southeast Asian relations after World War II without referring to the United States. One of the tenets of the Yoshida Doctrine was Japan's complete reliance on the American security umbrella. Much of what seemed to be independent Japanese diplomacy in Southeast Asia was fully anchored in the American scheme of building triangular relations between the United States, Japan, and Southeast Asia within the context of the cold war in Asia. However, for the analytical purposes of this chapter, it is important to make a distinction between the different ways in which the United States influenced the transition to peace between Japan and the Southeast Asian states. The first, and most often discussed, was the broad, strategic impact of the American military presence and American security guarantees for regional stability. The second has to do with the economic tools the United States used to bring these countries closer together. The third has to do with the indirect benefits that the involved parties saw as stemming from their renewed relations (via the United States).

The combination of the American-written peace constitution that Japan adopted (especially its Article 9, banning the creation of an army), the American security treaty with Japan, and the physical presence of American troops on Japanese soil played an important role in mitigating Southeast Asian concerns about a future military threat from Japan. As long as Japan was in a formal security alliance with the United States, it had little incentive and little ability to embark on threatening rearmament. This was, and still is, the perception in Southeast Asia. The overwhelming American security and political presence basically neutralized the otherwise viable political and security concerns with regard to future Japanese aggression. This situation, of course, created a strategic setting much more comfortable and conducive to economic diplomacy. Given those strategic circumstances, the realist dilemma of exposing oneself to the dangers of interdependence with the former enemy was less severe. By comparison, from the perspective of Egypt or Jordan, the active American involvement in the Middle East appeared to be in reality a strong commitment to Israel per se and not to maintaining regional peace.

Furthermore, the overwhelming American security presence in the Pacific region and the U.S. security commitment to Japan were a precondition for Japan's successful pursuit of its policy of separating economics from politics. (This was a luxury none of the states in the Middle East could ever enjoy.) We should not forget that, at the most basic level, it was the United States that decided to push forward a very liberal peace treaty with Japan and practically forced (and bribed) the Southeast Asian states into accepting it. Everything that happened after that, including the reparations negotiations, must be understood in that context.

This being said, one should not jump to the conclusion that the American security presence explains the relatively successful transition to peace between Japan and Southeast Asia. As the earlier discussion throughout this chapter has shown, Southeast Asian states still had serious concerns about dealing with Japan, regardless of the American presence. Also, by the mid-1970s, this American presence and commitment had weakened somewhat, after its failure in Vietnam. As I have shown, it is actually that time period of the 1970s when most of the advancement in relations between the regional parties was made. So while the strategic reality that the United States created in Asia in the early post–World War II years was clearly conducive to Japan's economic peace diplomacy, it was not enough to explain the development of the regional peacemaking process.

Beyond the general context of American influence in Southeast Asia–Japan relations, what is perhaps most striking are the Americans' early attempts to push Japan back into Southeast Asia through various economic schemes and their rather limited success. The only American move that directly contributed to the development of economic relations between Japan and Southeast Asian states was its insertion of the reparations clause into the Treaty of San Francisco and its suggestion that reparations would be paid in goods and services rather than in cash flows. This obviously had an important impact on the development of relations, but it is important to point out that it was the Philippines that actually was directly responsible for the inclusion of the reparations clauses in the peace treaty.[63]

The American motivation to renew and develop economic ties between Japan and Southeast Asia stemmed from both economic and strategic concerns. Economically, because the United States wanted to strengthen the Japanese economy, it was forced to open its markets unilaterally to cheap Japanese goods. This move caused great concern among American manufacturers, who put intense pressure on the administration. Some, like J. F. Dulles (who negotiated the Japanese peace treaty and later became secretary of state), argued that Southeast Asia was Japan's natural market and that therefore Japanese goods should be heading there, thus reducing the impact of Japanese goods in the American market. Reviving trade between Japan and Southeast Asia would also serve two other strategic goals. It would help to curtail the Japanese temptation to trade with mainland China, and it would help to strengthen Southeast Asia's noncommunist countries. The basic American expectation and hope was that, just as Germany was to become the "workshop for Europe," Japan was to become the "workshop for Asia."[64]

Even before the signing of the Treaty of San Francisco, the Americans came up with various plans to stimulate regional triangular trade. Some of these were quite blunt and could be interpreted as pushing forward Japan's initial goal of creating a greater East Asian "co-prosperity sphere." One such proposal, ultimately rejected, was made by Tracy Voorhees, the undersecretary of the army, who suggested that any loan or grant the United States gave to any country in Asia would be tied directly to Japan. Perhaps the most ambitious plan was to create the Yen Fund. This plan was based on the assumption that the main factor limiting Japan's exports was the inability of regional states desiring Japanese goods to pay for them. The proposal therefore suggested that Japan pay for its imports from the United States with Japan's own currency, the yen, which the United States would, in turn, give to its Southeast Asia partners, who would use it to buy Japanese goods, thus creating a form of reparations. This plan also never materialized. One of the main obstacles was the opposition of Southeast Asian states at that time to such regional trade plans. Any such plan, not surprisingly, smacked of renewed Japanese economic dominance. They preferred to strengthen their bilateral economic ties with the United States rather than with Japan or each other. The lack of enthusiasm among Japan's potential Southeast Asian partners helped prevent most of the U.S. regional initiatives from getting off the ground.[65] In the final analysis, Japan's return to Asia was not so much linked to these American efforts but to bilateral regional dynamics.

States involved in the transition to peace may move through the process with the hope of gaining indirectly from a third party, in this case the United States. Prime Minister Kishi, who initiated the first attempt to begin serious interaction with Southeast Asia and who, in 1954, was the first Japanese prime minister to go on a tour of the region, suggested later on in his memoirs that his emphasis on Southeast Asia was a tool for improving Japan's position vis-à-vis the United States by showing that Japan was the representative of all of Asia.[66] This was the indirect benefit to be gained from better relations with Southeast Asia. However, a central difference between this case and the Egyptian and Jordanian cases is that here, despite the strategic centrality of the United States, there were clear and important *direct* economic benefits to be gained from the new bilateral and regional relations, independent of benefits related to the United States. This, in turn, gave greater long-term viability to these relations. In fact, even into the 1990s, Japanese–Southeast Asian cooperation at times appeared to be both cooperation vis-à-vis the United States as well as competition against it.

Furthermore, the Southeast Asian incentive to cooperate with Japan was also strengthened by the appreciation of the very different economic ideology of the United States—the second potential source of economic development aid for Southeast Asia. Whereas the United States called for minimal government intervention and for reliance on private capital and enterprise, Southeast Asian governments wanted to pursue heavy industrialization with massive government involvement. This was much more compatible with the development model that Japan advanced, which came to be known as the model of the developmental state. Against this background, cooperation with Japan became more attractive, thanks in part to Southeast Asian governments' dislike of the U.S. development model.[67]

While the United States is clearly the prominent third party in this case, one could also point to the growing role of another regional actor: ASEAN. One of the reasons for the durability of Japanese-Indonesian and Japanese-Filipino relations is the nesting of those relations within the regional multilateral setting of ASEAN. I have already discussed how ASEAN has mitigated the negative consequences of power disparities between the states. Beyond that, Japan's institutionalized interaction with ASEAN over the years as a dialogue partner, as a participant in the Post Ministerial Conferences (PMC), and as a member of its security forum (the ASEAN Regional Forum [ARF]) has greatly improved, deepened, and strengthened relations between the states. Relations expanded to cover cooperation across various fields—economics, finance, and transnational challenges such as counterterrorism and antipiracy efforts, environmental protection, and measures to fight epidemics.[68] The two bilateral trade agreements between Japan and Indonesia and Japan and the Philippines, presented at the beginning of this chapter, are in fact part of the broader ASEAN-Japan Comprehensive Economic Partnership (AJCEP) that was completed in April 2008.[69] This nesting of bilateral relations in a broader multilateral cooperative arrangement helps to stabilize relations in the long run. This role of regional institutions is still nonexistent in the Israeli context. It is, however, of central importance in the two European cases discussed in chapters 6 and 7.

To CONCLUDE, in the cases discussed in chapters 2 and 3, I pointed out that sometimes there is no convergence between former enemies as to the priority of political or economic goals, thus increasing misunderstanding and frustration. In the case examined in this chapter, there was a convergence and an understanding between the parties on the priority of promoting economic development to achieve the political goal of regime survival and domestic stability. In fact, until the late 1970s, most of the Japanese attempts to pursue a regional political role met with suspicion and opposition.[70] In all three countries, there was close cooperation between government officials and powerful business leaders —cooperation that was based on the common economic development philosophies of these regimes. This relatively small number of powerful actors on both sides, each with a strong vested interest in peace, also made it easier to control the process of building new economic relations. This powerful domestic and cross-national coalition was the driving force behind the signing of the peace (and reparations) treaties and the development of economic ties among the three countries. In terms of the analytical framework of this book, this coalition was clearly a sufficient condition to reach the first stage of the transition to peace. It was also quite effective in bringing about the beginning of economic normalization (the second stage). However, this elitist process of normalization, combined with the popular sentiment in the Philippines and Indonesia that ordinary people would not benefit from the peace with Japan, led eventually to the violent riots of 1974. In this case as well, we find that the peacemakers were not democratic regimes but authoritarian ones. Here, as in Egypt or Jordan, this centralized decision-making structure was useful in manipulating a difficult transition to peace with a hated enemy but then posed problems at the second stage of the transition because the public simply did not trust its government.

While many scholars and practitioners point to the merits of Japan's economic diplomacy, the fact remains that in order to move forward in the second stage of peace, toward greater normalization, politics had to come back in. Indeed, Japan's true re-integration into Southeast Asian politics came only in the 1990s, once it began to pursue an active political regional role. Thus, there cannot be an exclusively economic road to peace building.

In terms of the impact of wide economic power disparities, this case raised several points. The extreme disparities played a positive role in the first stage of transition to peace, creating huge stakes in peace for the Southeast Asian states. However, these disparities were a crucial factor in generating wide popular fears of the threat of a Japanese economic invasion, thus generating wider opposition to trade normalization. This situation in Southeast Asia underscored the importance of looking beyond the raw economic data of each state. It reflects the importance of looking at public perceptions or expectations about developing dependence or asymmetric interdependence in specific economic issue areas and across them. While it was clear that trade and investment relations were going to be extremely asymmetric (in favor of Japan), the fact that Japan was extremely dependent on Southeast Asian natural resources was enough to mitigate concerns that Japan would abuse its relative power to exert unwanted influence on the regional states. Furthermore, this case demonstrates that the use of regional cooperation institutions can help mitigate the problems of power disparities, as was the case with ASEAN, and thus facilitate the development of normal, peaceful relations.

The U.S. presence in Asia, especially during the early post–World War II years, clearly played an important role in the story of this transition to peace. However, I hope to have shown that understanding the U.S. role is not enough to understand the transition process and that actual American efforts to get the parties to interact economically with each other showed surprisingly little success. The limits of a third party's ability to promote normalization are demonstrated most clearly in the case of Japan and the Republic of Korea.

5

GOVERNMENT AND BIG BUSINESS

Normalizing Relations between Japan and South Korea

UNLIKE THE OCCUPATION of the Philippines and Indonesia, which lasted only three years, Japan's occupation of Korea lasted from 1910 until 1945. It took twenty more years for a normalization treaty to be signed, in 1965. Even then, the treaty triggered massive domestic opposition in the Republic of Korea (hereafter ROK or South Korea). Economic relations between the two countries, however, developed and even flourished over the years. These intense and highly developed economic relations did not spill over into the cultural-social sphere until the late 1990s, however. This case raises several interesting issues that shed light on the role of economic factors in the transition to peace and also highlight some of the remaining questions. First, this case, perhaps more than the Southeast Asian case, resembles the Middle Eastern situations in the level of preexisting and deeply ingrained animosity between the parties. At the same time, the developments over time are quite different. Second, the Japanese-Korean case, at least until the 1990s, exhibits the limits of spillover from economic normalization to cultural-social normalization. It is quite impressive to see the gap between the extraordinary levels of bilateral trade and FDI, on the one hand, and the obvious animosity and resentment that persist. In light of that persistent animosity, exploring the developments in Japanese-Korean relations further accentuates the difficulty of defining "peace." How does one aggregate high economic interdependence with high levels of animosity and the heavy emotional baggage of history? Finally, this case has also raised the question of the appropriate historical cut-off. When can we say that the transition to peace has been completed? There is no simple answer because it depends, once again, on one's perception of what "peace" is.

An Overview of the Shift from Conflict to Peace

It is customary to begin any discussion of Korean antipathy toward the Japanese with the thirty-five years of Japanese colonial rule. However, this animosity runs much deeper and further back in history, to the sixteenth century and the invasions of the Japanese warlord Toyotomi Hideyoshi. Those incursions led to unprecedented destruction in the Korean peninsula (later matched by the devastation of the war in 1950–1953). In the nineteenth century, Japan fought both the Chinese (1894–1895) and the Russians (1904–1905) in order to establish its power and authority in Korea. Only then does the time line reach the long period of colonial rule. During that period, any internal resistance to Japanese rule was crushed, and even peaceful demonstrations for independence in 1919 were met with brutality. Beginning in the early 1930s, the Japanese tried to force the "Japanization" of the Koreans, not allowing them to learn their language in school or use it at home, forcing them to "Japanize" their names, and then abusing Korean resources to support the war effort in Japan.[1] During the war itself, the Japanese army abused many Korean women, forcing them to serve as "comfort women," which has remained a thorny issue in the relationship to this day.[2]

Unlike the Philippines and Indonesia, Korea was already a unified independent state before it was taken over by the Japanese. Consequently, Korean nationalism has fermented under Japanese rule, and, to a large extent, it came to be identified with anti-Japanese sentiments. This historical animosity and negative historical memory is deeply ingrained in the mind-set of Koreans and Japanese through formal and informal institutions. Even today the two main national holidays in Korea celebrate Korean patriotism by remembering the struggle for independence from Japanese rule.[3]

After World War II ended, the southern part of Korea regained its independence when the United States took control of that zone while the Soviet Union took control of the northern zone. Twenty years later, South Korea and Japan signed a treaty normalizing relations. (Korea was not a signatory on the Treaty of San Francisco because it was not an independent state during the war.) However, even beyond the very strong anti-Japanese sentiments that still prevailed when the treaty was signed in 1965, South Korea had several fundamental issues to resolve with the Japanese. One was the issue of property claims that Koreans demanded as compensation for the years of colonial rule and abuse. Related to that was the broad societal demand for an official and explicit apology from Japan for its wrongdoings. A separate problem was a dispute over fishing rights. This problem got worse following the unilateral declaration of South Korea's first president, Syngman Rhee, in January 1952, establishing the Rhee Line or Peace Line. This line of demarcation extended two hundred miles offshore at certain points, and within it the Korean government intended to exercise sovereignty over the fishery. A third problem, arising after 1953, was the issue of recognition for South Korea and not North Korea and consequently the whole issue of economic and diplomatic interaction with the North. A fourth problem had to do with the treatment of the approximately 600,000 Koreans living in Japan itself. The last thorn was the territorial dispute over the island group known as Dokto (in Korean) or Takeshima (in Japanese).[4]

Relations during this period were characteristic of either a very tenuous cold peace or, perhaps more appropriately, a cold war situation. On the one hand, early negotiations had already gotten under way in 1952, though with limited success. They ended with a decision to exchange notes for the establishment of diplomatic offices as of April 1952 and to extend the terms of the SCAP-Korean trade, financial, and shipping agreements.[5] On the other hand, this was a period of intense anti-Japanese sentiment and outright conflicts. Between 1952 and 1964, for example, 2,874 Japanese fishermen were captured and detained to serve terms ranging from a few months to more than a year for their intrusion into the area delimited by the Rhee Line.[6] In 1959, a serious crisis erupted after an earlier decision of the Japanese government to allow the repatriation of Koreans to North Korea. The South Koreans responded by enacting economic sanctions, including a ban on trade with Japan, and President Rhee actually ordered the military to destroy the Soviet ships on which the Koreans were to be returned to North Korea. The only reason this did not happen was that the military refused, arguing it could not operate without American help.[7]

The 1965 normalization agreement settled some of the open issues. The fisheries problem was resolved, as were as the Korean property claims. The ROK was to receive the total of $800 million from Japan, with $300 million in grants, $200 million in government loans, and up to $300 million in private commercial loans. To facilitate economic cooperation between the two countries, an agreement was made to hold annual South Korean–Japanese ministerial conferences, and within the next few years, various agreements were signed, including a double taxation pact. This government-level interaction was soon followed by private Japanese enterprise when, in 1966, the South Koreans for the first time allowed a Japanese company to own a 51 percent share in a joint venture with a local firm. In 1967, two Japanese banks began operating in Seoul.[8] By the mid-1970s, private-level institutional ties had developed in the form of the Korean-Japanese Economic Cooperation Committee, organized by leading business figures from both nations and meeting regularly, as well as the Korea-Japan Friendship Association and the Parliamentarians' League.[9]

After the signing of the treaty, there was a rapid increase in Japanese trade and investment in the ROK. South Korean exports to Japan jumped from $23.5 million in 1962 to $84.7 million in 1967, to $409.6 million in 1972, to nearly $3.4 billion in 1982, and up to approximately $12.7 billion in 1990. At the same time, imports from Japan surged from $109.2 million in 1962 to $443 million in 1967, to approximately $1 billion in 1972, to $5.3 billion in 1980, and up to $18.6 billion in 1990.[10] By the end of the 1970s, Japanese FDI in the ROK had reached $610 million on a cumulative basis, and Japan extended more than $1.1 billion in government-administered loans and more than $2.4 billion in commercial loans. Japan was South Korea's largest source of FDI, which by 1990 had reached nearly $4 billion.[11] Trade continued rising into the twenty-first century. Japanese exports to the ROK reached approximately $28.5 billion and nearly doubled by 2005 to nearly $46.9 billion. Imports from the ROK remained significantly lower but were also rising, from about $15.4 billion in 2002 to $24.5 billion in 2005.[12]

Despite various problems related to either the chronic trade imbalance or trade with North Korea, there is no doubt that Japan and South Korea have reached an impressive level of economic normalization. This impressive advancement of economic cooperation, however, was achieved without the normalization of other issues. Politically, relations between the two nations had their ups and downs. Cooler relations in the early 1970s, following Prime Minister Tanaka's decision to follow a more balanced regional foreign policy and the Japanese normalization of relations with China, replaced the initial period of cooperation. Relations reached a low in 1973, when Korean intelligence agents kidnapped Kim Dae-jung, the South Korean opposition leader (later to become president), from his hotel room in Tokyo, leading to intense Japanese criticism of this gross breach of its sovereignty.[13] The reader may recall that a similar incident greatly damaged developing Israeli-Jordanian peace relations, when Israeli Mossad agents tried to assassinate the head of the Hamas political branch, Khaled Mashal, in Amman.

ROK-Japanese relations improved against the backdrop of U.S. plans to disengage from Asia in the mid-1970s. After a crisis in 1982 over alleged amendments to Japanese history textbooks to reflect more favorably upon Japan's wartime behavior, relations once again improved in 1983–1984, following an exchange of visits by Prime Minister Yasuhiro Nakasone and President Chun Doo Hwan and the emperor's historic public apology for Japan's past aggression against Korea. Victor Cha argues that the ups and downs in political relations between Japan and South Korea are linked to their perceptions regarding the likelihood of American abandonment. Other scholars also stress that the political dynamics were the outcome of strategic conditions rather than anything else.

The most obvious gap in relations emerged between the high level of economic cooperation and the absolute lack of cooperation or, more precisely, the active ban on any Japanese popular culture products. A strict official ban on Japanese culture existed until the early 1990s. Performance of traditional Japanese arts, associated with the imperial tradition, was prohibited for decades. Japanese songs were banned from South Korean radio and TV. Until 1987, even Korean songs that were considered to be written in a Japanese style were banned. The only place in Seoul where it was legal to watch Japanese films was at the Japanese embassy's cultural center.[14] This is reminiscent of the absolute boycott of Israeli cultural activities in Egypt. However, whereas in Egypt this cultural boycott stemmed from below, from the active opposition of Egyptian artists and filmmakers, in South Korea it was dictated by the government. This cultural boycott reflected an ongoing feeling of distrust and resentment toward the Japanese, feelings that were periodically strengthened by such crises as the one over history textbooks, the visits of Japanese prime ministers to the Yasukuni shrine, where wartime Japanese heroes are buried, the issue of the comfort women, and what the Japanese perceived as a Korean obsession with the issue of a public apology.[15]

Only in the late 1990s did it seem that the underlying negative feelings toward Japan were beginning to weaken. The cultural ban gradually gave way to cultural interaction following the presidency of Kim Dae-jung. In the 1998 visit of Kim to Japan, he and Prime Minister Keizo Obuchi announced the decision to build a "new Japan-ROK Partnership toward the twenty-first century," and the Japanese prime minister offered a written apology to the Korean leader. Kim's successor, Roh Moo-hyun, followed in his footsteps.[16] There were more and more institutionalized channels of communication, as well as an expansion of popular channels of communication, and even on security issues there was cooperation at a functional level.[17] Both countries now engage in an ongoing strategic dialogue, have a joint committee on environmental cooperation, a joint history project, and a system of high-school student exchange via the Japan–East Asia Network of Exchange for Students and Youth. It is worth noting that of the foreign tourists visiting Japan in 2007, the largest number came from South Korea (2.6 million).[18]

The emerging security cooperation between the two states is especially impressive in light of the years of open hostility and mistrust. It has been argued that Japan-ROK security relations reached their adolescence in the late 1990s, with the development of military cooperation in various fields. This cooperation is now stable enough to withstand periodic crises on issues such as the history textbooks.[19] While not a warm peace, current relations between Japan and ROK can be characterized as relations of a stable peace.[20]

As with the previous chapters, the goal of the following analysis is not to offer a general explanation for the fortunes of Korean-Japanese relations but to examine the type of impact that economic factors and their interaction with politics had on the process. More specifically, while economic factors may not be currently central for understanding the overall relations between the two states, I suggest that they are very important for understanding the earlier stages of the actual transition to peace in the 1960s and that they are an important contributing factor in many of the current problems.[21] By looking at the economic stakes involved and at the nature of the domestic winners and losers from the transition to peace, we can explain the rapid economic normalization that occurred after 1965 despite the clear and overwhelming hostility toward Japan. Examining these domestic coalitions, together with an examination of the negative impact of the economic power disparities between South Korea and Japan, should help us understand why even extensive economic interaction was not enough to push forward deeper normalization. The relative narrowing of these disparities combined with the domestic shift in South Korea toward greater democratization help us in turn to understand the trend since the late 1990s.

While there is perhaps no direct link between the recent deepening of the relations and the growing security cooperation, such relations, in my opinion, could not have developed without the backdrop of intensive (even if at times conflictual) economic interaction over the years. The recent increase in security cooperation between the two states is not so much a response to a North Korean threat as it is a reflection of the shared goal of coordinating responses to low-intensity crises and maintaining regional stability. These shared goals, in turn, are a result of the intensifying economic interaction in the region, primarily the surge in maritime traffic, as well as shared responsibilities created by overlapping exclusive economic zones (EEZs) designated under the auspices of the UN Convention on the Law of the Sea (UNCLOS) of 1994.[22]

The Economic Peace Dividend

As in the cases discussed in previous chapters, the willingness of South Korea to sign a treaty with Japan to normalize relations was closely linked to the expectation of a major economic dividend for the country and for the regime. Unlike the two Middle Eastern cases, especially the one involving Egypt, here there was a direct economic dividend to gain from Japan for the economy as a whole. This economic peace dividend, however, was not apparent until the early 1960s. This delay greatly contributed to the extremely slow pace of the negotiations between the two countries.

After World War II, and much more so after the Korean War ended in 1953, South Korea was in a state of virtual devastation. More than a million civilians had died and more than 3 million soldiers had been killed. The country had no industrial base. Under colonial rule, the Japanese had built enormous hydroelectric stations on the Yalu River that generated 90 percent of the electricity used, but these plants were under the control of North Korea when the peninsula was divided after World War II. Similarly, the large chemical factories built by the Japanese were also on the northern side of the new border at the 38th parallel. All South Korea had was a cheap labor force, which had been undermined by the high human cost of war.[23]

During the 1950s, South Korea under Syngman Rhee followed an inward-looking economic approach, focusing on rebuilding infrastructure and producing enough consumer nondurables and construction materials for basic needs. Exports were very limited and existed only for a small number of primary commodities. Most of the reconstruction during that period was financed by the United States. At that time, therefore, normalizing relations with the hated Japanese did not appear to be important economically. This changed significantly in the 1960s with the coming to power of Park Chung-Hee, who adopted an export-oriented development strategy.

Park's strategy of export-led growth required for its success a significant amount of foreign capital to invest in new industrial projects, as well as a significant increase in imports of raw materials and machinery. At the same time, however, the United States was gradually reducing its aid to South Korea. Consequently, it became painfully obvious that a treaty with Japan was needed in order to utilize Japanese capital and know-how. Japanese economic assistance was regarded as crucial for the implementation of Park's five-year development plans. This logic led the Park government to almost unilaterally push through the normalization treaty with Japan, despite domestic opposition.[24] As described previously, this logic worked very well. After normalization, the huge amounts of Japanese capital, in the form of loans and investment, were crucial for South Korea's developmental take-off. In one very concrete example, one of South Korea's major steel companies, the Pohang Integrated Steel Works, would not have existed without the Japanese. When the South Koreans wanted to build the steel complex, both the World Bank and a consortium of European firms rejected requests to finance it. The project was saved only through substantial Japanese financial as well as professional assistance.[25]

Critics of these normalized relations argue that this economic benefit was accompanied by a very high cost for South Korea, which became a debtor nation chronically suffering from a trade deficit with Japan. Its development, they argue, was a dependent development.[26] Elaborating on this debate is beyond the scope of this chapter, but I do address an aspect of this question in my discussion of the impact of economic power disparities. This being said, even critics of these trade relations are likely to acknowledge the crucial role that Japanese capital played in the early period of South Korean industrialization.

In the transition to peace between Japan and the Philippines and Indonesia, it was clear from the outset that Japan had a vital economic interest in resuming normal economic relations with the Southeast Asian states, due to their abundance of natural resources. Such a strong economic interest did not initially exist in the Korean case. In the early postwar years, most Japanese knew very little about Korea and cared even less. While in North Korea there were minerals, South Korea had almost nothing to export but labor. Consequently, unlike the Southeast Asian cases, in which there was a concerted Japanese effort to advance the reparations agreements and resume trade, in this case Japan was in no hurry. It felt that time was on its side since it was clear that the South Koreans, sooner or later, would turn to Japan for help.[27] In fact, right after the 1950–1953 war, Korea was thought to have had a limited capacity to absorb capital, especially in the industrial sector. Many observers after the Korean War gravely doubted South Korea's chances of success in overcoming serious economic stagnation.[28] This situation explains the extremely long delay in signing a normalization treaty. Also in contrast to the Southeast Asian case, the initial Japanese interest in normalization was strategic. Since Korea was always perceived as "a dagger pointed at the heart of Japan," it was important to secure a stable regime there and to prevent the expansion of communism.[29]

Later on, however, Japan's economic interest in the ROK emerged. The Japanese economy enjoyed a boom during the Korean War, and once the war was over, the Japanese economy again faced problems. Japan's government concluded that long-term growth required secure export markets to finance necessary imports. For that purpose, South Korea had two useful assets: labor and land. In order to both maintain a competitive edge and deal with emerging domestic criticism regarding the environmental cost of industrialization, the Japanese became interested in transferring to South Korea the labor-intensive and processing sectors of key industries such as steel, aluminum, chemicals, and even shipbuilding.[30] As discussed below, it became possible to capitalize on this potential economic dividend only after the regime in South Korea adopted a different developmental strategy than the one Rhee had pursued.[31]

The Domestic Balance of Winners and Losers after Peace

The perception of the economic peace dividend from Japan, as described previously, emerged only after General Park Chung-Hee came to power. The first South Korean president, Syngman Rhee, did not believe he had anything to gain from normalizing relations with Japan. When Rhee came to power in August 1948, it was under the auspices of the American Military Government (AMG), which recognized an immediate need to stabilize the political situation. As a result, many individuals who had collaborated with the Japanese colonialists were brought into the government because they were the only skilled personnel available at the time. This lenient treatment of former colonial collaborators was seen as unjust by many nationalist Koreans who had been active in the struggle against Japan. Consequently, Rhee's regime suffered to begin with from a problem of weak legitimacy. In order to boost his legitimacy, Rhee mobilized two sentiments: anticommunism and anti-Japanism. The latter was a sentiment he strongly and personally endorsed, as he himself was known as someone with extreme anti-Japanese sentiments. On the economic front, Rhee did not feel he was sacrificing much by rejecting a treaty with Japan due to his strategy of import-substitution, which left little room for Japan. Furthermore, his economic focus was not on development but on strengthening his own position, and he worried mainly about his ability to fund the police and the military, which backed his regime. Given the predatory nature of the Rhee regime, little benefit was seen in normalizing relations with the hated Japanese.[32]

This calculus changed dramatically when General Park came to power. Park, who led a military coup in 1961, announced an ambitious program of economic development. The establishment of a self-supporting economy was one of the "six revolutionary pledges" of the military regime. Economic success was crucial for establishing the legitimacy of the Park government. This need grew even stronger after the 1963 elections, which were to transform his government from a military dictatorship to a constitutional government legitimized by popular support. Although Park won the elections, the results were inconclusive and did not provide him with the clear mandate to rule that he wanted.[33]

Unlike his predecessor, Park adopted a development strategy based on export-led growth. His first five-year economic plan (unveiled in 1962) aimed at developing labor-intensive and light industries with outward-oriented industrialization strategies. The success of this strategy, however, hinged upon a massive influx of foreign capital. The ROK economy was suffering under the heavy strain of maintaining standing armed forces of some 600,000 men since the signing of the Korean War armistice, and the government was spending more than 33 percent of its total annual budget for defense. The United States, which was the major source of capital after the 1950–1953 war, was reducing rather than expanding its foreign aid to South Korea. Consequently, Japan emerged as a crucial source of both the capital and technology needed for Korean industrialization and development.[34] As described previously, the massive influx of Japanese capital was a crucial factor in Park's being able to implement his economic plans and maintain his power.

Probably not by coincidence, Park's economic approach, which led to a strong interest in renewing formal ties with Japan, was enhanced by his own personal feelings toward Japan. Unlike Rhee, Park was educated in a Japanese military academy. He did not share Rhee's strong anti-Japanese emotions but viewed Japan as a model for development and modernization.[35] This view, combined with the critical need for Japanese capital, led Park to conclude that while signing the normalization treaty with Japan would have domestic costs (e.g., widespread opposition), it was still economically, and therefore also politically, the sensible thing to do. Park's own pro-Japanese feelings probably did facilitate the signing of the treaty. Indeed, after Park was assassinated in 1979, relations between South Korea and Japan cooled and suffered several crises. However, these ups and downs remained within the framework of the normalization treaty, and economic relations continued to expand.[36] Similarly, in the Jordanian case many observers have commented that the late King Hussein's personality and vision had been crucial in the effort to develop relations with Israel. Relations continued, though, even after his death.

Under the authoritarian system that existed in the ROK until the late 1980s, the president was the most significant political actor, and his own calculations consequently had a crucial impact on foreign policy. However, the pro-Japan coalition was wide and included many big business firms that were emerging in South Korea. The nature of their ties with the government is a topic of much debate among scholars studying South Korea's "economic miracle."

South Korea's large conglomerates, known as the *chaebol,* were a relatively new phenomenon that grew only after World War II. Unlike Japan, whose *zaibatsu* (business conglomerates) were well organized and active in the pre–World War II era, Korea had no significant independent major business firms. Korean capitalists during colonial rule were tightly supervised by the Japanese administrators and could not operate independently.[37] After the devastation of the two wars, very little capital remained in the country. No millionaire businessmen existed in South Korea in 1953. The majority of the *chaebol* developed after 1956, with their most intensive growth taking place between 1966 and 1970.[38] The growth of the *chaebol* indeed coincided with President Park's new economic strategy. According to the new strategy, the government encouraged and promoted the development of giant, Japanese-style trading companies to boost the export of labor-intensive goods. After nationalizing the commercial banks, the government became actively involved in the allocation of foreign loans. Consequently, the *chaebol* received most of the foreign capital.[39]

This emerging big business class had a direct stake in the success of Park's development strategy. Consequently, it also had a direct stake in the building of economic ties with Japan. These business and financial leaders organized the Korean Businessmen's Association (KBA). They saw great opportunities in the prospect of $800 million in Japanese capital that would come with normalization. Their monopolistic domestic market was already saturated beyond the point of further expansion, and better relations with Japan would open new opportunities to explore foreign markets with the help of Japanese capital, technology, and marketing skills. Korean business leaders also believed that the ROK could take over Japan's light industries and thus employ South Korea's large and low-paid yet skilled labor force.[40] Furthermore, top executives in Korea often were fluent in Japanese and were familiar with Japanese business practices.[41]

This strong coalition of government and business cooperated closely, creating a situation somewhat similar to that in Japan but in a more top-down manner, with the Korean president less dependent on business for political support than in Japan. Scholars differ in their characterization of government-business relations in South Korea, especially under the Park regime. While initially Park tried to crack down on the large and powerful *chaebol* by arresting their owners, he eventually became convinced that he could use them to advance his economic plans. From then on, a relationship of give-and-take developed between the state and big business.[42] The debate on whether the state exerted greater influence on big business or vice versa is less relevant for our purposes here. What is important is the fact that a very close relationship developed between these groups, and it was this strong, elitist coalition that was the driving force behind the normalization of relations with Japan. A lot of criticism has been directed over the years at the political corruption and collaboration between the government and the *chaebol.* This criticism, in turn, also influenced South Koreans' perceptions of the growing economic relations with Japan. For example, a common argument was that the intense economic interaction between South Korea and Japan was driven by and dominated by a triangular elitist group consisting of President Park, powerful Korean businessmen and politicians, and Japanese multinational firms. Such a perception clearly prevented these economic relations from spilling over to other issue areas and generating a positive cognitive change in perceptions of Japan.[43]

The perception that a corrupt relationship was emerging between South Korean elites and the Japanese government further enhanced broad societal opposition to normalization. The strong government-business coalition, which gained much in normalization, faced a strong and aggressive coalition of opposition parties, students, the press, and religious organizations, which clearly did not feel that there was much to gain from such a treaty. These various groups demanded an official, sincere Japanese apology to Korea for its misdeeds during the war. The money that Japan was to transfer to South Korea according to the treaty was not called "reparations" or "compensation" as was the case in Southeast Asia but rather "economic cooperation." Opponents argued that there was no legitimate reason to sign a normalization treaty without a proper Japanese acknowledgment of and apology for their past offenses. Opponents of normalization also argued that South Korea would become a market where Japan would dump its surplus and obsolete industrial goods, that Korean business leaders would become agents of monopolistic Japanese capital, and that the Japanese would control the politics of Korea.[44] As noted previously, the obvious winners of the economic development strategy of the Park regime were the *chaebol.* Small and medium-sized companies did not get to enjoy much of the foreign capital entering the country. South Korean labor was also paying the price of the pressure to increase exports. It was exploited and denied many of its basic rights (e.g., to attract Japanese investors, the government denied Korean workers employed in foreign-owned enterprises the right to strike).[45]

On a more fundamental level, the opposition to the normalization treaty reflected the public's deep distrust of both Japan and their own government. The hatred toward Japan was a national sentiment, not just one of the political opposition. It engulfed the elderly, who had lived under Japanese colonial rule, as well as the younger generation, which had been brought up under anti-Japanese indoctrination via the media and school textbooks. In fact, argues Victor Cha, parts of the Korean self-identity became constructed in polar opposition to Japan.[46] This antipathy toward Japan combined with the public's distrust of their own government. Distrust of a corrupt government made it difficult for many people to envision themselves as potential beneficiaries of the treaty in the long run. They were concerned that the ruling party would abuse the normalization and pocket the money given by the Japanese, and they feared that most of the public would receive no benefits or compensation whatsoever for the direct suffering it endured under Japanese rule.[47]

This opposition expanded aggressively. Hundreds of protest rallies and demonstrations took place throughout the campaign against normalization in 1964–1965, and more than 3 million students participated in protest activities. These protests were forcefully quelled. In June 1964, martial law was declared in Seoul, and in August 1965, the protest was crushed by a division of combat troops called into Seoul under a decree of "garrison state" (similar to martial law).[48] When the treaty was to be ratified in the ROK National Assembly, opposition members resigned en masse. The ruling Democratic Republican Party members then moved on to ratify the treaty in a one-party assembly.[49]

On the Japanese side, as described earlier, there was no urging needed to reach a formal agreement with South Korea until the 1960s. Still, by the mid-1960s, a strong coalition supporting normalization of relations had emerged. Pressure was coming from the Japanese Ministry of Foreign Affairs and from a group of powerful conservative Japanese politicians. They argued that, regardless of how much financial compensation Japan would end up paying, the Korean public would always want more. Consequently, it was best to strike a deal with Park, who was under intense pressure and whose authoritarian rule made him less susceptible to popular demands.

Another group pushing for the treaty in 1965 was the powerful Japanese business lobby that stood to gain from renewed official diplomatic relations along the lines described earlier. While as many as sixty major trading and industrial firms had offices in Seoul by the mid-1960s, the ROK still represented an untapped market, which became especially attractive in light of Park's ambitious development plans.[50] Some of the members of this conservative group pushing for normalization were former bureaucrats in the Japanese colonial government in Korea. They were comfortable with the authoritarian atmosphere there and developed close personal ties with Korean government officials in order to advance relations. Their behavior, however, alienated many intellectuals, as well as people within the business community.[51]

This "Korea lobby" spent a lot of money on propaganda in favor of normalization. Out of all of their former colonial markets, the ROK was a very comfortable one for them, especially in view of its geographic proximity and their vast knowledge of Korea. Also, the expanding investment by the United States, West Germany, France, and Italy in the ROK led to a concern that Japanese business would be eliminated from the Korean market unless diplomatic relations were established soon.[52] Although, as noted previously, Japan had a strategic interest in normalizing relations with South Korea, it was the business groups and economic interests on the Japanese side that pushed the deal forward. The ROK also clearly stood to gain politically from normalization, given its struggle for international recognition vis-à-vis North Korea, the worrying activities of North Koreans in Japan, and the need to improve the status of the large group of Koreans still living in Japan. Still, the analysis suggests that the economic gain was the most powerful one in this situation.[53]

Within Japan, however, there was also vocal opposition to the normalization treaty. By contrast, such loud opposition did not occur prior to the signing of the reparations agreements with the Philippines and Indonesia. Japanese opposition stemmed from several sometimes unrelated concerns. The Japanese Socialist Party was concerned that signing the treaty would serve American, rather than Japanese interests, and would eventually push Japan and South Korea into a northeast Asia treaty organization analogous to the North Atlantic Treaty Organization. They were also concerned about the moral aspect of signing a treaty with South Korea's repressive military junta. The communists, as well as the Koreans residing in Japan who supported North Korea through the active Chōsoren organization, opposed the treaty because it perpetuated the division between the North and the South and offered formal recognition to the South. The socialists played an important role in postponing the treaty until 1965, because they set up violent opposition to Prime Minister Ikeda Hayato when he raised the issue for discussion in the Diet.[54] Their intense opposition does help explain the length of the negotiations. However, it was not strong enough to prevent the treaty from being signed.

Among the general public in Japan, initial attitudes toward Korea ranged from lack of interest to contempt. Most Japanese did not think that they owed Koreans any apologies whatsoever. They held a paternalistic view of Korea, doubted that it had ever had an independent culture, and viewed Koreans as ungrateful for the contributions that the Japanese were making for their development.[55] Public opinion polls ranked Korea as one of the states most disliked by Japanese. While ordinary people in Tokyo did not go out to demonstrate against the treaty the way residents of Seoul had taken to the streets, the public's broad negativity toward Korea was seemingly impervious to alteration by the treaty and increased economic interaction between the two states.[56]

How can we link this discussion to the question of the different stages in the transition to peace? The Korean case does not neatly fall into the categories defined in the first chapter. Some trade existed even before 1965. The treaty signed that year was not called a peace treaty, since Japan and Korea were never officially at war, but it can be seen as the official act institutionalizing a cold peace, with the formal, mutual recognition of Japan and South Korea. The 1965 treaty, which was in fact called a "normalization treaty," did lead to a surge in economic interaction, as described previously. This government–big business-dominated process was extremely successful in bringing about economic normalization. However, as the first part of this chapter shows, this economic normalization did not automatically spill over to other issues. Almost twenty years after the treaty, when South Korean president Chun Doo Hwan made his historic trip to Tokyo, his visit was accompanied by large demonstrations in Korea, as well as some public opposition in Japan.[57] Similarly, in joint public opinion polls conducted in both countries in 1984, 1988, and 1990, there was actually an increase among Koreans in negative assessments of Japan's economic aggression against its neighbors and a strong emphasis on the past.[58] The lack of any real, positive social impact of the intense economic cooperation is easier to understand in light of the perceptions of the broader public in South Korea regarding their own regime and its interaction with Japan. This observation necessarily leads us to examine the impact of the democratization process that South Korea has been undergoing since 1987 on the warming up of the peace with Japan.

I argued in chapter 1 that progress on the normalization axis cannot proceed very far if broader segments in society do not feel that they are winners in the process. As the cases discussed in previous chapters clearly showed, under authoritarian rule, many segments in society are skeptical about their regime's intentions and about the likelihood of enjoying the fruits of major foreign policy shifts. The South Korean case appears to be no exception. Here, as in the Middle Eastern cases, the combination of enduring public memories of the enemy and mistrust of their own government generated great opposition to peacemaking. If that is indeed a logical truth, we should expect to find more normalization following the democratization process that the ROK began undergoing in the 1980s.

In 1987, Roh Tae-woo won the presidential elections, promising a restructuring of South Korean politics and the nation's political economy with greater liberalization. His successor, Kim Young-sam, followed his reforms. The biggest symbol of the transition in Korean politics was perhaps the election of the long-time opposition leader, Kim Dae-jung, to be president in 1997.[59] The democratization process had several consequences relevant to the discussion here. First, within the ROK, it helped change South Koreans' perceptions regarding the nature of the interaction between their government and big business. After democratization had begun to be implemented, the established informal ties between the state and big business were subjected to serious public criticism, and it became more difficult for the state to favor its client business leaders. One of the key slogans of the election campaigns was the promise to promote a "clean government" and to break the link between big business money and the government.[60] Second, greater political and economic liberalization was important in order to move Korean-Japanese relations to a greater level of normalization, because it enabled both South Koreans and Japanese at different societal levels to develop new and direct channels of communication and interaction. According to Cha's description, relations between the two states expanded to include more institutionalized channels of communication, which is typical of two liberal democratic states. This was an important change, because as described above, the previous relations, while quite advanced on the elite level, lacked public acceptance.

However, Cha makes a very important distinction between the positive impact of democratic consolidation on the transition to peace and the negative impact of democratic transition. The latter can make things worse because new political entrepreneurs are likely to use historical enemies to win political support. This, he argues, was evident in the late 1980s and early 1990s, when there were clear instances in which Japan-bashing served domestic political needs. Thus, for example, the Chun Doo Hwan regime (1980–1987) engaged in a variety of efforts to fuel anti-Japanese sentiments to divert attention from its military origins. Similarly, the Kim Young-sam regime (1993–1997) used the territorial dispute over Dokto (Takeshima) to gain votes prior to the legislative elections.[61] With democratization, public sentiments toward Japan were becoming an important factor in official Japan policy. Consequently, when, for example, the issue of the Japanese history textbooks was rekindled in the 1990s, there was a violent outburst of anti-Japanese sentiment that had previously been suppressed under the military regime. The ROK government itself also adopted a hard-line policy toward Japan on this issue.[62]

These developments present the same dilemmas that were raised earlier, in the Jordanian case. Contrary to the common assumption, democratization and transition to peace do not always go well together. In the Jordanian case, the initial transition to peace with Israel was facilitated by the fact that it was controlled by the Jordanian monarchy and its close business allies. Such strong coalitions of those who will benefit most from peace are effective in making difficult transitions work more smoothly. It is easier for such coalitions to change direction when given new and clear economic incentives than it is for the broader public. In Jordan, the domestic process of political liberalization clashed with the process of normalizing relations with Israel. The king then made a strategic decision (guided by a clear economic logic) to put normalization ahead of democratization. In the Korean case, the Park regime also chose to impose martial law to deal with wide opposition to normalization of relations with Japan (although, in this case, no political liberalization process preceded the tightening of authoritarian rule). The ROK has managed, under authoritarian rule, to move much further than Jordan in building significant economic relations with its former enemy, a fact attributed to the greater economic potential of the relations. However, even after South Korea became one of Japan's major trading partners, the elitist nature of the interaction served as a very powerful brake to the process of normalization at a broader public level.

This being said, the inability of continuous and intensive economic cooperation to generate greater goodwill among Koreans stemmed not only from the elitist nature of the process but also from the unequal nature that this economic partnership undertook.

The Impact of Economic Power Disparities

Compared to South Korea, Japan was an economic giant. In 1965, the year of the normalization treaty, Japan's GDP was approximately $92 billion, compared to South Korea's GDP of $3 billion. South Korean exports at the time reached only $251 million, compared to Japan's $10 billion.[63] Over the years, the South Korean economy has developed remarkably, becoming an advanced, export-oriented economy openly competing with Japan in various fields and markets. Both the change and continuity in South Korean–Japanese relations over the years can be attributed to this economic trend. On the one hand, the strengthening of the South Korean economy had some positive effects. On the other hand, the continued built-in disparity has led to persistent negative side effects. To illustrate this change, South Korea's GDP grew dramatically, to approximately $93 billion in 1984, then up to $345 billion in 1998, and to $970 billion in 2007. At the same time, though, Japan's GDP grew to nearly $1.3 trillion in 1984, to more than $3.9 trillion in 1998, and to $4.4 trillion in 2007.[64]

The problem, however, was not so much the persistence of the gap between the two states but the patterns of trade between them. While South Korea and Japan have become major trading partners, the emerging trade relations were extremely asymmetric, a fact that did not change despite South Korea's remarkable growth rates. Thus, in 1965, South Korea imported goods at the value of $175 million but exported to Japan only $44.6 million. In 1984, it imported goods at the value of $7.64 billion but still only exported to Japan goods worth $4.6 billion. By 1995, South Korea imported goods worth $32.6 billion and exported goods valued at a total of $17 billion.[65] These data have a double meaning. On the one hand, the numbers reflect a dramatic growth in the economic interdependence between the two states, quite remarkable in light of the unresolved emotional issues discussed previously. On the other hand, the great asymmetry is also very stark. This asymmetry is not likely to change much because it stems from a structural weakness of the South Korean economy. Because South Korea is dependent on the import of capital goods and technology needed to produce its export products (e.g., electronic components, general machinery), expanding the exports of manufactured goods also necessitated a corresponding expansion of the import content of export production. Consequently, when South Korea dramatically increased its exports to the American market, it had to increase its imports from Japan.[66]

The conceptual framework of this book suggests that economic power disparities cause problems in the transition to peace between former enemies for several reasons. Most prominent is the translation of such disparities into economic dependence and the concern over the consequences of such dependence. While this may be a problem for either an advanced or a developing country commencing trade relations, the South Korean–Japanese case nicely shows how the economic disparities become much more accentuated when they are combined with the heavy emotional baggage of the past. This combination of economic power disparities and emotional baggage creates two major problems. First, it leads the weaker side to attribute the economic success and expansion of the stronger side not to economic realities but to imperialist designs. We have seen this in the Middle Eastern cases, but this feeling was probably stronger in the Japanese case, given that Japan had actually tried to implement such imperialistic plans not so very long ago. This is reflected in much of the literature critical of Japan's growing ties with South Korea.[67]

Another problem in transitioning to peace is linked to the difficulty of agreeing on the meaning of fair mutual cooperation. As I argued in previous chapters, the power disparities in themselves create different expectations, with the weaker side often expecting a larger concession from the stronger former enemy. This issue is accentuated in the South Korea–Japan case by the emotional problem. The South Koreans' conviction that Japan should apologize for its past and their sense of what one author described as a "victim complex" led to very different expectations regarding the appropriate nature of economic cooperation. South Koreans are convinced that Japan's historical record obligates it to give Korea special consideration. The Japanese, for their part, consider the South Koreans ungrateful for the important role that Japan played in underwriting their remarkable economic growth. They are irritated, for example, by the South Koreans' habit of citing its trade deficit to Japan in cumulative terms, to stress how big it is.[68] The extent to which this Korean complaint is sincere is a question that is beyond the scope of this book. I should note that there is also an argument suggesting that by playing up the aggressor-victim memory of the past, South Koreans are able to take the moral high ground and instead of simply saying, "Japan is strong and Korea is still weak, so we would appreciate your help," they insist that Japan owes Korea a great deal of assistance.[69]

Going back to the initial stages of the transition to peace between the two countries, the wide power disparities were one cause of the opposition to the normalization treaty of 1965. The fear of a resurgent Japan was real. Many of the protestors in the streets believed that Korea was not economically (or politically) strong enough to withstand Japanese aggression or competition.[70] There was a genuine fear among some that if normalization occurred and the Korean market opened up to Japanese products, Korea would be subjected to Japanese economic exploitation.

One of the potential negative consequences of economic power disparities is the creation of an influence effect by the stronger party. The influence effect, as the reader may recall, refers to the ability to change the state's perception of its own self-interest by creating domestic groups that share the interests of the stronger state. This concern comes across clearly in a comment by a professor from Korea University in 1962, three years before the normalization treaty was signed: "Imagine the inflow of Japanese funds into Korean politics and the consequent rise of pro-Japanese political parties."[71]

While generating societal concern, the huge economic disparities on the eve of the normalization treaty also were a key factor leading to the treaty. Only Japan's major capital infusion into the Korean market could have justified a move that was otherwise so controversial. The wide disparities, therefore, played a positive role in the initial stage of signing the treaty but became an ongoing irritant and a source of resentment and conflict that definitely prevented the warming up of the relations.

With that in mind, it is interesting to examine whether or not the strengthening of the South Korean economy had the expected positive impact on its relations with Japan. The findings are ambiguous. In the late 1970s and into the 1980s, the South Korean economy emerged as a vibrant, fast-growing, and increasingly competitive economy. Its success was such that it began to pose real competition to Japanese products, especially in the shipbuilding industry, textiles, and consumer electronics.[72] This transformation of the South Korean economy had one significant positive impact on Korean attitudes toward the Japanese. It led to a growing self-confidence on part of the Koreans, which in turn mitigated their resentment of Japan. As Soong-Hoom Kil nicely puts it, the increased national confidence in light of the country's acknowledged economic success helped South Koreans transform their anti-Japanese feelings into something like a sporting "let's beat Japan!" spirit.[73] The rapprochement of the 1990s, culminating in Kim Dae-jung's visit to Tokyo in 1998, was facilitated by this growing Korean confidence, which stemmed from both the economic progress ROK has made as well as the concurrent recession in Japan. This perception of narrower disparities led to a more relaxed and pragmatic approach. Also, the rapid economic development of South Korea helped to change and improve the Korean image in Japanese eyes. This combination facilitated cooperation.[74]

The narrower economic gap between the two countries also had some negative consequences, however. It raised Japanese concerns about the impact of their cooperation with Korean companies on their future competitiveness. When power disparities were huge and South Korea posed no economic competition whatsoever for Japan, it was much easier to offer various economic incentives to build relations. As I argue in chapter 1, when wide power disparities exist, it should be easier for the stronger country to use economic tools for the political purpose of promoting peaceful relations because the economic stakes are not very high. These stakes, however, are higher when disparities are narrower. Under such circumstances, the logic of economic competition, often playing itself out via political pressure applied by powerful domestic companies, is likely to pose a greater challenge to a different political/strategic logic. In such a case, this dilemma is most apparent in the issue of technology transfer, a contentious ongoing issue between the Koreans and the Japanese. A good example of this dilemma is the story of Japanese involvement in the development of the Pohang Integrated Steel Works. Early on, New Japan Steel decided to help strengthen the Korean economy by selling its technology to establish the large steel plant at Pohang. This facility began producing in 1973, and by 1983, it had become a major producer. By the late 1980s, however, the South Korean steel industry had improved more rapidly than Japan had expected, consequently becoming its competitor. When it came to providing the Koreans with later technological developments, the Japanese became much more reluctant to share their technology.[75] Similar problems of technology transfer are found in other industries where Korean companies pose some threat, for example, in the automobile industry.

These ongoing tensions, however, are closer in nature to the tensions caused by fierce economic competition among advanced states with otherwise "normal" relations. It is true that the combination of economic competition and negative historical memories made the impact of such economic complaints more significant. On balance, however, I would conclude that the level of normalization had gone far enough to allow this economic conflict to remain, for the most part, an economic conflict, despite the ongoing use of images from the past.

The Role of Third Party Involvement

The case of the normalization of relations between South Korea and Japan reveals the limitations of third party involvement. Shortly after the end of World War II, both South Korea and Japan became strategic partners of the United States in its cold war struggle in Asia. With the ROK and Japan being mutual partners of the same large ally, it is impossible to understand their relations outside the context of their American connection. As Victor Cha, who has studied this triangle, argues, both countries shared fears of American abandonment and had to deal with the asymmetric nature of their security alliances with the United States. Cha argues that American influence on relations between the two states was mostly indirect, with any rise in the perceived risk of American abandonment leading to closer cooperation between the states, which spilled from the political into the economic arena.[76]

This dynamic, however, was still not obvious in the years leading to the normalization treaty. The role of the United States in Korea after 1945 was critical. Regarding the economic dimension of the U.S. role, it was American aid that literally sustained the weak and fragile Korean economy. Up to 1961, the United States offered unilateral aid to Korea. After the end of the Korean War, from 1953 to 1961 the United States donated 95 percent of all foreign aid that Korea received. Overall, up to 1976, U.S. military and economic aid alone reached $12.6 billion.[77]

Until 1963, the United States was somewhat ambivalent regarding the issue of Japanese-Korean reconciliation. It was very reluctant to get involved in the process, so as not to open the Tokyo and Seoul governments to the allegation that they caved to American pressure. As described earlier, one of the reasons for opposition to the treaty in Japan was exactly this tightening link with the United States. In Korea, there were concerns that the Americans were trying to re-sell their country to the Japanese. While a normalization treaty was in the Americans' interest, a low profile, at the time, seemed desirable. The Japanese government, as described previously, chose to take its time. And in Korea, Syngman Rhee did not pursue serious negotiations.

American interest in bringing about a Japanese-ROK agreement became more intense in 1964, in light of the changing strategic circumstances. The rise of the Chinese threat, China's mutual defense treaty with North Korea, and the growing American commitments in Indochina all increased the urgency of set-tling the relations between America's two regional allies so as to strengthen the anticommunist regional camp.[78] The Americans had a strong interest in closer re-lations between the two countries for not only strategic reasons but also because they wanted to shift some of the economic burden of resurrecting the Korean economy to Japan. Revisionist scholars argue that the United States had a grand scheme to make the economically backward South Korea dependent on Japan.[79] While I do not share their interpretation of such a grand design, clearly there was some official American consideration of the ability of Japan to reduce the economic burden of sustaining the South Korean economy. The American ad-ministration was constantly facing serious obstacles in Congress in their attempts to renew and enlarge aid to Korea. From the late 1950s on, there was increasing focus on how to reduce the costs of America's involvement in Korea. This found expression in the plans to reduce the number of American forces in the ROK, as well as in a gradual decrease in the level of aid since 1957.[80]

While the Americans wanted a settlement between their two antagonistic al-lies, they did not intervene in the process of negotiations for more than ten years. The South Koreans and Japanese had already had their first serious round of negotiations in 1951–1952. At the time, the Koreans approached the Ameri-cans and requested their good offices to facilitate the negotiations. While the Americans did offer their good offices, they were careful not to interfere di-rectly in the negotiations, although the parties did try to draw them in. Given the Koreans' tremendous dependence upon the United States at that time, one might wonder what the outcome of these talks would have been had the United States chosen to be more actively involved.[81]

The American pressure intensified after 1964. Interestingly, the Americans raised their level of involvement at that time in the face of the mounting student riots because "gradual Japanese cooling toward bailing out ROK made us look on 1964 as a year of decision."[82] Japan, which was highly dependent on the United States both economically and strategically, was not in a position to ig-nore such American diplomatic pressure. Similarly, President Park could not ig-nore the explicit American calls for signing a treaty. For his part, Park was urging the United States to involve itself more openly and extensively in the ne-gotiations, to allow him to overcome domestic opposition.[83] Officials in President Lyndon Johnson's administration made normalization the top priority in all of the bilateral meetings with the South Koreans and the Japanese. While unable to openly push for the treaty until a basic agreement was accepted, they did offer important support at critical points during the negotiations. For example, one of the main concerns of South Korean opponents of the treaty was that if they signed this treaty, the United States would place South Korea into Japanese economic hands and consequently disengage itself from South Korea. The student demonstrations in 1965 reflected anti-American sentiments, stemming from this feeling that the United States was trying to hand Korea over to Japan.[84] The Americans were aware of these Korean concerns. The Korean government turned to the United States, requesting its help in explaining to the Japanese government the domestic difficulties the Korean officials were facing and urging it to maintain its level of economic aid.[85] In order to quell such concerns and give strong backing to President Park, American officials invited Park to Washington in May 1965, and he received an official promise for a $150-million development loan fund along with a strong reassurance that the United States would not abandon the ROK.[86]

There is no doubt that the American military presence in Japan and South Korea, as well as its political and military commitment to both states, was a critical factor leading to a South Korean–Japanese treaty. The physical American military presence in Japan allowed South Koreans to focus on issues such as history, guilt, economic dependency, and fair distribution of gains while mostly avoiding issues such as the real concern over a resurgent Japanese military threat to South Korea. More specifically, on the process of transition to peace, it is also clear that the more subtle American involvement in the last stages of the negotiations process was important for its eventual success. Still, the normalization treaty and the serious negotiations leading to it were much more the result of changing domestic realities in South Korea, with the new economic agenda of the Park regime. Perhaps the most significant contribution of the United States to the eventual treaty was the American decision to reduce its aid to South Korea, as well as the strong pressure it put on the Park regime to adopt a new economic development plan. These two factors combined to create the urgent domestic need for another source of foreign capital, pointing naturally to Japan. This shows that a third party can best influence the transition to peace by changing the domestic incentives of the actors involved.

The United States did not use any economic incentives to push the process forward. To the contrary, it was a threat of reduced economic aid over time that did the job. This is a stark difference from the Egyptian case, in which the primary potential gain from making peace with Israel was capital from the United States, or the Jordanian case, in which the United States did offer economic incentives for bilateral cooperation in the form of the QIZs. Here, the potential economic gain from normalization was a direct gain from the bilateral relations, not from a third party. This fact helps explain why the economic interaction between the two states continued to deepen over the years, despite several often emotional crises and changes in leadership. Once the treaty was signed, very quickly Japan surpassed the United States as South Korea's major source of trade and capital. Once these bilateral relations began developing, the United States no longer played any direct economic role in pushing them forward. Unlike the Middle Eastern cases, there was enough of an economic logic built into the bilateral ties to allow them to develop their own dynamics. Whatever role the United States did play was less direct. Cha suggests that economic, political, and security relations intensified during periods when both the ROK and Japan were concerned about American disengagement from Asia.[87]

THE CASE OF THE NORMALIZATION of relations between South Korea and Japan reflects the various dynamics and problems addressed throughout this book. This case does not offer the clear distinction that existed in the previous cases between the first stage of peace (an official treaty with tightly controlled and limited economic interaction) and the second stage (actual normalization of relations). However, it is still quite easy to identify and trace the transition from the extremely tenuous cold peace (or even cold war) of the postwar period to the second stage of formal mutual recognition and official resolution of a large number of outstanding issues in 1965. It is also possible to trace the shift between the single-track high-intensity economic normalization and the broadening of normalization ties to cultural and security issues in the late 1990s. These transitions offer sufficient variation in the process of stabilizing peace for me to examine the impact of the three main explanatory factors.

The case of Japan and South Korea demonstrates how a strong authoritarian coalition of government and big business can play a decisive role in bringing about an official peace treaty (even if it was not defined as such). The same coalition was also able to push forward a remarkable process of economic normalization. However, the fact that this interaction remained very elitist and was identified with corrupt deals between top officials and rich business leaders greatly contributed to the emerging gap over the years between the intense and high-volume economic relations between the two states and the lack of progress on other normalization issues. The gap between the interests of the winners in peace and the rest of society came across most strongly in this case, in the form of the massive and dramatic protests against the normalization treaty in 1964 and 1965. The process of democratization in South Korea beginning in the late 1980s did have a positive impact on the normalization process, as people gained greater faith in their government's interaction with Japan and as a larger number of communication channels between the two peoples emerged. At the same time, the transition to democracy also created a stronger domestic incentive for politicians in South Korea to capitalize on unresolved anti-Japanese sentiments.

The ongoing economic power disparity between South Korea and Japan, which found its most dramatic expression in the large ongoing trade imbalance, also had a negative impact on relations between the two states. It further exacerbated Koreans' concerns about Japanese imperial intentions and about their own weakness vis-à-vis Japan. The strengthening of the ROK economy in the 1980s and 1990s, together with the Japanese recession, created at least a perception of narrowing power disparities. This new perception, in turn, led to the development of a new self-confidence in South Korea, which in turn led to a more relaxed approached toward the Japanese. At the same time, it is illuminating to see that as disparities narrow, the tough logic of economic competition kicks in and overwhelms any thoughts of making political use of economic tools.

Finally, the normalization of South Korean–Japanese relations was clearly nested in the broader strategic reality of their alliances with the United States. Still, a closer examination reveals that the United States played a relatively limited role in actively promoting the transition to peace between the two states. The main driving forces behind the transition, while indirectly linked to American behavior, were domestic forces in South Korea and Japan.

THE "CLASSIC" CASE IN PERSPECTIVE

France and Germany from War to Union

MUCH OF THE THEORETICAL LITERATURE on the logic of commercial liberalism, especially its early roots, either builds upon or is inspired by the Franco-German transition to peace after the end of World War II. One of the goals of this book was to move away from the Eurocentric bias of that literature by examining the role of economic factors in transitions to peace in other regions of the world, especially the Middle East and East and Southeast Asia. This chapter now turns back to the allegedly classic case of commercial liberalism. Unlike the cases discussed in previous chapters, cooperative activities between the French and Germans began early in the transition to peace. Consequently, the sharp distinction made before between the stage of cold peace and the shift to normalization is less clear in this case. Economic considerations did play a crucial role in each state's decision to invest in peace, since cooperation promised and delivered significant economic dividends for both countries. Even in this case, however, the role played by economic factors, especially in the early stages of the transition, was by no means the role envisioned by classic liberal economists. It was highly political, and it was manipulated and regulated by top decision makers in both countries. Consequently, it was the political economy behind the transition to peace that was important to examine, not a pure, apolitical, economic logic. The difficulty with this case lies in the fact that, in many ways, postwar Franco-German cooperation was overdetermined: economic incentives were intertwined with a strong and compelling geostrategic logic, given the new Soviet threat and the new American commitment to European security. Much has been written on these issues, but here I focus on the economic dimension.

Compared to the cases discussed in previous chapters, the economic power disparities between the Federal Republic of Germany (FRG) and France were the narrowest, which should have a positive effect on the dynamics of cooperation. This case also demonstrates the need for a more complex understanding of the impact of economic power disparities. The French did not consider the economic disparities vis-à-vis the FRG in a political vacuum, and for a long time German economic power was seen as being balanced by France's relative political power in Europe. A significant change in the economic power disparities developed in the 1970s, when the German economy showed impressive growth. The most dramatic change, of course, occurred in 1990, with the unification of Germany. This change provides a good test of the degree of "normalcy" in the relations. As for the impact of third parties, the key outsider in this case was once again the United States, and indeed there has been much debate among international relations (IR) scholars regarding the central role of the United States in the pacification of Europe (meaning first and foremost the pacification of Franco-German relations). Still, the unique aspect of this case is the introduction, at a rather early stage of the transition, of regional multilateral institutions within which Franco-German relations came to be embedded (namely the European Community and later the European Union, as well as their joint membership since 1954 in a military alliance, the North Atlantic Treaty Organization).

From Conflict to Peace

France and Germany share an impressive and bloody legacy of historic rivalry. The unification of a group of German states under the king of Prussia was closely associated with their defeat of France in the war of 1870, which created in France the bitter legacy of territorial loss (the provinces of Alsace and Lorraine). Then came the unprecedented bloodbath of World War I (1914–1918). Finally, there was the deeply tragic history of World War II and the occupation of France by Nazi Germany.[1]

After World War II, the transition to peace between France and Germany took five years, from the defeat of Nazi Germany until the birth of the new state of the Federal Republic of Germany and its recognition by France. When the war ended and Germany was divided into four occupation zones, the initial French policy was to keep Germany weak and divided. The French sought to split off the Saar region and the Ruhr valley and to annex them, along with their rich natural resources. This policy shifted only in late 1947, after it became apparent that this option was not feasible because of conditions imposed by America's Marshall Plan. It was only then that French decision makers began to consider a new and positive approach toward Germany, one of accepting the reality of a sovereign West German state with which cooperation was possible and even desirable.[2] The dramatic first agreement that symbolized the beginning of normalization of Franco-German relations was the creation of the European Coal and Steel Community (ECSC) in 1952, following the Schuman Plan. The ECSC was an ambitious agreement that put the production of coal and steel in France and Germany under joint supervision.[3] But even before the ECSC, trade relations were gradually reemerging, first on a private level and then on an official level, culminating in the Franco-German tariff agreement in February 1950, which allowed goods to pass freely from France into the French-controlled occupation zone in Germany and into German markets.[4] It is also important to note that while most (non-German) observers tend to focus on the French initiative (the Schuman Plan), in March 1950, in a journal interview, West German chancellor Konrad Adenauer proposed the political union of Europe, with a Franco-German pillar as its primary support.[5]

The next major step in the developing relations between the two countries took place in 1954, with the signing of the Paris Agreements, under which West Germany received most of the privileges of a sovereign state, France accepted its existence, and much more than that, it agreed to bring the FRG into NATO. In effect, France and the FRG had become military allies. In 1955, the two countries signed a commercial treaty and became each other's largest/second-largest trading partner.[6] The last remaining territorial conflict between the two states, over the Saar region, was resolved in October 1956, when France agreed to accept the local referendum, in which voters in the region chose to remain part of West Germany. In 1958, both the FRG and France signed the Rome Treaty, further institutionalizing their economic cooperation.[7] Perhaps the point that best symbolizes the completion of rapprochement between France and Germany was the signing of the Elysée Treaty in 1963, following the historic visit of French president Charles de Gaulle to Germany in 1962. During that visit, de Gaulle captivated the German public with a series of public speeches in which he stated that "today, what is happening in the Ruhr [i.e., production in German factories] . . . no longer arouses in my country anything but sympathy and satisfaction," and he called the Germans "a great people."[8] The Elysée Treaty, signed by

President de Gaulle and Chancellor Adenauer, institutionalized regular meetings between French and German officials, twice a year for the president and the chancellor and every three months for the foreign and defense ministers. The treaty also led to the creation of a Franco-German youth office, which concentrated on youth exchanges, conferences, and language instruction. The treaty also called for cooperation on the security front, with the objective of harmonizing defense doctrines and arriving at common principles. However, there was little concrete follow-up on the treaty until the 1980s. One must keep in mind, though, that the treaty represented the culmination of fourteen years' effort on both sides.[9]

During the 1980s and 1990s, Franco-German cooperation intensified under the guidance of President François Mitterrand and Chancellor Helmut Kohl, with the two states becoming the linchpin around which the whole Western European system consolidated. Despite ups and downs and various crises in the relations, the two states remained close partners in leading the process of European integration. A Franco-German commission on security and defense was created in 1982, leading to joint maneuvers and to the creation in 1990 of the Franco-German brigade. The German unification only intensified cooperation between the two states. Following the signing of the Maastricht Treaty, the brigade was transformed into the Eurocorps in 1991. In 1996, a Franco-German defense agreement was officially adopted and reported to NATO and the Western European Union (WEU).[10]

Translating this broad overview of Franco-German relations into the conceptual framework of this study, we can see how the relations between France and Germany have undergone the greatest possible transition—from archenemies to close partners, two states in a state of stable warm peace. Many even argue that the two have formed a pluralistic security community. Both Benjamin Miller and Norrin Ripsman have tried to identify more formally the stages in the Franco-German transition to peace. Miller suggests that the years 1945–1950 can be characterized as years of cold war. Indeed, during that period France was set on devising a harsh, punitive policy vis-à-vis occupied Germany, one aimed at keeping that country divided and weak and authorizing a takeover of its resource-rich areas. Miller identifies the subsequent period, between 1950 and 1954, as the period of transition to cold peace.[11] It is during this period that the two states recognized each other and signed various agreements and that France accepted German rearmament via NATO and the WEU. The Paris Agreements of 1954 symbolized the official transition to cold peace. Indeed, the efforts during that period to improve relations with Germany were driven by state actors and political elites, as the definition of cold peace would suggest. Miller then identifies 1954–1957 as the period of transition to "normal peace," facilitated by the resolution of the Saar problem, and the period of 1958–2005 as one of transition to "warm peace."[12] Ripsman offers a broader distinction between the period since the end of World War II and up to 1954, which he terms the actual transition to peace, and the period following 1954, which he terms the "endurance" of the Western European peace.[13] There is no contradiction between these two descriptions.

In terms of my distinction between the transition to cold peace and the stage of normalization, the Paris Agreements of 1954 offer a good landmark symbolizing the achievement of official peace. Developments from that year on reflect the process of normalization (which is close to what Ripsman means when he writes about the "endurance" of peace). This being said, the sharp distinction that appeared, for example, in the Middle Eastern cases between the cold peace stage and the stage of normalization is less clear here. Marc Trachtenberg, for example, argues that by 1954, given the changed strategic circumstances, French decision makers had already ceased to view Germany as a military threat and in fact saw German conventional forces as essential for security in Western Europe. This perception of a reduced threat is more characteristic of "normal peace" than of "cold peace." Such views, however, were held mainly by French political elites, not by the French public in general. The French public was still reluctant to accept German rearmament, but on economic and cultural issues there was already growing societal interaction.[14]

In the French-German case, much more so than in the other cases examined so far, one can find clear expressions of the different dimensions of normalization of relations. Political, economic, and cultural relations between the two states gradually expanded, and great effort was invested in institutionalizing various channels of cooperation. These relations were based on a complex mix of networks and structures—regular meetings of heads of states and ministers, both bilaterally and multilaterally, various informal networks of elite civil servants, and bilateral party-based contacts. As noted earlier, the Elysée Treaty established a series of such bilateral institutions, and by the late 1980s and into the 1990s, defense and security agreements had also been signed.[15] What is unique to this case is the institutionalization of the bilateral cooperation, also within a broader, multilateral framework.

The concept of normalization implies not only expanded state-level contacts but also a greater number of contacts and changed perceptions at the societal level. Unlike the Middle Eastern cases, in the Franco-German case, private efforts at normalizing relations began early, just after the end of the war, and were pursued not only by big business (as in the Asian cases) but also by various societal groups. Even before the treaty, many groups and individuals in France and Germany, including private associations and employers' federations, were working toward reconciliation and closer association between their two countries. One central source of such cooperation was the common vision of European integration, shared by federalist groups in both countries. Groups of politicians, business leaders, and representatives of all sectors of society met on a regular basis within different federalist groups, coordinated by the European Movement that was already in existence in 1948.[16] However, on balance, the early stages of the transition to peace were clearly dominated by state actors and big business in both states. Popular exchanges existed before, but after the 1963 treaty was signed, they were institutionalized and encouraged, largely through the Franco-German Youth Office, which successfully promoted youth exchange, conferences, and reciprocal language instruction.[17] Academic cooperation became very prevalent, and explicit attempts were made to negotiate on the disputed issues in French and German history.[18] On the economic front, both governments created a mechanism to facilitate trade in any possible way. Official bodies made every effort to facilitate private-level economic interaction. For example, in 1965, a joint committee was established to further industrial collaboration. In its various subcommittees, there was an emphasis on representation by the private sector. Indeed, there were also many private initiatives. Beginning in 1965, a summit of industrial leaders became a regular event, and leaders of smaller-scale enterprises also established close links with their counterparts.[19]

The normalization of relations between the two countries found its clearest expression in the dramatic changes in French public opinion over the years. In the early 1950s, French public opinion clearly opposed any notion of German rearmament. In 1950, 55 percent of the French opposed cordial relations with Germany, according to a Gallup poll.[20] In 1956, the French public still exhibited little or no confidence in West Germany. In 1964, a year after the Elysée Treaty was signed, an overwhelming majority of the French had a good opinion of the FRG, and by 1967, 52 percent of French respondents actually thought that German reunification (so vehemently opposed in the late 1940s) was in the French national interest. By March 1972, 86 percent of the respondents agreed that Germany no longer represented a danger to France.[21] Julius Friend argues that this perception of diminished threat from Germany already existed in the aftermath of the stormy European Defense Community (EDC) debate, during which there had been widespread opposition to German rearmament without it taking place within a broader multilateral framework that would ensure French security. Ironically, while the EDC debate effectively illustrates the security concerns of the French regarding Germany, Raymond Aron suggested in his memoirs that the EDC debate served as a catharsis, ridding the French of their resentment of the "hereditary enemy" that had accumulated over a century. Once the French National Assembly voted in favor of having German army troops integrated into NATO, neither the political class nor the public wished to continue the debate. On the German side, following Adenauer's official visit to France in July 1962, the German press wrote that "the hereditary enmity is dead."[22] Franco-German integration at the societal level made impressive progress over a decade's time. A detailed public opinion analysis demonstrates that between the mid-1950s and the early 1960s, there had been a remarkable increase in what he calls "net trust" of both French and German populations and in their mutual esteem, reflecting the emergence of a pluralistic security community.[23]

Improving relations between the two states were further institutionalized via the EC and later the EU. Perhaps the final event reflecting the "normalcy" of the Franco-German relations was the unification of Germany. This dramatic event is discussed in this chapter in the context of the changes in bilateral power disparities. While not without some concern, France greeted the collapse of the Berlin Wall and endorsed the process of German unification. Finally, Germany had returned to its natural size. While the current relations between the two states are not without discord, most scholars would agree that those are normal tensions between two leading regional powers engaged in a relationship of stable peace.

In light of this historical review, the rest of this chapter focuses on Franco-German relations up to the 1960s. It is in those years, leading first to the Paris Agreements of 1954 and then to the Friendship Treaty (the Elysée Treaty) of 1963, that the major transition in the relations between the two states occurred. Obviously, the normalization and subsequent deepening of relations continued later on through the two states' joint actions in the EC and EU. Thus, when the architect of Franco-German reconciliation, Chancellor Adenauer, was replaced by Chancellor Ludwig Erhard, the latter disagreed with most of the policies advanced by President de Gaulle but still felt that "reconciliation of the French and German people was an accomplished fact, that there was no danger of a revival of old enmities."[24]

The Economic Potential of the Transition to Peace

In the Franco-German case, the economic potential of the transition to peace was of major importance for both France and Germany. After the war, France found itself in poor economic shape. French industry had languished for four years, the occupation having disrupted and finally drained the economy and having cut off France from Britain, its main source of coal. France's early postwar vision of peace with Germany was based on keeping Germany weak and divided. The economic dividend of such an arrangement was to come from the dismantling of German factories and their relocation to France, as well as by internationalizing the Ruhr valley industrial region so that France (as well as other European economies) could use its vast resources. However, regardless of the geopolitical circumstances, this initial plan was not viable for economic reasons. The Monnet Plan (France's Modernization and Re-equipment Plan) strived to make the French economy more internationally competitive and to make France Europe's largest steel producer. However, this transformation could be achieved only by increasing inputs of German coal and coke into the French economy. Consequently, French reconstruction was from the outset tied to German economic reconstruction.[25]

Germany, for its part, stood to gain economically and politically from a transition to peace with France. As in the Middle Eastern cases, the benefits of peace were closely linked to the high cost of the previous conflict. Germans had a very clear and grave understanding of the cost of the very recent armed conflict. With Germany's defeat in 1945, the nation's economy lay largely in ruins. Communications and power supplies were disrupted, factories were destroyed or damaged, and with only one-fifth of all dwellings habitable, hundreds of thousands of residents were displaced and living under strict rationing.[26] The main price Germany had to pay for a peace treaty was the division, for the time being, of the country into East and West, a price that the German government was willing to pay at the time. West Germany's postwar strategy was based on an export-led growth strategy and as such was highly dependent upon the desire of the rest of Europe to trade with it.[27] Indeed, there were strong commercial interests on both sides that favored moving to peace so as to reap economic benefits. Andrew Moravcsik argues that it was those commercial interests, rather than any geostrategic considerations, that pushed France and Germany into each other's arms.[28] There was a basic complementarity in strategic and economic terms between France and Germany after the war, and normalized relations fulfilled specific functional needs: they served the French interest in gaining access to German energy resources and in playing a preponderant political role within the European Community, and they served the German interest in regaining independence and ensuring access to lucrative markets.[29] This is exactly the type of natural interdependence that gave the transition process its underlying logic and driving power and that did not exist in the Middle Eastern cases, in which the significant economic dividends from peace came from the United States as a third party.

The importance of the economic factor is reflected in the fact that the rapprochement with Germany did not occur until the economic goal of restoring prosperity became a central foreign policy goal for France. This did not happen until 1947, because in 1944 the expressed goals of the Fourth Republic focused on maintaining the status quo and security vis-à-vis Germany. The new economic logic was also backed by a new geostrategic logic, prompted by the rising Soviet threat and the need to invest in Atlantic security.[30]

Domestic Winners and Losers from Peace

The transition to peace between France and Germany went hand in hand with economic rapprochement. The strategic, political, and economic logics all pushed in the same direction of rapprochement, making it difficult to isolate the relative importance of each factor.[31] As opposed to the Middle Eastern cases, in the Franco-German case there was a compelling underlying economic logic for close cooperation between the two states, given the natural complementarity of their steel and coal industries. This complementarity was closer to that exhibited in the two Asian cases but even more compelling. Consequently, there was also an underlying consensus both in France and in Germany that rapprochement was to carry significant economic benefits. The process itself was not framed in the language of "transition to peace" but rather in the language of "European integration." In practice, though, the latter embodied the transition to peace between the two states.

Still, it would be a mistake to conclude that the process of Franco-German rapprochement was driven from below by economic considerations, following the standard commercial liberal principle. While standing on more solid economic ground, the transition process itself was clearly guided from above by state agents who perceived a clear link between building economic ties with the former enemy and establishing a more solid and reliable strategic partnership between the two states. The first dramatic initiative to promote the transition to peace, the Schuman Plan, along with the subsequent European Coal and Steel Community, reflected a political, managed economic approach that was far from a reflection of liberal economic rationale. Although French foreign minister Robert Schuman promised that his plan would make war between France and Germany unthinkable and materially impossible, its immediate appeal was still based on his claim that the establishment of common bases of economic development would bring major economic advantages to both countries.[32]

At the national level, as noted previously, there was a strong economic incentive to promote cooperation. France faced major economic challenges on the road to economic modernization envisioned by the Monnet Plan, challenges that greater trade with Germany could ameliorate. Germany's overwhelming dependence on foreign trade as a means to rebuild its economy, as well as its desire to achieve equal treatment from other European nations, suggested that cooperation would potentially bring major benefits to the German state, benefits that largely overshadowed potential costs (mostly the acceptance of German division and the loss of East European markets). This mutual state-level interest is thus reminiscent of the Asian cases discussed in previous chapters. In those cases, the government of Japan (the defeated, potentially powerful former enemy) attached tremendous importance to the building of economic ties with its neighbors for the purpose of promoting its export-led growth strategy. Similarly, the governments of its Southeast Asian neighbors, as well as the government of the Republic of Korea, viewed trade with Japan as a necessary strategy for promoting economic reforms and growth. A key difference here lies in the nature of the power disparities between those states, but this issue will be discussed later.

A second common characteristic of the economic profile of the transition to peace in Asia and in Europe has to do with a history of economic cooperation prior to the last armed conflict. Soon after the end of World War II in the Pacific, economic connections were rekindled between Japanese companies and Southeast Asian companies and local entrepreneurs. Those connections were made during the period when Japan occupied the Philippines and Indonesia. Once the war was over, it was much easier to build on those earlier connections. In the Franco-German case, there was an even longer history of elaborate economic cooperation in the interwar years. In fact, many of the post–World War II ideas of business diplomacy had their roots in the prewar era. Thus, by 1920, against the backdrop of the punitive Versailles Treaty, the French had already initiated the Seydoux Plan to create a revolving fund to commercialize the reparations debt in order to give German manufacturers an economic stake in French reconstruction. In 1926, the International Steel Cartel (ISC) was founded, encompassing France, Germany, Belgium, and Luxembourg. This was the first industrial agreement to be used to link the nations of Western Europe. It reflected a belief that market-sharing agreements could be worked into a new system of trade and diplomacy. The fortunes of the ISC shifted over time. Ironically, it was strengthened in the 1930s, even as Hitler seized power. Consequently, postwar discussions of building economic ties between France and Germany were already rooted in a long history of industrial cooperation.[33] The potential benefits of peace and economic cooperation were thus not just hypothetical visions, like those often mentioned in the peace-economics literature on the Middle East.

The German government, led by Konrad Adenauer, and Ludwig Erhard, his economics minister, adopted a growth strategy based on free market competition (with a social twist) and an emphasis on foreign trade. As was the case with Japan, German reliance on external markets for its economic rehabilitation after the war gave the export sector greater political power over the formation of economic policy dealing with foreign trade. That business sector's influence was further enhanced by the close links between business interests and Germany's Ministries of Finance and Economics. There were also strong links between industrial and trading bodies and the relevant ministries.[34] German coal and steel producers had a vital interest in achieving an agreement that would both halt the dismantling of German factories and open up foreign markets for exports. Immediately after the war, German industrialists began preparing for peace, stressing the importance of reestablishing and building upon Germany's foreign business contacts. Until such ties were restored, they argued, Germany could not be readmitted to Europe's economic sphere.[35]

By mid-1948, long before the Schuman Plan was announced, major German and French industrialists had already begun meeting and examining potential cooperative projects.[36] At that time, steel producers in the Ruhr region were facing the threat of physical destruction because only a month before Schuman announced his plan, the Allied High Commission adopted Law No. 27 (April 13, 1950), which gave the juridical basis for the deconcentration of the large German conglomerates, known as the *Konzerne*. German hopes that the law would not be implemented were dashed when six major steel-producing firms were liquidated in September 1950, followed by deconcentration of the mining industry. This process led to ambivalent responses on the part of German industrialists.

On the one hand, it made them more anxious to enter the ECSC pool so as to be rid of the postwar occupation controls, but on the other hand, they feared they would enter the ECSC in a very weakened position. While they claimed they supported the Schuman Plan in principle (which would be logical, given their underlying interest in market expansion), they opposed the details of the plan. Those details, they argued, reflected a French attempt to prevent the revival of German industry. The German trade unions initially feared that the ECSC and the High Authority, the new body that was guiding it, would become a new type of cartel, dominated by great capitalists. There was also concern that other related reforms would harm the interests of German employees. However, they decided that the advantages of the coal and steel pool outweighed the drawbacks, since Germany would gain a great share of the European coal market, and that an increase in employment in both coal and steel industries was likely to occur.[37] Support for the ECSC was also enhanced by the influence of independent economic and business institutions, which published many studies explaining the potentially huge benefits of the plan for Germany.[38]

Still, the Schuman Plan received its greatest momentum from and was pushed to ratification mainly by Chancellor Adenauer. Alan Milward suggests that the close cooperation between the government and industry was premised upon the latter's acceptance that the government had an overriding political interest to which industry must subscribe.[39] The central role played by key political leaders, mainly Adenauer and later de Gaulle, also reflects a recurrent pattern in all of the transition cases examined in this book, one in which leaders with a liberal-economic vision pushed the process forward despite generally negative public opinion about such economic cooperation.

The support of the German trade unions and academic institutes can be contrasted with the strong opposition of Egyptian and Jordanian professional organizations and unions to any economic interaction with Israel. In the Middle Eastern cases, ideological and religious factors played an important role in shaping this opposition. However, one cannot ignore the fact that, in the case of Franco-German rapprochement, the potential economic benefits from economic cooperation were dramatically larger and clearer. As illustrated in the Egyptian case as well, once clear and crucial economic gains became evident through the QIZ project, the relevant Egyptian textile companies were eager to come on board.

The same underlying desire to expand and institutionalize access to European markets also led German business to support the next dramatic step in institutionalizing Franco-German cooperation in a wider multilateral setting: the creation of the European Economic Community (EEC) in 1958. The impressive gains in productivity and in trade volume just two years after the creation of the ECSC converted many of its critics into supporters. By 1957, the major employers' associations were strong advocates, in principle at least, of extending the community to the whole European economy. Industrialists found the ECSC more rewarding than they had expected. Throughout the 1950s, various business organizations were working on promoting reconciliation, and they created numerous economic agreements (e.g., an agreement between Air France and Lufthansa, the creation of many chambers of commerce, and an agricultural committee to harmonize agricultural policies).

One of the central challenges in the transition to peace and normalization of relations was the need over time to go beyond peace dividends that are shared by a narrow government and business elite to peace dividends that are shared (or at least perceived as such) by broader segments of society. This aspect of transition did not occur in Egypt or Jordan, where frustrated populations had little faith in and saw little evidence of the trickling down of economic dividends from peace with Israel. For early postwar Germany, this was less of a problem for two main reasons, one being structural and the other, more circumstantial. First of all, the decade and a half after the beginning of rapprochement with France was a period of rapid economic growth and rehabilitation. To illustrate, GNP went from 98 billion deutsche marks (DM) in 1950 to approximately 303 billion DM in 1960, to 679 billion DM in 1970, to nearly 1.5 trillion DM in 1980. This dramatic growth was based largely on the country's industry, and about a third of its industrial production was exported. This tremendous overall growth of the national economic pie was also translated into a dramatic rise in workers' salaries. The average nominal hourly gross earnings of a German industrial worker rose between 1950 and the early 1980s almost tenfold, by about 300 percent in real terms.[40] The fact that the crucial decade of transition to peace was accompanied by dramatic economic growth and a dramatic rise in citizens' standard of living clearly facilitated the process of upgrading the peace. Regardless of the intricate causal links between economic cooperation with France, European integration, and German prosperity, it was easy to view the German society as a whole as a winner from peace. The notion of "peace dividends" was not an academic notion but a vivid description of reality for most Germans.

This understanding that peace dividends were not only to be realized by a small business elite was further strengthened by the unique nature of industrial relations in West Germany, characterized by collective bargaining and workers' participation in management. Such participation was prevalent in the coal, iron, and steel companies—three industries that were central players in the postwar economic game.[41] Such participation also created a greater sense of the involvement of German workers in the policy process and ensured that they would share in the economic benefits of peace and integration. This, combined with the impressive annual growth in workers' real wages, made the German labor unions part of the grand coalition supporting export expansion.[42]

This material evidence of the peace dividends was strengthened by the general public attitude favoring European integration in Germany. Surveys conducted in the early 1950s revealed that a substantial majority (70 percent) of Germans favored European integration and felt that Germany had much to gain from the integration of Western Europe. Such pro-European sentiments drew from different sources: a genuine European ideology, an impulse to "escape into Europe," and a kind of "crypto-nationalist" Europeanism, that is, a belief that German economic and political dominance could be attained through European integration.[43]

As for the French, it took several years for them to accept the fact that their initial goal of making sure that Germany remained weak and divided was not viable, both in light of the new international conditions and in light of France's own domestic goals. The Monnet Plan made it clear that the French steel industry could not be modernized without German coal and steel. The Schuman Plan can be seen as an attempt to rescue the Monnet Plan by providing the needed access to German resources, access that could not be sustained via the more convenient controls of the occupation regime (the Ruhr International Authority). The process leading to the formation of the ECSC in France was very much an elite-driven process. French leaders were constrained by the generally hostile attitude of the French public toward Germany. However, they were able to manipulate public opinion gradually and get the citizens to accept the need to move to a more liberal peace arrangement with Germany. Thus, the Schuman Plan was meant to reconcile French public opinion with the eventuality of German economic resurgence, and it did so quite successfully.[44]

Although there was a general sentiment of hostility and distrust regarding Germany, the public did not appear to have been mobilized to participate in the ECSC debate. In fact, as late as September 1952, 28 percent of the French population had not even heard of the coal and steel pool, and as late as January 1954, only 45 percent had any definite idea as to whether it was a good or bad institution and 26 percent had still never heard of it.[45] Craig Parsons suggests that the institutional process of Franco-German rapprochement, from the ECSC through the EEC, was an elitist process guided by Robert Schuman, who served as an "entrepreneurial coalition builder" to push forward his community strategy for dealing with the "German problem." Parsons demonstrates how clear preferences were barely articulated in the face of Schuman's ECSC project, both in the French political arena (where there was much opposition to the whole idea) and among interest groups. It was Schuman's political maneuvering and vision that led to the adoption of that strategy.[46]

French industrial interests, for their part, were at best ambivalent about the ECSC project. There was a widespread belief that a common market would lead to intense German competition that would overwhelm French industry. The steel industry's trade association led the opposition, and the chemical and engineering industries followed, since they too felt menaced by further pooling. All of these industries were concerned about the heavier social charges for labor welfare in France, that the French coal and steel industries would be fatally weakened, and that the plan would lead to unnecessary government intervention. Still, the industry was not united in its opposition and therefore did not lead an efficient campaign against the ECSC.[47] Part of this ambivalence stemmed from the fact that French industry understood that economic logic pointed clearly to an increase in supplies from Germany. The debate was not really about the necessity of expanding economic ties with Germany but about the best means for doing so. Most French trade associations resented the ECSC's provisions but were outmaneuvered. Their main concerns were that, once the community was functioning, a static France would be pinned against a dynamic Germany and the coal and steel community approach would spill over into other areas.[48] However, once the ECSC was operational, within two years it was performing so well that any doubts regarding cooperation disappeared and criticism was muted.

Unlike the early stages of the transition to peace in the Middle East, even though the Franco-German process may have been driven by elites, it did reflect an underlying economic logic that various interest groups basically accepted. This is a significant difference from the Middle Eastern cases, and it played a key role in the relatively rapid expansion of relations and normalization.

While the ECSC project was particularly relevant to the French steel industry, the next dramatic step in rebuilding Franco-German relations, the creation of the EC in the Rome Treaty of 1957, was clearly supported by another powerful group in French politics and economics: the agricultural sector. All over

Western Europe after World War II, the agricultural sector was gaining political importance, and there emerged an unprecedented consensus on the need to protect agriculture (in light of the fresh memories of food shortages during and immediately after the war). In France, the agricultural sector was especially powerful since it employed 25 percent of the French workforce.[49] The key to understanding agricultural interests is the fact that within Western Europe, the French and Italian agricultural sectors had the greatest export potential, compared to German agriculture, which was less developed. However, these agricultural sectors were not highly competitive in the global market. Consequently, when France wanted to become an exporter of wheat, dairy products, sugar, and meat, it had to find and open up another regulated market with prices higher than its own. French agriculture was concerned over any limited market liberalization on a broader European level, where it would have to compete with Italian agriculture. For French farmers, the perfect solution was to open up the German market. German agriculture also feared wide liberalization, and the German government, while aggressively pursuing market liberalization for its industrial sectors, excluded agriculture from that effort.[50] This Franco-German understanding was at the heart of the emerging Common Agricultural Policy (CAP), which was to be a central pillar in the new European Economic Community initiated in Rome.[51] The basic bargain struck between France and Germany as they entered the new community was a trade-off between the French insistence on the CAP and the German insistence on opening up industrial markets. Finally, it is telling for our purposes to note that throughout the parliamentary debates leading to the Rome Treaty, there was hardly any mention of the "German problem" or geopolitical issues.[52] Debates revolved only around economic matters. This is a significant sign that at that point Franco-German relations had already reached an advanced level of normalization.

Milward nicely summarizes the nature of Franco-German relations after the creation of the ECSC. He suggests that this association

> was in many respects a shotgun wedding. The German bride, although her other choices were not very enticing, had nevertheless to be dragged protesting by her aged father to the altar while numerous members of her family staged noisy protests on the way and an equally large number of the bridegroom's friends and relations prophesied disaster. Yet the knot once tied this surprising union soon settled into a safe bourgeois marriage in which the couple, rapidly becoming wealthy and comfortable as passions cooled, were held together, as such couples are, by the strong links of managing their complex joint economic affairs.[53]

The Impact of Economic Power Disparities

One of the central arguments of this book is that economic tools can play a useful role in transitions to peace when the economic power disparities between the states involved are small or moderate. I have argued that the combination of wide economic power disparities and a history of hostility and conflict create serious obstacles in the transition. While economic logic may point otherwise, the weaker party in such a situation is likely to be much more concerned about developing a dependence upon its former enemy and to view any such economic cooperation as an attempt by the more powerful party to impose its will and dominate the relationship in nonmilitary ways. This problem was prominent in the two Middle Eastern cases examined, where pure economic logic called for an exchange of Israeli know-how for low-wage Egyptian or Jordanian labor. This rational economic option was not politically viable. The return of Japan to Southeast Asia, however, presented an apparent anomaly, because the very broad economic power disparities between Japan and the Philippines and Indonesia, while generating public anxiety and concern, did not deter Southeast Asian elites from rebuilding ties to Japan. That case demonstrated the importance of understanding how power disparities and their implications are perceived by the relevant actors. A key factor was the extent to which actors thought that economic power disparities necessarily translated into economic dependence, with its political implications.

The Franco-German relationship is a case in which the power disparities between the two parties at the outset of the transition were relatively narrow, particularly in comparison to the past (when Germany was much more powerful) as well as to the more distant future (when German reunification occurred). It is a case that illustrates the benign impact of moderate power disparities and reflects concerns stemming from the potential of German dominance. The combination of its size and location at the heart of Western Europe along with its rich natural resources and skilled workforce has historically given Germany the potential to be the most powerful actor in the region. The combination of this potential power and a history of aggressive foreign policy created the "German problem" for all of Europe but particularly for France. Immediately after World War II, France faced a war-torn Germany, occupied and divided into zones controlled by four nations and on the verge of an economic crisis. While the French did foresee the economic resurgence of Germany, it was easier to negotiate the terms of peace and of economic cooperation from the victor's stand. Thus, the initial French instinct was to try to maintain the immediate postwar power disparities by keeping Germany divided, preventing its return to using its full industrial capacity, and dismantling factories and equipment and moving the works to France.

However, as was the case with Japan, it became clear that the war's damage would not and could not be allowed to have a lasting effect. In fact, despite the wartime devastation, one finds upon closer inspection that Germany's economy emerged from the war in better shape than one would think. German industry, especially the steel industry, actually got stronger during the war. As a result of the rearmament effort, the lack of serious damage to capital equipment, and a high rate of investment, German industry emerged from the war with better machinery and in better shape than any major producing nation except for the United States.[54] On the economic front, as opposed to the military front, France was the loser and Germany the winner. During the years of Nazi occupation, France was cut off from its traditional source of coal in Britain and was therefore more dependent than ever on coal from the Ruhr valley. French industry languished during the occupation, which drained and disrupted the economy. In effect, the Franco-German imbalance of economic power after the war was even greater than before the conflict.[55]

This imbalance did lead to concern in France that economic cooperation with Germany via an institution such as the ECSC might be dangerous for France. When the plan was made public, many participants in French industry were uneasy about it. As one French economist put it, "Germany, with its industry, its capacity for work, and its creative energy, is aspiring in an almost spontaneous way to become the dominant economy on the continent, and by this expansion alone is a threat to the other nations of Europe."[56] Similar concerns also existed before France joined the Common Market project. Those who opposed the treaty feared that the Common Market would benefit the German economy at the expense of France. As noted before, however, no mention was made of the contribution of the treaty to resolving the German problem or to the reconciliation between the two states.[57]

One might wonder why these concerns did not hinder actual economic cooperation between France and Germany. The answer may be that the nature of the two economies was such that a natural interdependence existed between them. This interdependence was indeed asymmetric across time. Germany remained by far France's largest trading partner, and France was less important for overall German trade, but both were each other's most important trading partners. There has long been a complementarity between the French and German economies; a strong French surplus in the agricultural sector was offset by a strong German surplus in machine tools and industrial goods.[58] This interdependence and the clear mutual gains from economic interaction outweighed any concerns about the existing power disparities between the states.

Concern over economic power disparities was also mitigated by two noneconomic facts. First, Germany was divided and was to remain divided for the foreseeable future (as it seemed in the early 1950s). Second, under the Paris Agreements that led to the creation of the sovereign Federal Republic of Germany in 1954, the FRG instituted various safeguards to prevent German militarism. For example, it promised not to produce atomic, biological, or chemical (ABC) weapons, guided missiles, or other strategic weapons, and its military forces were to be part of the Western European Union, which, in turn, was to be put directly under the authority of the Supreme Allied Commander in Europe or SACEUR (i.e., the United States).[59] This commitment by the FRG was enhanced by the American commitment to maintain ground forces in Germany. As was the case in Japan's transition to peace, it is impossible to ignore the fact that the FRG's decisions to forgo offensive military operations and limit its armies, as well as the American security presence, mitigated the concerns of its neighbors. Still, these guarantees on their own would not have provided the necessary fuel for a full transition to peace. The fuel, in this case, was the strong economic logic of cooperation and the clear gains for both parties.

Furthermore, due to Germany's unique political condition after regaining its sovereignty, what developed over the years between the two states is a special partnership in which German economic power was balanced by French political influence. While relations were asymmetric, they were clearly complementary. Despite their relative economic weakness compared to Germany, the French did not feel like a junior or more vulnerable partner (especially at the early stages of the transition and under de Gaulle) because Germany was clearly dependent on France in political terms.[60]

Although the transition began when economic disparities were relatively small due to the occupation regime, the Germans expected to become economically much stronger in the future. Consequently, Adenauer was more willing to acquiesce to the French in their efforts to realize the Monnet Plan. Adenauer believed time was on his side and that the real danger was that a stronger Germany moving too fast would rekindle old fears and suspicions and prolong the occupation regime.[61] As mentioned previously, one brand of Europeanism within Germany, which Gabriel Almond terms "crypto-nationalism," reflected an appreciation of the pro-German power disparities and assumed that if Europe were integrated, Germany's economic power and energy would be sufficient to regain the position of dominance in Europe to which it was entitled.[62] This finding, in addition to the findings from the Southeast Asian case, points to the importance of examining how material economic power disparities translate into a sense of vulnerability and an expectation of dependence. When dependence in one sector is offset by dependence of the other party in another sector or another important issue area, the overall concern over dependence and vulnerability will be smaller.

Although the transition to peace had been completed by the time of the Friendship Treaty signing in 1963, one should not ignore the French attitude toward German unification nearly thirty years later. It is an important case since, with Germany returning to its larger size, unification had a significant impact on the power disparities between the two states, despite the economic challenge that unification posed for the West German government. It is interesting that, in late 1966, de Gaulle already supported the German desire for reunification and did not think that a unified Germany would again pose a danger to peace, as long as it did not develop nuclear capabilities and if there was agreement between East and West.[63] This stance has been the basic French foreign policy ever since. When unification eventually occurred, France's basic approach did not dramatically change. Concerns clearly existed in France (and elsewhere in Europe), but those were never concerns regarding an increased likelihood of German aggression vis-à-vis France (i.e., the concern one would expect to find between former enemies that have not yet completed their transition to peace). On the contrary, the French were concerned that a unified Germany would drift into neutralism, its new geopolitical reality perhaps weakening its ties to the European Community and to NATO. As for unification's direct impact on France, many French politicians and experts assumed that the resurgence of German political influence would directly affect France's own standing in Europe.[64] An issue that did resurface in public opinion polls was concern about future German economic strength. While more than 60 percent of respondents thought that unification would be a "good thing" when the Berlin Wall was finally breached, this figure dropped to 37 percent a year later. During the campaign preceding the French referendum on the Maastricht Treaty, this concern was raised by the "'No' camp" (i.e., those opposed to the treaty). Opponents argued that the treaty would give Germany the means to dominate the continent through the monetary union.[65] Such arguments suggest that traditional sentiments and stereotypes die hard. However, the crucial point to remember is that despite such arguments, openly debated, the French eventually did approve the Maastricht Treaty and choose to further upgrade their relations with the unified Germany through the European Union. In spite of the changing balance of power, the Franco-German partnership remained the most important relationship within the European Community.[66]

On the German side, many scholars focus on the impact of unification on the German motivation to invest more in European integration in order to reassure its European neighbors to accept the new Germany.[67] This brief discussion of European integration leads directly into a discussion of the impact of third parties on the process, the third hypothesis of this study.

France, Germany, the United States, and European Integration

There is no doubt that the Franco-German transition to peace was greatly influenced by the strategic conditions that arose with the onset of the cold war, mainly the Western powers' insistence that Germany had to be revived and that its resources ought to be mobilized to defend the West against aggression by the Soviet Union.[68] This position helped change the initial public sentiments and official policy in France, which had been calling for another punitive treaty with Germany and for keeping it weak and divided. France knew it would be impossible to stand firm against the Anglo-American coalition, which, beginning with the merger of its occupation zones into the "Bizone," was pushing for German rehabilitation. For American decision makers, it became clear that Germany had to be rehabilitated, both to strengthen the West and to avoid any possible drift toward the Soviet Union and the Eastern camp.[69] In the minds of many scholars, the American position on Germany and the United States' willingness to offer the Europeans firm security commitments in the form of a continued military presence in Europe were crucial in getting the Franco-German peace process under way.[70]

This book, however, focuses on the economic role of third parties in promoting transitions to peace. Such a role was indeed played in this case by the United States, which initiated the Marshall Plan.[71] I have argued that third parties can use economic incentives in order to establish or strengthen domestic beneficiaries of the peace. I also argued that in order to make a more significant and lasting contribution to the transition to peace, the third party should create a mechanism through which the former enemies will have an ongoing incentive to cooperate with one another so as to receive the desired benefits (e.g., the QIZ strategy applied in the Jordanian and Egyptian cases). The Marshall Plan is perhaps the classic example of using economic tools to promote peace. The very decision to offer rehabilitation aid and to include the then-occupied Germany in the program was crucial in shifting the French belief that Germany must remain in a weakened state. After U.S. secretary of state George C. Marshall made his historic speech proposing the plan, France came to realize that it would be unfeasible to try to separate the Ruhr resources from those of Germany. It can be argued that the Marshall Plan was mainly an attempt to dovetail German economic recovery with general European recovery so that the former would be politically acceptable to France.[72] Furthermore, the terms of the Marshall aid strongly tied Germany to the process of European integration and therefore also to a process of institutionalized reconciliation with France. The Americans refused to offer aid to individual Western European states and insisted that all Western Europeans work together to devise a European recovery plan. It was this American condition that forced Western European states to come together for arduous discussions in the Paris conference (July–September 1947) to try to bring their often conflicting national economic goals into harmony. The Americans pushed the Europeans to create a supranational body to manage the aid and to think in terms of rehabilitating and recreating an integrated Europe. After several months of European debates, the United States was forced to intervene itself in order to help the Europeans come up with a reasonable plan, one that the American administration could then defend and push through Congress. The American administration argued that, by creating a supranational body, it would be possible to revive the German economy but not the German threat to Western European security. Furthermore, supranational institutions would help harmonize national economies so that natural market forces could operate across the ERP (European Recovery Plan, or Marshall Plan) area as a whole.

The American supranational aspirations were defeated at the time due to strong British opposition. Instead, what came into being in April 1948 to manage the aid program was the intergovernmental Organization for European Economic Cooperation (OEEC). The issue on which the Americans had greater success (indeed, due to strong cooperation with Britain) was on reviving Germany. Both the United States and Britain worked together to create the rudiments of a West German government, introduce a new German currency, and increase the level of German industrial production. France found it extremely difficult to push back this Anglo-American move.[73] However, the Americans themselves were divided over the question of Germany. A special National Security Council subcommittee was formulated to address this debate, and it concluded in March 1949 that (as argued by the State Department) Germany had to be reintegrated into a "strong common structure of free Europeanism" because a "segmented" Germany might again dominate the continent economically. Once this conclusion was reached, the Americans worked hard to convince their French counterparts.[74] As described earlier, similar thoughts were entertained by French foreign minister Robert Schuman, but they were not particularly widespread in France. Consequently, the ongoing American effort to both convince and pressure the French to accept this new line of thinking was very important. The United States also took practical measures to tie its aid to increased economic interaction with Germany. In its bilateral agreements with individual European states, the United States managed, after hard bargaining, to insert a clause forcing the European countries to offer most favored nation (MFN) treatment to German trade (though the clause was limited in its effect to two years, after which any German government would have to bargain for itself).[75]

However, it is also important to qualify the impact of the American economic involvement on the nature of the Franco-German transition to peace. While creating the initial window of opportunity, the United States had limited impact on the exact nature of the transition and on the political-economic strategy used by French and German decision makers to advance their bilateral relations. The type of economic strategy envisioned by the United States to help promote reconciliation between France and Germany was rooted in classic liberal economic ideas of free trade. It was indeed the basic logic of commercial liberalism that guided American economic policy makers regarding Europe.[76] However, the course actually pursued by France and Germany bore little resemblance to the American liberal vision and received only a partial blessing from the United States.

To begin with, the Americans were concerned about the French Monnet Plan, fearing it would lead to the restoration of the old steel cartels so prevalent in the 1920s and so detested by the United States.[77] This concern was in place since, as described earlier, many industrialists in both France and Germany were interested in reviving those cartels. The Schuman Plan also created a major challenge for the Americans. On the one hand, it appealed to the United States because it met the four basic American policy objectives of advancing the formation of a single market in Europe, integrating the new West German state into Western Europe, advancing peace between France and Germany, and promoting the federal principle in unification.[78] On the other hand, the United States was very critical of the Schuman Plan as being too mercantilist in its approach. What France and Germany had in mind was to cooperate to create a common regularized market on coal and steel, not to advance a liberal vision. Earlier, when France and Germany signed their first trade agreement in 1950, the treaty included provisions for regular negotiations between industrial and agricultural groups within both countries to request adjustments to the agreement whenever necessary, as well as various provisions for managing agricultural trade between the two countries. The United States at the time voiced strong objections to these provisions, which led to some changes in the agreement but did not erase its managed-trade spirit.[79] The actual course of Franco-German economic reconciliation was therefore influenced mainly by European considerations and politics, not by the United States. This became clearer as economic and political cooperation between France and Germany was further institutionalized through the creation of the EC.

While at the early stages of the transition to peace the United States was the major relevant third party, from the early 1950s on, with the creation of the ECSC and then the EC (in 1957) and even later, Franco-German relations came to be nested in the broader context of European institutions. It is beyond the scope of this book to examine this complex process, that is, the story of the progress in European integration, from community to union (in Maastricht) to its recent expansion eastward. But as Julius Friend puts it, Franco-German relations became and still are the "linchpin" of the European integration project. Institutionalizing Franco-German relations within this broader European context helped ameliorate the concerns stemming from Germany's overwhelming economic power and the concerns regarding its political ambitions, and it gave both states a role and a stake in the management of European affairs.[80] It also created additional grounds for Franco-German cooperation in managing Western Europe's economic affairs, thus cementing and accelerating reconciliation. French and German decision makers were obliged to think in collaborative terms, and at the personal level, cooperation within the European Community often brought them into closer contact.[81] At the earlier and perhaps more crucial stages, in terms of the trajectory of Franco-German relations, the creation of the European Community also had a significant impact by institutionalizing the existing understandings between the two states, thus ensuring their underlying continuity. Thus, for example, when the very traditional Charles de Gaulle came to power in 1958, his rally to the EEC reflected the institutional consequences of the EEC itself. The EEC did serve his broad foreign policy goals of leading France to a third way between the superpowers, which necessitated broad support from Germany and the exclusion of Britain from Europe. However, had it not existed, there was little chance that de Gaulle himself would have initiated it.[82]

THE FRANCO-GERMAN TRANSITION to peace after World War II is often presented as a good example of the logic of commercial liberalism. Critics of the commercial liberal approach tend to focus instead on the overwhelming role of geostrategic factors in making this transition possible. The analysis in this chapter suggests that, on the one hand, economic factors did play a very important role in facilitating the transition to peace, but on the other hand, the role they played was very political. What was driving the process were political-economic considerations on both sides rather than some neutral, purely economic force. This is apparent when examining the background of the Schuman Plan, the ECSC, and the road to the Rome Treaty.

Clearly, one of the key reasons that the transition was relatively rapid and that normalization began early on was the fact that there was a clear and present economic gain for both sides. In this respect, when comparing this case, for example, to the Middle Eastern cases, it is clear that here most of the French and Germans, as opposed to most Egyptians or Israelis, felt that at least economically they stood to gain a great deal from reconciliation with their neighbor. The success of the ECSC further entrenched the sentiment that both Germany and France were "winners from peace," since nothing succeeds like success. As in the Asian cases, close cooperation between national governments and big business was evident in the transition process. However, unlike those cases, in the Franco-German case it was evident from very early on that it was not only the elites who were the big winners from the transition but that broader segments of society felt that the peace dividend was trickling down to them as well. One can logically conclude that the democratic nature of the regime in France and in the new FRG played a role in creating from an early stage public expectations to share the gains from peace.

Furthermore, because there was some societal interest in reconciliation through the various pro-integration movements in France, the distinction between the first and second stages of transition was not as clear-cut in this case. Conceptually, I argued that in order to move to normalization, broader segments in society need to feel like winners as a result of peace. In this case, such sentiments did exist in part already but were also generated anew at relatively early stages of the transition. This being said, it was evident that, at least in the early years, the normalization process was driven by French and German political and business elites and not by societal pressures. Leaders are more flexible than publics in adjusting to changing strategic, political, and economic needs, as all the cases so far demonstrate.

The economic power disparities in this case were narrower than in the previous four cases, as both France and Germany were advanced industrialized states. Still, one of the sources of the chronic "German problem" for France (and the rest of Europe) did stem from the underlying geostrategic, geopolitical, and geo-economic factors that made Germany inherently the most powerful economy in Europe. Concern over German economic domination was indeed raised in France, but it was less problematic than in previous cases for several reasons. First, the fact that the transition began from the starting point of a (partially) French occupation of Germany did give the French greater self-confidence. Second, economic power disparities did not translate in France into a serious concern about asymmetric dependence on Germany. This was due to the fact that Germany had an existential interest in foreign trade as well as the fact that Germany's economic superiority was balanced over the years by France's perceived political superiority in Europe. This finding further strengthens the findings of the Southeast Asian case, suggesting that we should focus less on the objective economic power disparities and more on the factors and process that determine whether those disparities translate into concern over dependence and vulnerability. When Germany finally unified, thus returning to its natural size, its relations with France were so institutionalized and normalized that, while concerns over the power shift were still heard, they had a limited impact on the continued partnership between the two states.

The Franco-German case also provided what seemed to be the ultimate use of an economic strategy by a third party to promote peace: the American introduction of the Marshall Plan. Yet, while the Marshall Plan (together with American political pressure and security guarantees) did play an important role in facilitating the transition, much of the actual process of transition and its economic character were driven and shaped not by the United States but by decision makers in France and Germany. Scholars like Ripsman and Miller are right to stress the importance of the United States (and the Soviet threat) at the initial stages of the transition. However, I conclude that the strong economic logic of peace for both France and Germany, while not a sufficient condition, was a necessary one for the transition to peace. Without it, U.S. pressure may have led to some cooperation but not to a transition that produced sustainable, long-term relations.

To the extent that initial U.S. policies also played a role in promoting the European integration process, one could argue that the United States also helped bring about a second and crucial mechanism within which Franco-German relations came to be nested: the institution of the European Community and, later, the European Union. The lack of such an institutionalized environment over the years, both in the Middle East and in East and Southeast Asia, made an ongoing and expansive process of cooperation between the relevant states much more difficult.

FROM ENEMIES TO PARTNERS

The Polish-German Transition to Peace

THE TRANSFORMATION OF German-Polish relations since the end of World War II has been dramatic. Relations between these two countries have a history of bitterness dating back to the late eighteenth century, when Germans ruled over Poles. German rule may have brought technological progress, but it also crushed Polish insurrections and tried to "Germanize" Polish children.[1] The period of Nazi Germany's occupation of Poland between 1939 and 1945 was a brutal one. Mass expulsions of Poles from territories annexed to Germany were conducted, more than 6 million Poles perished during the war, and Polish culture was destroyed. To complicate things further, in the aftermath of the war following Germany's defeat and the creation of the new border with Poland along the Oder-Neisse Line, close to a million of the Germans who lived in Poland were expelled. Many perished during the expulsion, and others found themselves as refugees either in the German Democratic Republic (GDR) of East Germany or in the FRG. Despite being ethnic Germans, many of those who were expelled still dreamed of returning to their homes in areas that had become part of Poland.[2]

Despite this difficult history in German-Polish relations, most observers acknowledge that economic factors played a central role in the two nations' transition to peace, though somewhat differently for each party. For Poland, even under Communist rule and more clearly after the democratization process, there was a clear and strong economic incentive to develop peaceful relations with Germany. For Germany, while normalizing relations did hold economic benefits, the driving force behind the process was political, and economic tools were utilized to promote Ostpolitik in Eastern Europe in general and in Poland in particular.

After the end of World War II, the two states found themselves in two diametrically opposed ideological camps. Their relations were marred by a host of thorny problems. While Poland insisted that, according to the Potsdam resolutions, the Oder-Neisse border was the final and permanent border with Germany, the Germans insisted that it was not and that German "lost territories" should be returned. This call was picked up and repeated by the masses of German expellees who found their way to West Germany. Germany also demanded that the Polish government acknowledge the existence of the German minority in Poland and ensure its rights, something the Poles refused to do. Finally, the Germans were intent on recovering various cultural artifacts that the Poles had confiscated after the German withdrawal. The Poles, for their part, demanded sizable financial compensation from Germany for Polish victims of forced labor, as well as an apology for Germany's behavior. During the 1950s, Chancellor Adenauer adhered to the Hallstein Doctrine, which meant an official boycott of all of Eastern Europe in light of their recognition of the GDR. However, by the early 1960s, economic relations between the two states had begun to develop once again. Thus, for example, while official diplomatic relations were not possible at the time, in 1963, the FRG did open a trade mission in Warsaw, which in practice served as a sort of embassy.

The first major official breakthrough in renewing relations between the two states was the Warsaw Treaty, signed in 1970, which followed the German policy shift known as Ostpolitik, introduced in the mid-1960s by Chancellor Willy Brandt. The treaty affirmed that the Oder-Neisse Line formed the western frontier of the People's Republic of Poland and that neither side had any territorial claims against the other. This in itself was a major accomplishment, given that this westward shift of the Polish frontier came at the expense of nearly forty thousand square miles of formerly German territory that had been home to about 8 million Germans. Still, this crucial border issue was not fully resolved because West Germany argued that actual recognition (a word that did not appear in the treaty) could be granted only by a unified Germany. The Germans thus stressed in the aftermath of the treaty that they would respect the border as long as the FRG existed. Final resolution of this issue would not take place for twenty years.[3]

The part of the treaty emphasized by the Germans was that calling for the normalization of economic and cultural relations. The treaty (ratified in West Germany only two years later, in 1972) was indeed followed by a mutual effort to facilitate and institutionalize wide cooperation. For example, Polish imports from West Germany had grown by more than 80 percent by 1972, West German business subsidiaries were formed in Poland, and permanent Polish business representatives were living in the FRG. Official visits between government leaders grew significantly, and following the Helsinki Accords in 1975, there was also an increase in contacts and formal meetings between labor groups, scientists, educators, and others, as well as an increase in the number of tourists.[4] Against the setting of the Helsinki Accords, a specifically political-economic deal was made between the FRG and Poland. Chancellor Helmut Schmidt signed a package of agreements with Polish Communist Party secretary Edward Gierek, among them a German loan of 1 billion DM at a low interest rate in exchange for the consent of the Polish authorities to allow up to 125,000 Germans to leave Poland over the next four years.[5] Throughout the 1980s, economic relations between the two states continued to develop, though further warming was difficult because of the political realities of the region. Many authors note the elitist nature of this transition process, especially since, on the German side, political considerations played a significant role and therefore involved the government, whereas on the Polish side the prominent economic logic driving normalization was closely guided by the Communist Party. Even after the crushing of the Solidarity movement and declaration of martial law in Poland in December 1981 under General Wojciech Jaruzelski, the Germans tried to continue a business-as-usual approach toward Poland. This, of course, did not generate much societal support for Germany in Poland.[6]

The next dramatic milestone signifying the upgrading of relations between the two states came only after the historic events of 1989–1990: the fall of the Berlin Wall, the beginning of talks about German unification, and the fall of the Communist Party government and the inauguration of the first democratically elected government in Poland. On November 14, 1990, Poland and Germany signed a treaty permanently fixing their border along the Oder-Neisse Line.[7] On June 17, 1991, Poland and Germany signed the Treaty of Good Neighborliness and Friendly Cooperation after eight months of arduous negotiations. In it, Poland finally acknowledged the existence of a German minority and agreed to grant it rights, while Germany committed to help Poland enter the European Community and other multilateral organizations, including NATO, and deal with its foreign debt issues. Since the signing of the treaty, there has been an intensification of cooperation between the two states, including a significant growth in bottom-up cooperation. There has also been an explosion of trade and travel across the border, with more than 100 million people crossing the Oder-Neisse border in 1993 alone.[8] A wide variety of institutions and bilateral consultation mechanisms were created to further institutionalize the relations, drawing on the Franco-German model. At the local level, cooperation has been particularly apparent along the border, with the most prominent example being the developing Nysa Euro region.[9] Germans and Poles made efforts to advance the resolution of the compensation issue for victims of the Nazi occupation of Poland. Thus, for example, Germany created in 1999 a "Remembrance, Responsibility, and the Future" fund of approximately 3 billion DM to be financed by German companies, which would distribute money to victims from Central and Eastern Europe. Similarly, a foundation for German-Polish reconciliation was created, into which the Germans paid 500 million DM for Polish victims. The Poles, however, were dissatisfied by the treatment of this issue, especially in light of the generous assistance the German government was providing to the German minority living in Poland.

Beyond these enduring questions, cooperation also developed on the military front, especially after Poland's entry into NATO. Joint German-Polish military maneuvers took place on Polish soil, Polish troops were being trained in Germany within a NATO framework, and a joint Polish-German-Danish military force was created. Such broad cooperation is remarkable when one considers both the distant and recent past of German-Polish relations.[10] From bitter enemies, especially from a Polish perspective, Poland came to see its relations with Germany as a "community of interest."[11] On December 20, 2007, another historic step was taken, when Poland joined the European Schengen Area (within which no visas are required) and the once contentious Oder-Neisse boundary became an open border.

Despite this progress, several issues remained unresolved between the two states, including reparations for Polish victims of forced labor, ongoing demands of the German expellees, German demands for the return of its cultural artifacts, problems relating to the management of the German-Polish border crossings, and the issue of free sailing on Pomorska Bay. While relations are solid, these issues create periodic crises, which have become more apparent since the mid-1990s.[12]

Translating this brief overview of Polish-German relations into the language of the conceptual framework of this book, we find that, as in the Franco-German case, there is no clear-cut temporal distinction between the achievement of a cold peace and the process of normalization. In an attempt to characterize the different stages in the transition to peace between the two countries, Adrian Hyde-Price argues that since the end of World War II and up to the mid-1960s (the beginning of Ostpolitik), relations were characterized by a precarious peace. Beginning in the mid-1960s, a state of conditional peace developed between the two countries but could not warm up any further until after the demise of bipolarity and the democratization of Poland. Consequently, in the 1990s, relations between the two states began moving in the direction of stable peace.[13] As noted previously, I prefer using Benjamin Miller's typology of cold-normal-warm peace stages. In light of the above description, I would suggest that until the mid-1960s, relations between Germany and Poland were characterized by a cold peace. The underlying conflicts between them were not resolved but definitely reduced, given the overwhelming defeat of Nazi Germany, the creation of the democratic FRG closely tied to the West, and the positioning of Poland under the Soviet security umbrella. Concerns regarding the German acceptance of the Oder-Neisse border were evident, and in fact, during the 1950s, both the United States and Britain supported the German claim for a revision of Germany's eastern border.[14] The Warsaw Treaty of 1970 in many respects brought relations closer to a state of "normal peace" à la Miller because it partially resolved the border issue and tried to deal with the issues of the expellees and compensation. As I explained in chapter 1, it is more useful to try to identify the process of normalization (i.e., movement toward normal and then warm peace) than to dwell on trying to define the level of peace at a given time. A process of normalization may be characterized by an expansion of cooperation between governments, expansion of cooperation between societal actors (among whom there is supposedly very little cooperation in a situation of cold peace), expansion of cooperation into various issue areas, and an observable process of institutionalization of such cooperation. Such a process is clearly observable in this case, though not without some complications. Since the signing of the treaties there has been impressive institutionalization of cooperation, on paper and in practice. Such institutionalization took place on both the bilateral and multilateral levels. Bilaterally, institutionalized cooperation was evident, for example, in regular meetings of German and Polish parliamentary committees on social affairs, close cooperation between the German ministry of agriculture and its Polish counterpart in preparation for Polish entry into the EU, close cooperation between the ministries of foreign affairs and environmental protection, and so on. Following the 1991 "neighborliness" treaty, hundreds of treaties were signed among bodies at different government and local levels in both countries, a figure that can be starkly contrasted with the very limited number of treaties that were signed (and never implemented) following the peace treaty between Israel and Egypt.[15]

The clear distinction between cold peace and normalization is undermined by the fact that even before official relations were established between the two states, even during the late 1950s and in spite of Adenauer's policies, commercial relations already existed.[16] Furthermore, the official policy of Ostpolitik was preceded and partially inspired by a societal-level initiative, which came in the form of an impressive exchange of letters between the Polish and German Catholic bishops who attended the Vatican Council in Rome in November 1965. The Polish bishops wrote to their counterparts, "Let us try to forget. . . . We stretch our hands to you, who sit on the benches of the Council that is about to end; and we forgive and we ask you also to forgive." The German bishops responded by acknowledging the horrors inflicted upon the Polish nation by the Germans and concluded by saying, "This is why we also ask for forgetfulness, more, we ask for forgiveness." This represented the first conciliatory step by a major West German group toward Poland since the end of World War II. At the same time, one should note that the Polish bishops were heavily criticized in Poland for their letter.[17]

Still, most of the interaction between West Germany and Poland once Ostpolitik was adopted as an official policy was driven by governments and not by society. In the aftermath of the 1970 treaty, and more intensely after the 1990–1991 treaties, both governments invested in wide institutionalization of economic, political, and cultural cooperation. The official goal of the German government was to develop any possible tie—political, social, cultural, academic, or scientific—with Eastern Europe. But as in the other cases examined in this book, reconciliation between governments and politicians came long before such a process began to take hold at the level of the general public.[18]

What is also striking is the fact that, despite the significant economic aspects related to the 1970 treaty, the long debates over its ratification, both in the FRG and in Poland, did not mention economics at all and focused on the very political and symbolic question of recognition of the Oder-Neisse border. In fact, most speakers in the Polish parliament prior to ratification expressed the feeling that the treaty itself was only the first step on a new and long road toward normalization.[19] This top-down approach, however, proved relatively successful. In the spring of 1995, a Polish survey showed that 70 percent of Poles considered Germany to be their best neighbor, and in 1996, a majority named Germany as their preferred partner for close cooperation economically (77 percent), politically (74 percent), and even militarily (67 percent).[20] From the perspective of 2007, opinions are mixed regarding how successful this normalization process has been, and they reflect the difficulty of assessing objectively the level of normalization or the quality of the peace. Some scholars stress the half-full glass perspective and the fact that relations have never been so good in the past 250 years. Beyond the highly institutionalized relations, Germany is Poland's major trading partner and Poland is Germany's main partner in Central and Eastern Europe. Bilateral trade in 2007 reached €60.2 billion. Germany is also among the top investors in Poland. Significantly, such investments are being made not only by big business but also by small and medium-sized companies in border regions.[21] Other scholars and practitioners stress the half-empty glass perspective, focusing on the lingering impact of historical animosities and unresolved disputes and the continuation of misperceptions and negative stereotypes, especially at the societal level. Skeptics point out that the process of normalization is still driven by elites.[22]

This complexity is exemplified in the crisis in relations between the two countries that occurred in June 2007, which stemmed from the Polish refusal to accept the German plan to reform the voting system of the EU in a manner that was to privilege the states with larger populations (i.e., Germany). Poland became the only EU member state that threatened to veto German chancellor Angela Merkel's proposed plan for the treaty to replace the EU draft constitution. The German press characterized relations at that time as reaching a level of animosity not seen since before the end of the cold war. The German media interpreted Polish behavior as driven once again by a perceived "German threat" and a perception that the EU had become an instrument of German domination.[23] This crisis was resolved only in October 2007, when a compromise was reached that allowed the signing of the new treaty, which came to be known as the Treaty of Lisbon. Once it was signed on December 13, 2007, Poland wanted to be the first to ratify the treaty, reflecting its willingness to play a productive leading role in the EU.[24]

Even before that particular crisis, whenever conflicts of interest emerged, the Poles were quick to invoke painful memories of past German behavior to reprimand Germany. For example, another bone of contention was the agreement between Germany and Russia to construct a natural gas pipeline through the Baltic Sea, therefore decoupling gas supply to Western Europe from gas supply to Poland and potentially allowing Russia in the future to withhold gas supplies from Poland without affecting the gas supply to other parts of Western

Europe. The Poles criticized the agreement, and Polish defense minister Radosław Sikorski was fast to compare the treaty to the Molotov-Ribbentrop Pact, which divided Poland between Germany and Russia prior to the German invasion of Poland in 1939.[25]

The complexity of German-Polish relations is further demonstrated by the fact that only six months after that disturbing low in the relations, on December 20, 2007, Poland officially joined the Schengen Area, within which EU citizens can move freely without the need for a visa or border inspections. Thus, the troublesome Oder-Neisse boundary, around which so many debates had taken place over the years, suddenly became an open border. This is clearly a significant step, indicative of the stability of the peace between Poland and Germany. Still, old stereotypes die hard. This apparently ideal ending to the chronological review of German-Polish relations to date is marred by the observation that this historic event received only limited media coverage in Germany, and most of the media coverage it did receive focused on Germans living close to the border and their preparations for the "Polish invasion"—installing metal shutters, putting up barbed wire, and even buying guns in anticipation of a surge in crime.[26]

These unique dynamics of Polish-German relations found their most recent expression in the Euro 2008 soccer competition that was taking place as this book was being completed. In the match between Germany and Poland, one could hear old World War II–related metaphors being shouted by fans. However, when Germany won the game, it was its Polish-born star, Lukas Podolski, who had clinched his team's victory. Podolski, following the match, refused to celebrate because of his Polish roots.

The Economic Logic of the Transition to Peace

In the Franco-German case, there was a clear, powerful, and urgent economic logic for Germany to normalize its relations with France; German industry could not survive without access to French markets. In this case, while an economic rationale for normalizing relations did exist, it was not the driving force for Germany. Germany was motivated to normalize its relations with Poland, as well as other states in Eastern Europe, first and foremost for political reasons—to demonstrate its benign intentions to the larger international community and to support reform in Eastern Europe. Economic cooperation was used to advance these political goals.[27] By contrast, Poland's interest in improving relations with the FRG was largely driven by economic factors. We have already seen this type of asymmetry in motivations in the two Middle Eastern cases. Still, it should be stressed that for Germany as well there was a real economic logic for reconciling with Poland, one that, even if not overwhelming, did converge with Germany's political interests. There were basic economic complementarities between the FRG and its Eastern European neighbors, especially Poland. The FRG was able to supply manufactured goods and technology that Poland needed. Furthermore, especially after its division and the loss of its raw material and energy supplies in the eastern territories (e.g., coal in Silesia), the FRG needed to import natural resources and other primary goods (e.g., natural gas and basic chemicals).[28] For the Germans, improving relations with Poland also offered the opportunity to enter a large consumer market with a relatively high demand for industrial and consumer goods. Furthermore, by 1962, there was a growing competition among Western European states for Eastern European markets.[29]

The policy of reconciliation with Poland was not one that the FRG originally pursued. When the policy was initiated in 1966, the potential benefits of such a strategy were weighed against the experience accumulated since the 1950s, during a time when Germany maintained a more hostile and conflictual attitude toward its eastern neighbors. The public feeling by the mid-1960s was that the long boycott of Eastern Europe did not bring anything useful to the FRG. On the Polish side, despite Communist Party rule, the need for an outlet for Poland's products and the dire need for technology created a strong incentive to trade with the FRG. In a pattern that is similar to the Jordanian case, a prolonged domestic economic crisis in Poland created ongoing social restlessness, which was endangering the regime's stability. Consequently, even the Communist Party rulers encouraged some economic interaction with West Germany.[30]

Although the underlying German motivation was political, the West Germans believed that economic statecraft would smooth the way to normal relations with Poland. For the FRG in the late 1960s and 1970s, "normalization of relations" with Poland meant the development of normal economic relations. The Germans wanted first to advance normalization and only then talk about formal ties. Conversely, the Poles wanted first to resolve all the basic problems and then move on to normalization.[31] These differing attitudes toward the nature and timing of "normalization" should remind the reader of a similar gap in the understanding of normalization between Egypt and Israel. The former signed the official peace treaty but made any normalization contingent upon the resolution of the major outstanding political issues. The latter wanted to move on the normalization issues in order to solidify the official peace. The difference in this regard stems from the fact that while Egypt could afford holding economic normalization hostage to further political developments, Poland was too dependent on the economic gains from normalization of relations with the FRG and thus held a much weaker bargaining position

Domestic Winners and Losers from Peace in Germany

The central factor characterizing the political economy of the transition to peace in the FRG was the close cooperation between government and private business. This situation arose because primarily political goals were driving the West German policy of Ostpolitik in the 1960s and 1970s and its post–cold war cooperation with Poland and Eastern Europe more generally. Specific branches of West German industry were quite dependent on eastern trade. For example, in the mid-1970s, as much as 20 percent of the iron and steel exports went to Eastern Europe. Leaders of those industries, together with the banks that supported them, acted as an important lobby in Bonn. It is estimated that the number of jobs directly dependent on this trade varied from 100,000 to 300,000. Thus, even if the original interest in developing trade with Eastern Europe was mainly political, the effect of this politically driven expansion was to increase economic interest in Germany as well.[32]

The long history of economic cooperation (and, at times, exploitation) between Germany and Poland, despite its negative implications, created an almost natural expectation of larger economic interaction with the Eastern Europe market in the future. The extent of trade with Eastern Europe before World War II (between 15 and 17 percent of German trade) created positive trade expectations after the war as well.[33] This perception is reflected in a speech given in 1972 by Walter Scheel, Willy Brandt's foreign minister, to the leaders of the iron, tin, and metal-processing industries. Scheel noted that for centuries "the German businessman in the East has realized our natural role as the mediator between the products and needs of West and Central Europe on the one side and of the Balkans and Eastern Europe on the other." This mediation was a function that, argued Scheel, German businessmen were again coming to fulfill, a function "given them by nature."[34]

Expansion of trade with Eastern Europe also served another goal of both German business and the government, which was to reduce their dependence on the United States for imports.[35] Furthermore, German business was skeptical regarding the American "open door" policy of free trade that it was trying to establish. They thought this policy would be very vulnerable to crises and that in such a case Germany would need a backup—its Eastern Europe trade.[36]

Most scholars who analyze German foreign economic policy stress the crucial role of West Germany's neocorporatist institutional structure, which yielded a smooth and efficient process of government-business cooperation. The German commercial sector was able to exert significant influence over policy thanks to its efficient organization through peak associations and its developed and institutionalized links to the bureaucratic ministries and to government. German business leaders could use the various "parapublic institutions," as Peter Katzenstein calls them, that were open to centralized interest groups as well as party leaders and senior civil servants.[37] The most politically active interest group in the FRG was the Federation of German Industry, a peak association representing all service and production industries. This peak association is actively involved in policy formulation; it evaluates proposed legislation that is related to business, follows it during all stages of policy making, and maintains close ties to the government. German banks also play an important role in coordinating foreign economic policy. They exert influence on the industry through their sources of financing and their substantial ownership of stocks in corporations. Leading banking and industry executives were always included as members of official state delegations traveling to Poland.[38]

This general pattern of activity found its clearest expression in the creation of the Eastern Committee of German Industry, already functioning in 1952, and the Poland Committee. The Eastern Committee included the official representatives of private German business interests in Eastern Europe. Due to the fact that, until the mid-1960s, the FRG did not have official diplomatic ties with Poland, the creation of a German commercial mission in Warsaw (as well as in other East European capitals) and the working of the Eastern Committee served the purpose of carrying out quasi-diplomatic relations without undermining the official West German policy of the Hallstein Doctrine. More specifically, the Poland Committee included about 130 representatives from German industry (including the banking and trade sectors). It also performed quasi-public functions and was responsible for promoting contacts between leading economic figures in both countries and facilitating the exchange of information.[39] This semiofficial role of business is very similar to the role that Japanese big business played in the development of trade relations prior to official normalization of relations with the People's Republic of China in 1972. The close and well-organized cooperation between government and business, though, was also reflected in the two Japanese cases and serves to further vindicate the argument that such cooperation is an important factor in making possible the productive use of economic tools in promoting peace.

The economic logic for cooperation between Germany and Poland was not as compelling as the economic logic driving German cooperation with France. This is due to both the power disparities between Germany and Poland and the perceived high risk of investing in Poland, especially in the volatile times after 1989. For this reason, the German government had to take action to assure private business owners that they would indeed have the opportunity to reap major benefits. The government encouraged economic cooperation by participation in various trade fairs in Poland. It also offered private German business leaders export credit guarantees (known as Hermes guarantees) in order to reduce the risks involved. If one contrasts this case with the limited normalization between Egypt and Israel, one finds that in that case, the Egyptian government, for its part, was unwilling to support its business leaders in their dealings with Israel, whereas the Israeli government, for its part, was not well coordinated with its private sector.

Despite the fact that there was a broad consensus among both public and private officials that economic cooperation with Poland was in their interest, there were also several groups that stood to suffer losses from normalization of relations. On the economic front, the main concern was that the expansion of trade with Poland, with its low-wage labor and low-cost products, might lead to dumping in the West German market and thus hurt domestic producers of consumer goods. These concerns were dealt with in the Treaty on Trade and Economic Cooperation of 1970, which paved the way to the political normalization declared in the Warsaw Treaty in December of that year. While the October treaty lifted most of the barriers to exports to Poland, it also provided protection for domestic producers in Germany since all Polish imports were to be subject to a "price clause," which was designed to prevent dumping by Polish firms. The treaty thus opened the way for export expansion to Poland while restricting import expansion.[40]

The other economic group that traditionally had set the limits of Germany's trade with Eastern Europe was the agricultural sector. Throughout the years of German interaction with Eastern Europe, this sector allowed expansion of trade with the East only if and when imports from the East did not threaten domestic

German agricultural price levels. Expansion of trade with the East after the creation of the FRG was possible in part due to the fact that under Communist Party rule, East European, including Polish, agriculture, no longer posed a real threat to West German agriculture.[41]

The main political group that perceived the normalization of economic relations with Poland as extremely costly was the group of ethnic Germans who were expelled from the western part of Poland at the end of the war. Beginning in the late 1940s, these expellees had formed various organizations to advance their interests, mainly of course to call for the return of the lost eastern territories of Germany. Although the expellees' demands were unrealistic, successive West German governments and political parties all had to cater to their claims because one-fifth of the West German voters were expellees. They were united into an overall union, which became one of the FRG's most powerful lobbies. Over time, their political power declined with Brandt's Ostpolitik and the rise of a younger generation that was already well integrated into the prosperous West German economy.[42] Still, their vocal opposition created major difficulties for German chancellors trying to reach agreement with Poland regarding the Oder-Neisse border and to offer an official and final recognition of it, as it was extremely difficult for a leader to state publicly that the eastern territory was permanently in another's hands. This issue was not resolved, consequently, until German reunification.[43]

Poland's Winners and Losers in the Transition to Peace

On the Polish side, the early stages of normalization took place under Communist Party rule and therefore did not involve an independent business or labor sector. The Polish government, however, was under serious pressure to develop its economic relations with the FRG in light of its dire economic situation. There was a basic understanding that in order to improve economic conditions (and ultimately save the regime), expansion of trade and especially the import of modern technology were inevitable and that West Germany was the most logical and accessible partner.[44] The enduring economic crisis led eventually to the fall of Władysław Gomulka, who was replaced by Edward Gierek. Gierek's power elite was composed of a relatively young group of pragmatic leaders having administrative experience and not born in the "womb of revolutionary struggles." Gierek understood that the absence of sustained economic growth was dangerous and increased the volatility of public protest. Consequently, his economic blueprint for 1970–1975 proposed a dramatic upgrading of commercial relations with capitalist countries. His logic was that commercial relations with developed countries would ease the economic and political situation in Poland. It is interesting that even the directors in the Soviet Union agreed that Poland should establish limited business relations with the industrialized West.[45] While the commercial treaty was signed in October 1970 and Gierek came to power only in December, there is no doubt that his outwardly oriented economic policy provided the treaty with a good tail wind. It is thus possible to identify this Polish government as a constrained version of a liberalizing coalition. Once again we find that such a coalition is more likely to cooperate for the purpose of advancing its economic goals.

This fledgling liberalizing coalition turned into a fully mature liberalizing coalition after the fall of the Communist Party government. The new Solidarity government embarked on the dual process of democratization and economic liberalization, two processes aimed at leading Poland "back to Europe." The new democratic government endorsed ideas that were developing among the Polish opposition throughout the 1980s. Especially after the 1980–1981 interlude in which the Solidarity union movement ended with its repression by the government, opposition leaders came to realize that a decisive reorientation to the West was an indispensable part of their desired domestic reform. This orientation, first and foremost, led to West Germany, for, as the new slogan of the time put it, "the road to Europe runs through Germany." A key motivation in the opposition's desire to support closer ties with Germany was economic. Germany was Poland's largest governmental creditor and source of private credit, so its cooperation was crucial for debt reduction. Also, Germany was seen as a partner that would facilitate Polish links to other Western economic bodies such as the IMF, the World Bank, and, obviously, the EC. Finally, the direct benefits of bilateral links to Germany would be of huge importance for any new reform government, since Germany was already Poland's most important Western trading partner.[46] In the 1990s, a new element was added to this situation when unemployment in Poland rose dramatically (from 1.5 percent in 1990 to 11.5 percent at the end of 1991). The Poles were thus also interested in Germany as an important center of employment for Polish workers, especially in the construction sector. The Germans, for their part, had since the late 1980s faced shortages of skilled workers, especially in the construction industry, which skilled Polish workers could fill. This led to a bilateral labor agreement between the two states in 1990.[47] Still, over time Germans grew more concerned over cheap Polish labor and announced a ban on Polish workers freely entering the German labor market. Polish workers found their way elsewhere, especially to Britain and Ireland.

In recent years, growing openness to the EU and to Germany is becoming unsettling for a broad segment of Polish society. Polish politics is divided in two camps. One camp is internationalist and promoting the "return to Europe." It views Germany as a bridge between the West and Poland and therefore as positive factor in pulling it westward. The second camp may be called nationalist or "isolationist." It views closer links with the integrated Europe as a threat. This camp includes artisans, shop owners, and their employees, who are concerned about their future in the onslaught of foreign investment and massive foreign-owned department stores and shopping malls popping up all over the country. These people, according to the German periodical *Der Spiegel,* are the ones who voted into office the brothers Lech and Jaroslav Kaczynski (president and prime minister), two nationalist conservatives who clearly viewed Germany as a threat.[49] In recent years, a growing number of Polish companies are also increasing their investment abroad, with Germany and especially Berlin becoming a major target.[50] However, at the same time, findings also show that in both Poland and Germany, large sections of society are convinced that their political and economic elites act behind the people's backs and against their most vital interests. This is a dangerous finding since it implies that many in the respective societies are still not grasping the economic peace dividend.[51]

The Impact of Economic Power Disparities

Most books examining German foreign policy stress Germany's structural economic advantage vis-à-vis its eastern neighbors as an underlying theme. Despite having a population half as large as Germany's, Poland has an economy only about 10 percent as large. It exports low value-added raw materials and semi-finished products to Germany while importing machinery and other high value-added products. Trade with Germany has been at least ten times more important for Poland than it has been for Germany.[52] This underlying asymmetry has not changed dramatically over the years, despite the significant changes that Poland has undergone. In the 1970s, Poland's trade with the FRG accounted on average for 6.3 percent of its exports and 9.4 percent of its imports, whereas its share of the total foreign trade of the FRG was very low, averaging 1.3 percent for exports and 0.8 percent for imports.[53] After the 1991 agreement, this asymmetry was only exacerbated, with Germany accounting for about half of Poland's trade with the EU (27 percent of its total trade in 1992) whereas Poland accounted for merely 1.1 percent of Germany's foreign trade in the same year. This happened even though in absolute terms Poland, for example, greatly expanded its exports to Germany (from $28.2 billion in 1998 to $41 billion in 2002).[54]

Despite the political motivation to cooperate, the development of more advanced forms of economic relations, especially in the fields of finance and investment, has been disappointing. Germans perceived the risks of investing in such forms of cooperation to be relatively high and preferred to wait for the Poles to make reforms and improve their efficiency first.[55] Włodzimierz Borodziej argues that the economic asymmetry between the two states has indeed been greatly reduced since the 1991 treaty as a result of the fast growth of the Polish GNP and the tripling of its higher education index. But at the same time, its quality has grown and it actually became more pronounced in the sphere of perception and mentality. He argues that whereas Polish prejudices among the general public about Germans are slowly waning, there is no change in the typical German's ignorance and sense of superiority.[56]

This underlying economic power disparity created both advantages and disadvantages for the process of the transition to peace between the two countries. On the down side, we find all the problems that characterize such asymmetric relations, especially between former enemies. The structural economic power disparities created a "psychology of asymmetry," which created a large gap between the two countries. The Poles view Germany as very important, whereas Germans think of Poland as a medieval rural state. This gap in perceptions leads, in turn, to the basic problem of German lack of interest on the one hand and Polish mistrust on the other.[57] Obviously, the history of the highly politicized economic relations between Germany and Poland prior to World War II feeds into these current suspicions. These concerns created problems for devising practical cooperation. One such example is the Stolpe Plan, a proposal for regional cooperation that was put forward in July 1991. The proposal was to create a cooperative zone along the entire German-Polish border, extending one hundred kilometers into Poland and fifty kilometers into Germany. Development in that zone was to be promoted by a joint German-Polish development bank, with Germany providing 70 percent of the capital and having a majority on the board of directors. The Germans were surprised at the outrage that the proposal created in Poland. Poles saw it as unfair, disproportionately favoring

Germany, and a threat to Polish sovereignty in these regions. The specializations assigned to German and Polish regions also seemed unfair to Poles, because they still had Germany specializing in modern manufacturing projects while Polish tasks would include simple processing of food and raw materials. This would "exploit uncompromisingly the low land prices and labor costs" in Poland. Similarly, the proposed development bank was seen as an instrument of economic penetration by Germany. The plan was consequently scrapped, and the bank never materialized.[58]

An abundance of similar problems can be observed when analyzing German-Polish cooperation at local levels. A close inspection of cooperation problems in the Nysa Euro region (established in 1991) also shows the detrimental impact of the wide economic disparities. The supposedly large Polish trade exports to Germany actually reflect a large share of exports from German subsidiaries located in Poland. Furthermore, many Polish producers in the region have been discouraged from direct trade with Germany by the onerous requirements placed on them by German manufacturers. This, in turn, created dependency relations between Polish producers and their German distributors.[59] This example closely resembles the Israeli experience vis-à-vis Egypt and Jordan. There, as well, we saw that in a case of significant economic asymmetry, following the strictly economic logic of cooperation (i.e., utilizing the comparative advantage of each side) may be rational, but it is definitely not conducive to the development of peace and cooperation.

Even though relations have normalized to the extent that Poles are not concerned about a German military attack, economic and cultural threats have persisted. A Polish newspaper article suggested that while the intelligentsia and the younger Poles no longer fear a "new blitzkrieg," they are "more concerned over the prospect of an economic superpower which could gradually buy up the entire country and could use a network of hardworking German directors to threaten Poland's national and cultural independence."[60] Once again, the concern over cultural penetration and neo-imperialism was also very strong among Egyptian and Jordanian intelligentsia. Such threat perceptions appear quite reasonable when one reads the various books written in recent years to examine Germany' successful economic diplomacy vis-à-vis all of its Eastern European neighbors, including Poland and even the more challenging neighbor—Russia. Analytical reviews of these relations indeed establish how a state can use its economic strengths to create positive economic linkage to win political concessions. Newnham goes as far as arguing that the economic imbalance helped shape the poorer state's foreign policy preferences.[61] This, of course, is exactly Albert Hirschman's "influence effect" at work.[62]

These same reviews, however, also reflect the *positive* potential of dyadic economic power disparities in promoting a transition to peace, if the more powerful state is indeed committed to using its economic leverage to lure its neighbor into cooperation, to change its negative perceptions, and to build a powerful domestic lobby supporting such cooperation. This worked very well in the German-Polish case, in which, at least in the long run, the economic dimension of Ostpolitik did have a positive impact on the Polish perception of Germany and its intentions. Such linkage was clearly made in the 1991 treaty as well. This being said, two points are worth stressing. First, the various economic benefits that Germany could offer Poland could not influence the Polish position on the Oder-Neisse border. An official and explicit German commitment to the permanent nature of that border could not be replaced by economic aid or trade credits. Only after the Germans conceded on this point could the economic dimension kick in again. This is important since it shows that even very big economic incentives cannot overcome what are perceived to be existential political and security concerns. Second, despite the centrality of economic considerations in the normalization of Polish-German relations, both Poland and Germany wanted to avoid a direct and public economic linkage. Such a linkage would have led to accusations that Polish leaders were sacrificing Polish national interests for financial gain.[63] This accusation is likely to be more acute given the power disparities between the two states.

I argued in chapter 1 that wide economic power disparities pose an obstacle to the use of economic tools in transitions to peace.[64] While evidence of such difficulties is abundant, the fact remains that economic cooperation, as well as political cooperation between the two states, did develop significantly over a decade, even though problems did arise. Such cooperation developed even under Communist Party rule, despite the diverging ideologies and political East-West rivalry. If, for Egyptians or Jordanians, the specter of an Israeli economic invasion and its negative implications was an imaginary one, for Poles this was not only a concern regarding the future but a strong memory of the recent past. Consequently, the decision to renew economic relations with Germany should not be treated lightly. What then can explain the Poles' decision?

The most important factor that existed here but not in the Middle Eastern cases is the obvious potential for strong economic gains that such cooperation could bring to Poland. One could therefore argue that Poland did not have much of a choice but to turn again to Germany. Aware of the dangers, as outlined by Hirschman, Polish officials charged with developing trade policy vis-à-vis West Germany initially tried to avoid a deficit in foreign trade and to maintain a balanced trade as a guarantee that Poland's development would not again become dependent on the economically stronger partner. In practice, however, this attempt failed, and Poland once again found itself dependent on West Germany.[65] The point is, though, that despite the asymmetries, Polish business leaders and the Polish government still perceived the potential for important economic gains from interaction with Germany. It is interesting to note the differences in attitude toward Germany expressed by Poland and the Czech Republic. The latter was much more apprehensive about developing relations with Germany and had several reasons for that apprehension, but the fact that the Czech Republic is much smaller than Poland is important. As the larger Eastern European country, Poland feels less physically overshadowed by Germany than does the smaller Czech Republic.[66] I made a similar observation regarding South Korea, which was economically much weaker than Japan, but South Korean business leaders felt the gap was such that they could still effectively compete in certain fields and make a meaningful profit. By contrast, for a country like Jordan that is economically much weaker than Israel, concerns over the adverse effects of this asymmetry, should free trade take place between the two states, were not mitigated by a clear expectation for significant economic gains from such trade.

The second factor that ameliorated Polish concerns regarding the potential negative implications of the wide power disparities with West Germany and later Germany has to do with the embedding of their bilateral relations in the wider, multilateral setting of the European Community and later the European Union.

The Role of Third Parties in the Transition to Peace

During the first round of the transition to peace between Poland and Germany, there was no positive role for third parties, especially not an economic role, which is the focus here. Obviously, relations were developing within a very difficult international environment. West Germany may have had more leeway to interact with Poland, given its membership in an alliance of democratic states. But the Poles were obviously operating within a much more constraining environment. It is doubtful that Poland would have been able to sign the Warsaw Treaty and pursue it without Moscow's blessing. Indeed, as the reader may recall, the Warsaw Treaty came about only after the signing of the Moscow Treaty between West Germany and the Soviet Union. New archival material offers evidence that the change in Polish first secretary Gomulka's hard line vis-à-vis the FRG stemmed from changes in the policies of the Soviet Union and the GDR. Gomulka was willing to consider a deal with West Germany only after it became clear to him that the GDR had decided to improve its relations with the FRG (by signing a long-term trade agreement in December 1968) and that the Soviets as well were negotiating a bilateral deal with the Germans. Moscow's perceived willingness to compromise Poland's security interests compelled it to obtain an independent West German guarantee for Poland's western border.[67] Bonn, for its part, could pursue its Ostpolitik more easily in the general atmosphere of détente. These, however, are all background conditions and do not deal directly with the economic processes involved in the transition. These processes, to a large extent, were driven by West Germany and Poland themselves.

The transition and especially the potential adverse effects of the wide power disparities on Polish concerns about Germany were very much influenced by the initial embedding of German foreign policy within European multilateral institutions and, consequently, the embedding of German-Polish bilateral relations within that multilateral setting. In the previous cases, the third parties being discussed were states, but the key third party here is the multilateral institution —the EC, then the EU, NATO, and the Weimar Triangle (a forum of security cooperation between Germany, France, and Poland). Of the three, the EU factor is the most relevant for this discussion. The German dominance in power, especially since unification, is attenuated by the evolving multilateral relationships linking Poland, as well as other Central European countries, and Germany to an increasingly integrated Europe and to the Atlantic Alliance. Embedding the relations within this regional institution had two positive effects: it reduced concerns over Germany because German foreign policy was now constrained by the EU, and, at the same time, it provided Poland with new opportunities to actively reduce the power disparities and to play a politically more significant role in shaping the future of Europe. The feeling in Poland was that Germany had become Europeanized and that, consequently, the fear of German hegemony or of political dependence on Germany had vanished.[68] The Polish ambassador in Germany explained that for Poland, embedding its neighbor's policies in a wider European framework was the only way to ensure it would not fall again victim to great power politics in Europe, as it had done several times in the past. Poland, therefore, pursued a pro-Europe foreign policy.[69]

A debate has taken place in Poland regarding the question of whether EU membership would serve to moderate German power. On the economic front, Poles are aware of the clearly uneven economic relations with Germany and hope that EU membership will help tackle that disparity. Expectations about the implications of EU membership for Poland's security arrangements are strongly related to the "German factor." It is interesting that the political parties (i.e., the Christian National Union or ZChN and the Peasant Alliance or PSL) that were skeptical about EU integration related their attitude to a fear of Germany. Along the same lines, the Euro-skeptic part of Polish public opinion sees that EU membership would compromise Poland's security against Germany.[70] Membership in multilateral European institutions thus was seen as a way to mitigate the asymmetry vis-à-vis Germany, but at the same time cooperation with Germany was seen as a crucial element in the strategy for rejoining Europe. A circular logic was created linking cooperation with Germany to getting into the EU to reduce asymmetries to better deal with Germany. In 1997, an official government statement declared that "we can overcome our historical backwardness and become an equal partner for the developed countries only through the adroit and effective inclusion of Poland in the economic and political integration processes of Western Europe. Self-isolation . . . will inevitably lead in time to marginalization of the Polish economy . . . which may in turn lead to a loss of freedom and sovereignty."[71]

This Polish perspective, in turn, was compatible with Germany's own postwar strategy that stressed the use of power only via multilateral institutions. Germany has adopted initially for instrumental reasons the European option in the 1950s, but over time its interests were fundamentally shaped by the institutional context of Europe and the Europeanization of the identity of the German state that had taken place in the preceding decades. It has become, as Katzenstein describes it, a "tamed power."[72]

Embedding German-Polish relations within multilateral integration also facilitated the emergence of a stable peace by encouraging habits of mutually beneficial cooperation based on deepening trust and common interests.[73] Within EU institutions, Poland and Germany interact on a regular basis, and within those institutions, their very asymmetric relations appear more balanced. As a relatively large state, Poland can become a meaningful actor in the EU, and, indeed, its positions on the EU constitution and European security and defense demonstrate that it has no hesitation to behave in an independent manner.[74]

Joint activities of Poland and Germany within the EU also enhanced cooperation. Both states, for example, cooperated to obtain beneficial solutions in the Growth and Stability Pact. Thanks to their joint efforts, Germany did not have to include the costs of unification in their budget deficit, while the Poles were exempt from including the costs of their pension system reform.[75]

The crisis in June 2007 between Poland and Germany surrounding Poland's refusal to accept the German reform plan for EU voting reflects the independent Polish behavior and its anxiousness to use the EU framework, as much as possible, to maximize its voice. This crisis, and the negative feelings it rekindled between Poland and Germany, demonstrates how institutionalization, even in a successful and well-developed multilateral setting, does not really resolve the asymmetry problem. Poland eventually did have to withdraw its opposition. At the same time, Poland was able to secure a guarantee that small groups of countries would be able to delay EU decisions they do not like.[76] Furthermore, when looked at from a somewhat different perspective, this crisis, described in the newspapers as the lowest point in Polish-German relations since the 1970s, also reflects the strength and virtues of embedding the potentially explosive bilateral relations in a wider multilateral setting. The broader setting allowed for other European states to become involved and to defuse the crisis. It is this nesting in the complex web of European institutions that lends the relations, despite the crisis and negative tones, an enduring quality. This quality, of course, found expression in the historic opening of the borders on December 20, 2007, only half a year later. The following statement by Chancellor Helmut Kohl, in June 1997, suggests that this was not a matter of chance but of design: "[We] must draw a decisive lesson . . . that there will never again be border problems in Europe. . . . We must make borders porous, as between Germany and France. . . . For this reason we want Poland . . . to become a part of the European Union."[77] Ten years later, this strategy proved itself.

SEVERAL CONCLUSIONS EMERGE from a survey of the German-Polish transition to peace. First, trying to characterize the current "level of peace" between the two states accentuates the difficulty of peace typologies, whichever typology we choose to use. How do we weigh the tremendous advances in the relations, on all fronts, with the lingering problems, tensions, and periodic crises? It is this difficulty that led me to put more emphasis on the process that moves states toward higher levels of peace rather than on describing static conditions and providing them with proper labels. Indeed, when one examines the process of transition from the 1950s to the present day, there is no doubt that a dramatic shift has taken place.

This case offers a good example of the complex interaction between the economic logic and the political logic of transitions to peace. Throughout the years, German foreign economic policy toward Poland was mostly driven by political motives. It used economic tools (aid, generous loans, trade agreements, foreign investment, facilitating Polish access to multilateral economic institutions, etc.) in order to promote its political goals. Achieving peace was important, first politically and then for economic purposes as well. Poland, on the other hand, was motivated to improve relations with Germany, especially before German unification, for economic reasons. After German unification, the political goal of permanently resolving the border issue and facilitating Poland's return to Europe became more prominent. For both states, especially after German unification, the political and economic logics reinforced each other. The use of economic tools worked so effectively because there was indeed a direct bilateral stake involved.

The successful use of economic tools to promote the transition to peace was closely linked to the fact that, on balance, there was a supportive domestic coalition that stood to gain economically and politically from the process in both states. This case, as well as the Franco-German case study, highlights once again the importance of domestic institutions and efficient cooperation between the government and the business community. The German neocorporatist structure clearly facilitated the development of an effective foreign economic policy of peace building. While somewhat counterintuitive, it was facilitated in the 1970s by the fact that Germany had to deal with a centralized regime in Poland. This, of course, was only true once the Communist Party regime in Poland became threatened by the terrible state of the Polish economy and was therefore motivated to pursue economic reforms to ensure its survival. This underlying motivation was present in all of the cases previously examined here. I have raised the problematic question of the interaction between democratization, economic liberalization, and transitions to peace in the case of Jordan's relations with Israel. In the Polish case as well, this dilemma became apparent and found perhaps its clearest expression in the German reaction to the revolutionary efforts of the Solidarity movement in 1980. While obviously supportive of the attempt to advance democracy and human rights in Poland, the German government was also very concerned lest the Solidarity revolution create such havoc that it would sabotage Germany's carefully crafted Ostpolitik and also have a detrimental effect on its developing relations with East Germany and the Soviet Union. Consequently, Germany chose to accept and endorse the declaration of martial law in Poland at the end of 1980 as a peaceful internal solution to a domestic Polish problem.[78] This German reaction demonstrates how it is easier to craft a cold peace or even a normal peace at the state and elite level, whereas societal interaction is much harder to carefully manage from above. I would also suggest that the use of economic tools to promote peace is easier between two stable states, democracies, or nondemocracies and that, consequently, the difficulties in advancing Polish-German relations in the early 1990s were related to the flux in which the democratizing Polish political system found itself.

This case reflects the dual impact of power disparities on the transition to peace. On the one hand, it was the economic power disparity that created a Polish motivation to reconcile with Germany, despite the heavy historical burden, and it was the same economic power disparity that enabled Germany to offer generous help that would promote relations. On the other hand, the Polish concerns stemming from those disparities and intensified by the burden of history did not disappear even after peace and cooperation had been institutionalized.

The unique aspect in this case was the role of the multilateral setting within which the German-Polish bilateral relations came to be embedded. This case has shown the added value of linking the transition to peace to the EU. It had an important role in ameliorating the negative implications of the economic (as well as other) power disparities between the two states, in creating a new and varied setting on which Germany and Poland could interact and cooperate on a regular basis, and in providing a multilateral framework that could be used to cushion the lingering tensions and problems that still exist on the bilateral level and prevent them from having a damaging impact on relations. Embedding German-Polish relations in the European setting is no panacea, as the recent crises have demonstrated, but it does provide this relationship with a much stronger, enduring quality than one that could be offered by a third state providing economic and political incentives, which could easily change over time. Consequently, such an institutionalized solution to increasing the bilateral incentives to cooperate is more conducive for further advancement and deepening of peace between former enemies.

POLITICS, ECONOMICS, AND PEACE

Setting Realistic Expectations

IN THE ONGOING DEBATE between proponents of commercial liberalism and realism over the role of economic logic in making peace with erstwhile enemies, we are likely to find instances that support either one of these approaches. There will be some cases in which economic factors are used to promote transitions to peace but are based on a political rather than liberal-economic logic as well as instances in which a pure economic logic is driving the political decision to move toward peace. Furthermore, the dominance of economic or political motivations may differ on both sides and may also change over time. This complexity must be acknowledged and studied if we are to understand the role of economic factors in the transition-to-peace process.

The six cases presented here illustrate the importance of identifying the nature of the motivation for developing economic interaction (economic or political). If the process is driven by an economic motivation and a real economic incentive is built into the bilateral relationship, then it is easier for the commercial liberal argument to kick in (e.g., Japan and Southeast Asia, or France and Germany). If economic incentives drive the move to peace, but the incentive is an indirect benefit from a third party, this could be a good enough incentive to sign a peace treaty, but the commercial liberal logic will have a hard time kicking in within the bilateral relations. Spillover is more likely to be in the wrong direction, improving relations with the third party instead of with the former enemy. This type of spillover occurred in Egypt's decision to move toward peace with Israel. Both in that case and in the Jordanian case, the natural pressures are for increasing economic interdependence and improving relations with the United States rather than Israel. This is problematic in terms of advancing normalization of relations with Israel. Israel, in turn, also ends up seeing the United States and the EU as its natural markets rather than looking to its Arab neighbors for customers.

If the main motivation for peace is political, then economic cooperation can be used to help foster peaceful relations and normalization, not on a liberal-economic but a political logic. For example, Israel came to realize that, given the broad economic power disparities with its neighbors, it would actually be dangerous to follow the straightforward economic-liberal logic of comparative advantage to promote normalization. The general problem of economic cooperation that is driven by a political logic, however, is that economic relations will remain hostage to political developments. In the Middle East, Israeli politicians and economists were highly aware of the need to foster economic cooperation according to a political logic. On the Israeli side, the political logic was overwhelming. On the Arab side, the initial logic for achieving cold peace was economic, but the logic driving (or largely preventing) normalization was very much political. The German-Polish case also illustrated a transition in which each side followed a different logic. The main German motivation was political, whereas the main Polish motivation (at least until German unification) was economic. In that case, as well as in the two Middle Eastern cases, it was the economically more powerful state that pursued a political goal. Consequently, the more powerful of the two was able to use economic tools for advancing its goals. The greater success of Germany stemmed from several factors, the most important of which was the nature of the economic benefits that the other party stood to gain. In Poland, the expected economic gains were so overwhelming that they helped override political limitations. Even in that case, however, the Poles were willing to forgo economic benefits when crucial political matters (e.g., the border dispute) were at stake.

The Possibility of Separating Economics and Politics

In the cases involving Japan, a clear separation could be observed between the economic and the political rationale, with the former guiding Japan's policy. This separation was convenient for Japan, as well as for the Southeast Asian regimes (e.g., Indonesia) that desired Japanese capital but did not necessarily endorse its foreign policy. Japan used this principle of separating economics and politics or *seikei bunri* to advance its economic relations with the People's Republic of China (PRC) in the post–World War II period, up to the two countries' official normalization of political relations in 1972. Japan was able to achieve this separation because of the very special strategic circumstances of U.S. control over its foreign and security policy in the immediate postwar period. A separation strategy is difficult to pursue in the long run, however, and is not useful for advancing normalization. Despite its initial success, Japan encountered problems in its relations with Indonesia similar to those encountered by the Israelis vis-à-vis Jordan and Egypt, only later. The Southeast Asian case, with the 1974 riots, shows the limits of separating the political and economic logic of economic interaction and the futility of trying to maintain such separation in the long run. The South Korean case also shows the difficulty of maintaining the convenient separation as a long-term policy. The broad protests against the normalization treaty in 1965 reflected the public's resistance to this separation. The ROK government's argument that there was an urgent economic need to foster close relations with Japan did not sit well with the public. Such resistance is common, especially after protracted conflicts during which the public is fed a steady diet of nationalist slogans and reasons to hate the enemy; suddenly switching gears and promoting good relations for rational economic reasons becomes problematic. By contrast, in the German cases, the economic and political logics were intertwined, facilitating long-term normalization.

A second factor limiting the likelihood of successful separation of economics and politics over time is that this strategy can work only if it serves the interests of both sides. It will run into trouble whenever one of the parties no longer wants to maintain this separation. In the Middle East, for example, many Arab states believe that increasing their economic interaction with Israel would be a bonus to Israel. They reject what they perceive as an Israeli attempt to separate economics and politics, to reap the economic gains without making any political concessions on the Palestinian issue. Ironically, when Egypt was finally forced to sign the QIZ agreement with Israel, for economic reasons, Israelis were quick to interpret or present this move as a political one. In the ROK-Japan case, while periodic political crises did not severely undermine the improving economic relations, they were used by the South Koreans to exert additional pressure on Japan (e.g., the textbook controversy). It also follows, quite intuitively, that the ability to separate economics and politics will be weakened if the more political issues remain unresolved. In the German-Polish case, for example, the Poles were willing to go along with the West German economic strategy while still under Communist Party rule, but when the border issue came to the forefront just before German unification, politics was again on the front burner. Once we look at the political economy of failed or more problematic peace processes, like that between Israel and the Palestinians, we see how difficult such a separation can be under more severe conflictual conditions. Thus, in 1994, after the Oslo Accords were signed but little significant political progress had taken place, Palestinian business leaders argued that, from a national perspective, it was wrong to do business with Israelis and that top priority should be given to developing an independent Palestinian economy, detached from Israel.[1] Another example of the separation policy is South Korea, which, since 1998, has tried to separate economics from politics and pursue a conciliatory policy toward North Korea. This "sunshine policy" had a central economic component but has not achieved significant gains, and it faced much criticism because North Korea was not willing to adhere to the separation principle.

The Domestic Balance of Winners and Losers from Transitions to Peace

All six cases showed that economic factors played an important role in leaders' decisions to sign a peace treaty with their former enemies. Economic pressures threatening the leader or his regime and potential economic gains played a key role in Egypt's and Jordan's decisions to make peace with Israel. They were also a very important factor pushing Southeast Asian states to normalize relations with Japan, given its ability to help them on the road to development. In Southeast Asia as well, it was clear to leaders that economic development was key to their political survival. This was also the case for President Park of South Korea, who desperately needed Japanese capital in order to finance his ambitious development plan, upon which the legitimacy of his regime rested. Similarly, the German economy could revive itself only through foreign trade, which necessitated a transition to peace with its neighbors. The French Monnet Plan, in turn, hinged on access to German raw materials. Finally, the Polish government faced such a severe economic crisis that even its Communist Party bosses in Moscow acknowledged that, if it wanted to survive, it had to trade with West Germany.

A central difference between the Asian and European cases on the one hand and the Middle Eastern cases on the other was the strong support of powerful business groups in the former. Powerful Japanese and Southeast Asian business elites all cooperated to push forward both the initial treaties and then actual normalization and expansion of trade. A similar coalition of the regime and the *chaebol* existed in the Korean case. In Germany as well, close cooperation between the government and well-organized business elites was a driving force, especially in its policy toward Poland. Such support existed in the Middle Eastern cases only on the Israeli side, and even then it was not very strong.

All of the case studies illustrated the importance of a ruling coalition with a liberalizing orientation, as Etel Solingen suggests. They also illustrated that such a coalition need not be democratic, as was the case in Egypt, Jordan, Indonesia, and Poland under Communist rule.[2] Furthermore, the effectiveness of translating economic motivations into bilateral cooperation depended, in turn, on the institutional setting within which the various winners from peace operated. Most conspicuously, the concentrated nature of big business and the tight, institutionalized nature of their interaction with the government in both Japan and Germany were important factors in facilitating their policies of economic statecraft. This implies that we need to examine not only the structure of existing coalitions but also the nature of the institutional arena within which they interact. This is partly related to the regime type, as discussed below, but is also related to the specific institutions connecting government and business. The comparison of efficient state-bureaucracy-business cooperation in Germany and in Japan, in contrast to the various bureaucratic difficulties facing Israeli business leaders in pursuing cooperation with Jordan and Egypt, is illuminating in this regard.

At the same time, there was strong societal opposition to normalization in both the Middle Eastern and the Asian cases examined. Even in the Asian cases, we saw that, on a popular level, there was great hostility toward Japan, with public opinion unenthusiastic or even hostile to the signing of a treaty. In both Egypt and Jordan, similar and more negative feelings existed. In the Western Europe cases, there was more public receptivity to the transition process. Still, as the opinion polls cited indicate, at the societal level, old stereotypes and resentments tend to endure longer than at the state level. This is a finding worth pursing in future research.

The domestic balance of power between winners and losers in economic interactions with the former enemy was thus important. In the first stage of peacemaking, state interests and big business interests played the most important role. This was the case for France and Germany, even though societal reconciliation initiatives did exist, yet a strong interest on part of the ruling elites was insufficient to lead to further normalization of relations. The Asian cases show that a strong elitist coalition of government and big business can effectively push forward significant economic normalization. But in these cases as well, as long as the process remained elitist, it had a limited impact on normalization in other issue areas. Some scholars argue that in authoritarian regimes like the ones in the Middle East, both leaders and third parties can afford to ignore public opposition. Leaders, it is argued, can easily manipulate public opinion, but this assumption is dangerous and misleading.[3] As both the Egyptian and Jordanian cases show, while the government (president or king) did have overwhelming power, it was either unable (in the Jordanian case) and/or unwilling (in the Egyptian case) to force normalization upon society. This is especially striking in the Jordanian case, in which the monarchy did make an active effort to promote normalization.

These conclusions are helpful in understanding why the growth of economic interaction between Israel and the Palestinian Authority after the Oslo Accords did not contribute to the advancement of peaceful relations between the parties. Economic cooperation clearly created big winners in the Palestinian Authority, but those winners were only a small group of PLO officials who returned to the West Bank and Gaza from Tunisia, together with a small number of enterprises representing the Palestinian diaspora. This small group was closely linked to Chairman Yasser Arafat, received beneficial concessions and favorable licenses from the authorities, and basically dominated the economy of the Palestinian Territories. The structure of the Paris Protocol, signed between the Palestinian Authority and Israel in 1994, enabled the former to create at least thirteen monopolies under the control of no more than five individuals who were members of the authority's inner circle. Meanwhile, for the majority of the Palestinian population, economic and social circumstances did not improve, and living conditions deteriorated even further. The majority of Palestinians, therefore, never felt like winners following the Oslo Accords.[4] The economic dividends of the Oslo peace process were thus enjoyed primarily by a very small elite. On the Israeli side as well, post-Oslo economic growth was far less evident in the periphery, where the general belief was that peace would largely benefit elites.[5]

A study by Jodi Nachtwey and Mark Tessler published in 2002 suggests that economic considerations influence Palestinian as well as Israeli attitudes toward the peace process in two ways. One is the standard cost/benefit analysis supposedly made by individuals. If individuals are satisfied with their economic condition or believe that peace will advance their economic position, they will support negotiations and compromise. The second influence mechanism is perhaps more interesting. Nachtwey and Tessler suggest that disenchantment stemming from one's economic condition translates into lower levels of confidence in political leaders and that lower levels of confidence in political leaders work against support for negotiations and peace.[6] This finding supports my earlier assertion that if the public perceives the regime to be corrupt, it is unlikely to believe that it could trust that regime to sign a peace treaty that would genuinely improve the economic conditions of the people.

This discussion highlights the importance of developing among society's members a broad vested interest in enabling peace to advance and stabilize. This, in turn, leads me to one of the interesting and potentially controversial findings of this study regarding the question of democratization and transition to peace.

Democracy, Democratization, and the Transition to Peace

From this study, I have drawn two conclusions regarding the linkage between democratization, democracy, and the political economy of transitions to peace. One has to do with the tension between these processes, whereas the second points to the necessity of democracy for upgrading peace relations.

The naïve belief that democracy, economic development, and peace all go together is a recurrent theme in American foreign policy. Most recently, we have witnessed the American campaign to promote democracy in the Middle East: in Iraq, in Egypt, in Jordan, in the Palestinian Authority. Clearly, the expectation is that democratizing the region will also help pacify the region. This belief is based on the theory of democratic peace (i.e., that democracies do not fight one another) and the academic research of its proponents. Commercial liberalism has also been added to the group of academic research programs that are influencing American foreign policy. Proponents of both concepts often use the classic case of Franco-German rapprochement after World War II to validate their theoretical claims. Commercial liberalism's most recent policy product is found in the grand American scheme to create a Middle East Free Trade Area (MEFTA).

However, the findings of this book cast doubt on the democratization thesis as a ready-made solution for successfully navigating transitions to peace. The cases examined here all suggest that, in fact, the initial transition to peace is more easily handled by nondemocratic regimes with economic liberalization aspirations. If societal groups had participated in the early negotiations for the peace treaty in Jordan or in South Korea in the 1960s, chances are that the treaty would not have materialized. An even more disturbing finding is that the establishment of peaceful relations was accompanied in some of the cases by a tightening of authoritarian rule or by the limiting of political liberalization reforms. Political liberalization initiatives, in turn, allowed suppressed opposition to the transition to peace to resurface and also created a temptation to use lingering hostility toward the former enemy for domestic political gain (as was seen in South Korea). Even the classic Franco-German rapprochement process was initially characterized by tight management by the governments involved. The German-Polish case even more clearly demonstrates how the transition to peace via the economic track was delayed and slowed down by the process of democratization in Poland and the internal confusion that inevitably was part of it.[7]

This being said, the second important finding of this study is that the lack of democracy was also a significant barrier to the process of peace building and normalization. In the long run then, democracy increases the likelihood of achieving a stable peace. In an authoritarian regime, broad segments of society do not feel they are likely to share the dividend of the transition to peace. They observe the transition to peace as an elitist process to which they are not a party. Furthermore, their resentment toward their own government is likely to become intertwined with their resentment of the transition to peace itself, complicating matters even more. The conclusion is, therefore, that in order to move toward warm peace, a process of political liberalization that would make citizens more involved in their own state, as well as facilitate a larger variety of communication channels between the two societies, is necessary. In the long run, the expectations of broad segments of society about reaping the peace dividend are crucial. Of course, these expectations and their realization are not only a matter of regime type but also of the economic realities and potential. However, the nature of the regime will influence the expectations of the public for a fair division of the "peace dividend pie," as well as allow more citizens and not just state-favored big business to conduct direct economic interaction. The Franco-German case illustrates this point very well, as we find broad public support for the transition to peace that is deeply influenced by the fact that the economic pie is constantly expanding and that everyone is benefiting from this expansion. The South Korean case also demonstrated that while significant levels of normalization of relations with Japan were achieved under military rule, it was only after the transition to and stabilization of democracy in South Korea that further deepening of the relations was possible. To illustrate this po using a different geographic region, the transition to peace between Chile a Argentina also began under authoritarian rule in Chile. However, it was o after Chile's return to democracy in 1990 that cooperation expanded and peace became stabilized. The success of that transition was also closely rela to the fact that the public, in both Chile and Argentina, viewed the transition part of their respective governments' liberal economic development strate; which generated new opportunities for economic growth and the spreading the new wealth.[8]

These two findings, unfortunately, create significant dilemmas for poli makers, who must choose the best way to promote regional peacemaking ar use policy tools in the correct sequence. The case studies in this book sugge that promoting regional economic liberalization as a first step is wiser th; pushing first for democratization. The most recent actions of the Palestini; Authority (PA) serve to highlight the importance of this question and the con plexity of the answer with respect to a whole array of current events. The Amer can administration insisted that the PA permit democratic elections, despi rising doubts over the likelihood that the Fatah movement could actually w; them and despite European suggestions to postpone the elections. The Amer can administration was shocked when free democratic elections brought to powe the radical Islamic Hamas movement.

The results of the recent elections in the PA demonstrate the danger of in vesting too much or for too long in supporting elitist economic cooperation Many commentators interpret the widespread vote for Hamas in the PA as vote of protest against the corruption of the existing Palestinian leadership. Thi reality exposes the difficult dilemma of building economic ties with narrow elite as an engine to peace and then trying to expand the benefits to the broader publi before it becomes disillusioned about the notion of a public peace dividend. would suggest that one possible solution for this dilemma is to emphasize in the future the crucial importance of good governance rather than democratization.

The Impact of Economic Power Disparities

A common critique of liberal arguments is that they downplay or ignore the fact that economic interaction is rarely symmetrical. Asymmetric economic interaction can cause several problems, all of which are accentuated when the relevant dyad has experienced a protracted or recent violent conflict. Examining the negative impact of economic power disparities also highlights the very different logics of economists and political scientists. The former would stress that in any economic interaction between an advanced and a weaker economy, the latter is likely to benefit a lot. The political scientists would stress, as I do here, the negative political implications of such interaction.

In the Middle Eastern cases, broad economic power disparities played a clearly negative role. These disparities did have some positive impact on the signing of the initial peace treaty, especially in the Jordanian case, where direct benefits from interaction with Israel were perceived. However, economic disparities caused serious problems in the attempt to advance normalization. The combination of the economic disparities and historical animosity intensified either or both realist and neo-Marxist concerns regarding the danger of dependence and exploitation. The Middle Eastern cases also demonstrated most clearly that if the goal was to advance peace, then the pure economic logic of comparative advantage had to be ignored. The negative impact of asymmetric economic relations was also quite clear in the case of Japan and South Korea. In that case, however, the disparities narrowed over time, leading to a more positive attitude of the South Koreans. The narrowing economic power disparities allowed for the channeling of lingering historical animosity into a more positive outlet: fierce economic competition. The German-Polish case also illustrated a situation of wide economic power disparities. Those disparities did, on the one hand, create the underlying Polish desire (or need) to reconcile with Germany but also created a negative "psychology of asymmetry." Given Germany's basic economic power preponderance in Europe, the French willingness to initiate the transition to peace was facilitated by the overwhelming nature of the German defeat in World War II, which for the short run (but at a crucial timing of the transition) ameliorated the concern over the negative consequences of economic normalization.

One may rightly ask how wide economic power disparities have to be in order to have a significant detrimental impact on the process of a transition to peace. I would argue that economic power asymmetries render the economic tools for peace-building purposes useless or even harmful when the asymmetries are wide enough to lead domestic actors in the weaker state to think that they cannot compete with their counterparts in the stronger state and that they therefore have nothing to gain and much to lose from closer economic interaction. Even if economic power disparities exist, as long as domestic actors believe they can successfully compete in certain sectors and reap some (absolute) economic gains, this will be enough to promote peace. This was the case both for South Korean industrialists, who believed they could eventually compete with their Japanese counterparts, and for Polish entrepreneurs, who, despite the obvious wide disparities, did believe they had much to gain from opening to the West German market.

The Japanese–Southeast Asian case served to highlight the need for a more complex understanding of the impact of economic power disparities. Although economic power disparities were very wide, they did not have a particularly strong negative impact on relations. I suggested that the negative impact of the huge economic disparities was mitigated by Japan's strong dependence on raw materials that could be bought in Southeast Asia. This implies that it is important to examine in a more nuanced and issue-specific manner the nature of economic power disparities. For the politics of peacemaking, it is not so much the objective economic power disparities as it is the perceived implications of those disparities that matter. States make a distinction between the implications of cooperation in different economic issue areas. The Japanese reparations money in the Philippines and Indonesia was used mainly to develop infrastructure that did not exist in the money-receiving states. Such infrastructure was crucial for basic state building and industrialization in Southeast Asia and was therefore easier to accept politically. However, when it came to the issue area of trade, we saw that there were stronger concerns regarding the dangerous consequences of opening the domestic market to Japan. In the Middle Eastern cases, we have seen that economic agreements were signed in specific issue areas where concerns over dependency were smaller and that they were not signed on issues where such concerns were greater (e.g., there was no banking agreement with Jordan). The QIZ agreements also helped mitigate the impact of the broad bilateral economic power disparities because they were trilateral arrangements of managed trade.

The fact that Japan reentered Southeast Asia via reparations agreements also made things easier. This is because the initial postwar economic interaction clearly came in the context of a Japanese recognition of its wrongdoings, thus ameliorating some (but not all) of the anti-Japanese sentiments. Indeed, the fact that the aid that Japan gave to South Korea after the 1965 treaty was defined as "economic cooperation" and never as "reparations" did cast its shadow over economic relations. These observations suggest that we need to go beyond the material face value of aid or economic interaction and to further study how such economic interaction is framed and perceived.

The level of sensitivity in different cases to the implications of economic power disparities is also influenced by perceptions of how the other side will take political advantage of those disparities. Obviously, the continuation of unresolved political disputes between the two states will increase such concerns. It is impossible to ignore, for instance, the basic fact that in Japanese–Southeast Asian interactions there were few thorny political issues that had to be dealt with. Similar mitigating strategic circumstances existed in the South Korean case, although not all political issues were resolved, leading to, for example, the ROK's constant concern about Japan's economic and political relations with North Korea. In sharp contrast, in the Middle Eastern cases, while bilateral peace treaties were signed, these pacts remained inextricably linked to the ongoing Israeli-Palestinian conflict. Consequently, sensitivities to the political effects of asymmetric economic deals were much higher.

Once again, by applying these findings to the current problems of Israeli-Palestinian relations, one can see how problematic the wide power disparities between Israel and the PA are. Israel dominates the Palestinian economy by being the stronger party in terms of the economic power disparity and in terms of the legal institutional arrangements that bind the two economies and provide Israel with full control over the PA's external economic relations. It is possible to argue that such asymmetry should be conducive to peace, due to the great dependence of the Palestinians on Israel. However, as the al-Aqsa or second intifada demonstrated, this was not the case. Instead, the wide economic disparities are widely interpreted as a situation of one-sided exploitation by Israel, generating ill will and resentment.[9]

The combination of wide economic disparities and ongoing political disputes is likely to undermine the ability to use economic tools to promote peace in other cases as well. Thus, for example, recent discussion about the potential of economic interaction for promoting peace between India and Pakistan is also undermined by the concern of different groups in Pakistan that India's strength will mean that Pakistan becomes an economic appendage. This belief persists despite the fact that, in both countries, there is a shift toward greater economic liberalization, given the pressures of globalization. The economic power disparities, in turn, also affect the domestic balance of winners and losers from economic normalization. Thus, in Pakistan, the economic power disparities with India turn its textile industry, which employs half of Pakistan's labor force, into a potential loser if it opens up to India, a fact that clearly does not contribute to this tenuous transition process.[10]

Economic Interaction, Cultural Penetration, and the Influence Effect

With hindsight, we can see in the Southeast Asian case that, despite the initial popular opposition to economic interaction with Japan, in the long run Japan has come to hold overwhelming influence over popular culture in Southeast Asia.[11] This type of cultural penetration is exactly the nightmare scenario feared by many Arab intellectuals and Islamist groups who believe that exposure of their markets to Israeli goods would lead to such an outcome. On the cultural issue, an interesting parallel emerged between the Middle Eastern cases and the ROK-Japan case. In the latter case, until the late 1990s, cultural normalization was not only unwelcome but also illegal. The relaxation of the cultural ban in the late 1990s cannot be understood outside the combined context of the democratization process of South Korea and the gradual long-term impact of the intense and institutionalized economic cooperation over the years. While I admit that this point was not established here beyond doubt, the decision to relax the cultural ban would not have had the immediate impact it did without extensive, long-term economic relations.

The Impact of Third Party Involvement

Much has been written about the involvement of extraregional powers in the process of regional peacemaking. In this book, however, I focused on the impact of third parties specifically on changing the economic incentives in the transition to peace. The cases showed that it is important to make a distinction between different ways in which third parties can be economically involved in facilitating transitions to peace. In the Egyptian-Israeli case, the United States played a crucial role but a problematic one. The economic benefits it had to offer Egypt played an important role in bringing about the peace treaty. However, because the peace treaty was based on potential economic benefits to be gained outside the bilateral relations with Israel, it was difficult to push normalization forward and there was little reason for the commercial liberal logic to start working. In the Jordanian-Israeli case, on the other hand, the United States played a more constructive role by conditioning the gains of duty-free access to the American market upon direct cooperation between Jordanians and Israelis in the QIZs. The Egyptian case shows that expectations of economic gain from peacemaking by a third party may influence one side to make the dramatic move of signing a peace treaty, but the third party's involvement is less helpful and perhaps even detrimental in the second stage of peacemaking, when the normalizing and expanding of bilateral peaceful relations occur. In the Asian cases, the United States played a crucial role in fostering an environment that would be strategically conducive to peacemaking between Japan and the states it had recently occupied. It is not at all clear that such moves would have been possible had Japan not been tightly linked to the United States and had the United States not played such a central role in guarding the stability of noncommunist Asia. The overwhelming American presence resolved a major part of the security dilemma facing the Southeast Asian states vis-à-vis Japan. Its role in providing regional security was less obvious in the case of Israel. The United States was indeed a central strategic actor in the region, but it was perceived by Arab states to have a biased, pro-Israeli policy.

However, the strategic role of a third party was not the focus of this study. When narrowing our discussion to the involvement of third parties in the economic aspects of peacemaking, one clear difference appears between the Middle Eastern and Asian cases. Whereas in the former, the main peace dividend stemmed not from bilateral economic interaction between the two former enemies but from economic benefits made possible by a third party (the United States), in the Asian cases there were direct economic benefits stemming from renewed economic relations within the region. These were the potential gains driving the process, not potential benefits provided by the United States or another state. Similarly, it was the bilateral economic gains that drove the process of Franco-German rapprochement rather than American pressure. Indeed, the American Marshall Plan did create the important set of constraints and incentives for European cooperation, but it did not shape the nature and depth of bilateral Franco-German relations. Quite to the contrary, as illustrated in chapter 6, the Americans were rather unhappy about the evolving nature of Franco-German economic cooperation.

What are the policy implications of this observation? A third party wishing to promote the transition to peace through economic tools should avoid providing all of its economic incentives with the signature of a peace agreement. It can use economic incentives to shift the balance in favor of a transition to peace, but if it wants to actively support the ongoing process of peace building and normalization of relations, it must use strategies that link its lucrative economic incentives to direct economic interaction between the two former enemies.[12] This strategy was embodied in the Marshall Plan. In that case, one could easily identify the economic complementarities between the relevant states. In cases in which a natural economic complementarity does not exist, as in Egypt, Jordan, and Israel, a more creative strategy is required in order to actually build over time an economic incentive for direct bilateral or regional interaction between those states. The limited success of the QIZ project between Israel and Jordan and between Israel and Egypt, however, reveals the limitations of a politically driven economic scheme. Because the natural economic incentives were not there, politically designed economic incentives were likely to generate a limited level of cooperation and were not very likely to generate the desired spillover effect.

This discussion is not merely academic these days. The 9/11 Commission Report that was issued in July 2004, in the aftermath of the events of September 11, 2001, recommended that "a comprehensive U.S. strategy to counter terrorism should include economic policies that encourage development, more open societies, and opportunities for people to improve the lives of their families and to enhance prospects for their children's future."[13] In this spirit, the Bush administration proposed in May 2003 a plan to create by the year 2013 a Middle East Free Trade Area (MEFTA). To advance this plan, the United States has already signed five FTAs with Middle Eastern countries (Israel, Jordan, Morocco, Bahrain, and Oman) and fourteen Trade and Investment Framework Agreements (TIFAs) with regional states (Israel, Jordan, Morocco, Bahrain, Egypt, Algeria, Tunisia, Saudi Arabia, Oman, Kuwait, the United Arab Emirates, Yemen, Qatar, and Iraq). The grand scheme of the American administration exhibits the practical implications of the link between domestic economic liberalization, growing international economic interaction, and peace. While all of these agreements except the QIZ scheme are bilateral, the final goal of the United States is to eventually knit all of these agreements together, either subregionally or, ultimately, into one large free trade agreement.[14]

The MEFTA scheme leads me to another observation regarding third parties and the political economy of peacemaking. The two European cases introduced another type of third party interaction, namely, the nesting of the bilateral process of a transition to peace within a wider multilateral institutional context. Franco-German relations clearly developed, expanded, and were stabilized by becoming the central axis of the European Community and later on the European Union. The normalization of Poland's relations with Germany as well was greatly facilitated by the multilateral EU context within which it took place. This multilateral nesting facilitated normalization by mitigating the negative impact of the bilateral economic (and political) power disparities, by facilitating issue-linkage and therefore the expansion of cooperation and of the potential coalitions of winners in each state, and by creating shared expectations regarding future cooperation. This type of institutional setting did not exist during the transitions to peace in Asia, although it would be worthwhile to examine the positive impact of the development of ASEAN and its institutionalized dialogue with Japan, as well as of the Asia-Pacific Economic Cooperation (APEC) forum, on the strengthening of those bilateral relations. The Middle Eastern cases, in comparison, also reflect the least institutionally developed environment. It remains to be seen whether the bringing together of regional states, indirectly, into extraregional multilateral arrangements (via the MEFTA scheme or via EU association agreements) will be enough to create a similar dynamic.

Peace as a Process Rather Than an Outcome

One of the goals of this book was to convince the reader that the standard dichotomy between war and peace is insufficient if we are to understand how states move from conflict to building peaceful relations with one another. After surveying different typologies of types of peace, I concluded that it was more productive to study peace not as a specific end condition but rather as a process. For this reason, I made the distinction between reaching the first stage of signing a formal peace treaty and the second stage of normalization. Within that second stage, it is possible to identify movement toward warmer peace (normal peace or warm peace, according to Benjamin Miller, or stable peace, according to Arie Kacowicz et al.). I suggested that this distinction is important because economic factors play a different role during different stages of the transition process.

In the first stage, the support of political authorities and powerful business leaders was crucial. However, while peace can be made between leaders, normalization requires broader societal involvement. In the Egyptian case, government policies gave little chance for official economic interaction to move down and spill over to the broader societal level until recently. In Jordan, government interest in pursuing economic interaction and peace with Israel could not overcome wide societal opposition. In both the Philippines and Indonesia, a clear distinction was made between signing the peace treaty (combined with the reparations agreement) and the actual normalization of relations. In the Asian cases, we saw that intensive big business economic interaction had a limited spillover effect, as the riots of 1974 highlighted the limits of Japan's purely economic diplomacy. In South Korea, there was indeed a dramatic expansion of economic interaction with Japan, which was dominated by big business in both countries. One could argue, consequently, that broader societal involvement was not necessary for moving along the normalization process. However, in that case as well, it was evident that despite extensive economic ties, up to the 1990s these elitist connections could not ameliorate the negative feelings toward Japan and clearly were not followed by broader societal rapprochement. This experience can serve as an important lesson or warning sign for Israel, in the currently unlikely yet optimistic scenario of increased economic interaction with its Arab neighbors.

The focus on peace as a process, however, still does not resolve some fundamental questions that leaders and the public should be asking about the goal they wish to reach. This question can be seen as a deeply philosophical, moral, and normative question regarding the meaning of peace and the type of relations between states we wish to advance. Is the notion of a warm peace, which is basically a description of the conditions in Western Europe, the ideal type of peace to which states in other parts of the world should aspire? Or is it an exceptional condition that we can admire but not really use for assessing "normal" interstate relations in the international system?

This question also has very practical implications. When two former enemies hold very different perceptions of what "peace" actually means, or what it ought to be, at least one party is likely to be disenchanted. There is greater likelihood of frustration and mutual misunderstanding. In that regard, the Israeli-Egyptian case is quite indicative. In Israel, people automatically expected that the 1979 peace treaty would lead to a warm peace. As someone who grew up in Israel, I vividly remember the idealized view of "peace" that was described to us at school, in terms of pigeons bearing olive branches, mutual soccer games, trips to the pyramids, and shopping in Cairo markets. On the Egyptian side, as I describe in chapter 2, peace was understood in terms of mutual diplomatic recognition and an end to hostilities and the use of force to manage bilateral relations. This gap in the fundamental understanding of "peace" has led to much frustration on the Israeli side, which could not be properly appreciated on the Egyptian side.

The question of what peace really means also becomes relevant for third parties that wish to help promote "regional peace." If the arguments presented throughout this book are correct, then third parties need to decide which part of the transition-to-peace process they wish to promote. Also, they should be more aware of the fact that peace is a dynamic process and that the type of economic tools they use to promote one stage may not necessarily be conducive for the next one.

The Limits of a Rationalist Analysis of the Economics of Peacemaking

The goal of this book was to address the ongoing and central debate surrounding the thesis of commercial liberalism and its relevance to transitions to peace. As such, it confined itself to addressing a debate that is conducted within a rationalist framework that focuses on rational actors making cost/benefit calculations. Consequently, it unraveled the mechanisms through which cost/benefit calculations can push actors toward cooperative interaction. There was little evidence in the cases that growth of economic cooperation spills over directly to the resolution of political conflicts (as a strong liberal argument would expect). However, ongoing economic cooperation that becomes meaningful and important can facilitate a faster movement along the transition-to-peace axis once thorny political issues are resolved or when changing strategic circumstances push the two sides closer to one another. Furthermore, if a separation strategy can operate for a considerable period of time, then once a significant mutual economic stake exists, ongoing political conflicts are more easily contained. This comes very close to the commercial liberal argument tested by scholars such as Bruce Russett and John Oneal, namely, that high levels of interdependence will create a vested interest in peace that will prevent crises from deteriorating to violence. Furthermore, the expansion of economic interaction between the former enemies also provides them with greater flexibility in times of crisis for showing their resolve or discontent in ways that do not involve the military. While the fact that Egypt holds further normalization with Israel hostage to developments on the Palestinian-Israeli front is lamentable, we should also appreciate the value of this strategy in allowing Egypt to express its discontent with Israeli policies in ways that do not put the peace treaty itself at risk. I suggested somewhat similarly that their joint membership in the EU allowed Germany and Poland to engage in harsh disputes without risking irrevocable damage to their bilateral relations. What this book suggested, though, was that these liberal mechanisms are only a part of a broader set of aspects that need to be considered when discussing economics and peace.

This rationalist approach is often criticized by regional experts who stress the overriding importance of ideology, culture, and religion or by international relations scholars from the constructivist school, who point to the need to focus on understanding the processes of social learning and identity change that are inherent in the transition-to-peace process, rather than focus on material incentives. As I argued in chapter 1, my goal was neither to offer a vehement defense of rationalist theory nor to suggest that economic incentives can overcome all other problems in transitions to peace. Indeed, throughout the case study chapters, I attempted to point out situations in which potential or actual economic benefits were not enough to produce a deeper social change and greater societal normalization. Thus, there were domestic groups who were willing to forgo economic benefits on ideological or religious grounds, economic power disparities acquired different meanings in different contexts, and even intense economic normalization between Japan and South Korea was insufficient in itself to bring about broader societal interaction.

However, for both academic and practical reasons, I strongly believe that it is important to examine *how* potential economic incentives can help move states closer to peace, as well as *how far* such economic incentives can take us. As the liberal argument suggests, increased economic interaction is not in itself the solution but rather a mechanism with which to enhance trust building between elites and societies, something to serve as a conveyor belt for ideas. The development of economic interaction can create an opening for social learning and change. Such change can occur on an individual level, as the personal examples from the Egyptian Delta employees demonstrate, but it also needs to be guided from above, through changes in official rhetoric, change in the education system, and greater official support for cultural and other types of engagement. These mechanisms deserve a separate book. This book, however, unraveled the possible roles and impact of material economic incentives, which may be easier to manipulate and use for advancing peace, both by the parties themselves as well as by third parties. Hopefully, after reading this book, decision makers wishing to promote peace will not only use economic incentives more wisely but also adopt realistic expectations about what those incentives can achieve.

NOTES

Preface

1. The term "in peace" is a direct translation from Hebrew.

Chapter 1. Beyond Commercial Liberalism

1. On the security debate, see Benjamin Miller, "The Concept of Security: Should It Be Redefined?" *Journal of Strategic Studies* 24, no. 2 (2001):13–42; Barry Buzan, Ole Weaver, and Jaap de Wilde, *Security: A New Framework for Analysis* (Boulder, CO: Lynne Rienner, 1998). For recent volumes that discuss the links between security and economics, see, e.g., Jean-Marc Blanchard, Edward D. Mansfield, and Norrin M. Ripsman, eds., *Power and the Purse: Economic Statecraft, Interdependence, and National Security* (London: Frank Cass, 2000); Peter Dombrowski, ed., *Guns and Butter: The Political Economy of International Security* (Boulder, CO: Lynne Rienner, 2005); Edward Mansfield and Brian Pollins, eds., *Economic Interdependence and International Conflict: New Perspectives on an Enduring Debate* (Ann Arbor: University of Michigan Press, 2003); Padideh Ala'i, Tomer Broude, and Colin Picker, eds., *Trade as Guarantor of Peace, Liberty, and Security? Critical, Historical, and Empirical Perspectives* (Washington, DC: American Society of International Law, 2006).

2. For a thorough review of the literature, see Katherine Barbieri and Gerald Schneider, "Globalization and Peace: Assessing New Directions in the Study of Trade and Conflict," *Journal of Peace Research* 36, no. 4 (1999): 387–404. See also Katherine Barbieri, *The Liberal Illusion: Does Trade Promote Peace?* (Ann Arbor: University of Michigan Press, 2002), chap. 1.

3. Ruth Arad, Seev Hirsch, and Alfred Tovias, *The Economics of Peacemaking: Focus on the Egyptian-Israeli Situation* (London: Macmillan, 1983), 5.

4. Richard Rosecrance, *The Rise of the Trading State: Commerce and Conquest in the Modern World* (New York: Basic Books, 1986).

5. For this argument, see James D. Morrow, "Assessing the Role of Trade as a Source of Costly Signals"; Arthur A. Stein, "Trade and Conflict: Uncertainty, Strategic Signaling, and Interstate Dispute"; Jack Levy, " Economic Interdependence, Opportunity Costs, and Peace," all in *Economic Interdependence and International Conflict,* ed. Mansfield and Pollins; and Erik Gartzke, Quan Li, and Charles Boehmer, "Investing in the Peace: Economic Interdependence and International Conflict," *International Organization* 55, no. 2 (spring 2001): 391–438.

6. Dorrette Corbey, "Dialectical Functionalism: Stagnation as a Booster of European Integration," *International Organization* 49 (1996): 253–84; Ernest Haas, *The Uniting of Europe: Political, Social, and Economic Forces, 1950–1957* (Stanford, CA: Stanford University Press, 1958); Shimon Peres and Arye Naor, *The New Middle East* (New York: Henry Holt, 1993).

7. These ideas are represented by the Manchester school of thought, best represented by the classic writings of Karl W. Deutsch, Sidney Burrel, Robert Kann, Maurice Lee, Martin Lichterman, Raymond Lindgren, Francis Loewenheim, and Richard Van Wagener in *Political Community and the North Atlantic Area: International Organization in the Light of Historical Experience* (Princeton, NJ: Princeton University Press, 1957). For a

critical review of the Manchester view, see Geoffrey Blainey, *The Causes of War,* 3rd ed. (New York: Free Press, 1988), chap. 2.

8. Emanuel Adler and Michael Barnett, "A Framework for the Study of Security Communities," in *Security Communities,* ed. Emanuel Adler and Michael Barnett (Cambridge: Cambridge University Press, 1998), chap. 2.

9. Joseph A. Schumpeter, *Capitalism, Socialism, and Democracy,* 3rd ed. (New York: Harper and Row, 1950), 121–30, 296–98.

10. Blainey, *Causes of War,* chap. 2.

11. See Kenneth Waltz, "The Myth of National Interdependence," in *The International Corporation: A Symposium,* ed. Charles P. Kindleberger (Cambridge, MA: MIT Press, 1970), 203–23; Albert O. Hirschman, *National Power and the Structure of Foreign Trade,* 2nd ed. (Berkeley: University of California Press, 1980). For an interesting application, see Rawi Abdelal and Jonathan Kirshner, "Strategy, Economic Relations, and the Definition of National Interests," *Security Studies* 9, no. 1–2 (1999–2000): 119–56.

12. Solomon W. Polachek, "Conflict and Trade," *Journal of Conflict Resolution* 24, no. 1 (1980): 55–78; Bruce Russett and John Oneal, *Triangulating Peace: Democracy, Interdependence, and International Organization* (New York: Norton, 2001); Barbieri, *Liberal Illusion,* chap. 6.

13. Examples include Solomon Polachek, John Robst, and Yuan-Ching Chang, "Liberalism and Interdependence: Extending the Trade-Conflict Model," *Journal of Peace Research* 36, no. 4 (1999): 405–22; David H. Bearce, "Grasping the Commercial Institutional Peace," *International Studies Quarterly* 47, no. 3 (2003): 347–70; Patrick McDonald, "Peace through Trade or Free Trade?" *Journal of Conflict Resolution* 48, no. 4 (2004): 547–72. Quantitative researchers also recommend examining the trade/peace issue through qualitative case studies. See Edward D. Mansfield and Brian M. Pollins, "Interdependence and Conflict: An Introduction," in *Economic Interdependence and International Conflict,* ed. Mansfield and Pollins, 20.

14. Dale C. Copeland, "Economic Interdependence and War: A Theory of Trade Expectations," *International Security* 20, no. 4 (spring 1996): 5–41. See also Dale C. Copeland, "Trade Expectations and the Outbreak of Peace: Détente 1970–74 and the End of the Cold War, 1985–91," in *Power and the Purse,* ed. Blanchard, Mansfield, and Ripsman, 15–58.

15. Paul Papayoanou, "Interdependence, Institutions and the Balance of Power: Britain, Germany, and World War I," *International Security* 20, no. 4 (spring 1996): 42–76.

16. Norrin M. Ripsman and Jean-Marc F. Blanchard, "Commercial Liberalism under Fire: Evidence from 1914 and 1936," *Security Studies* 6, no. 2 (winter 1996–1997): 4–50.

17. Paul Papayoanou and Scott L. Kastner, "Sleeping with the (Potential) Enemy: Assessing the U.S. Policy of Engagement with China," *Security Studies* 9, no. 1 (1999–2000): 157–87.

18. Norrin M. Ripsman, "Two Stages of Transition from a Region of War to a Region of Peace: Realist Transition and Liberal Endurance," *International Studies Quarterly* 49 (2005): 669–93. This argument is addressed in chapter 6.

19. See Beth Simmons, "Pax Mercatoria and the Theory of the State," in *Economic Interdependence and International Conflict,* ed. Mansfield and Pollins, 31–43. For examples of the quantitative literature, see Håvard Hegre, "Development and the Liberal Peace: What Does It Take to Be a Trading State?" *Journal of Peace Research* 37, no. 1 (2000): 5–30, and McDonald, "Peace through Trade or Free Trade?" The best example of a qualitative-comparative study unraveling the political process is Etel Solingen's *Regional Orders at Century's Dawn: Global and Domestic Influences on Grand Strategy* (Ithaca, NY: Cornell University Press, 1998), discussed later in this chapter.

20. See, for example, Conrad G. Brunk, "Shaping a Vision: The Nature of Peace Studies," in *Patterns of Conflict, Paths to Peace,* ed. Larry J. Fisk and John L. Schellenberg (Toronto: Broadview Press, 2000), 20–22.

21. Kenneth E. Boulding, *Stable Peace* (Austin: University of Texas Press, 1978), 12–13.

22. See his categories in Arie M. Kacowicz and Yaacov Bar-Siman-Tov, "Stable Peace: A Conceptual Framework," in *Stable Peace among Nations,* ed. Arie M. Kacowicz et al. (Lanham, MD: Rowman and Littlefield, 2000), 19–20.

23. Arie M. Kacowicz, *Zones of Peace in the Third World: South America and West Africa in Comparative Perspective* (Albany: State University of New York Press, 1998).

24. See Benjamin Miller, "Explaining Variations in Regional Peace: Three Strategies for Peace-Making," *Cooperation and Conflict* 35, no. 2 (2000): 158–59; Benjamin Miller, "When and How Regions Become Peaceful: Potential Theoretical Pathways to Peace," *International Studies Review* 7 (2005): 231–32.

25. Adler and Barnett, "Framework for the Study of Security Communities," 30.

26. Ibid., 50–57.

27. James P. Klein, Gary Goertz, and Paul F. Diehl, "The Peace Scale: Conceptualizing and Operationalizing Nonrivalry and Peace," *Conflict Management and Peace Science* 26 (2008): 67–80.

28. Kacowicz and Bar-Siman-Tov, "Stable Peace," 11. See also Yaacov Bar-Siman-Tov, "Dialectics between Stable Peace and Reconciliation," in *From Conflict Resolution to Reconciliation,* ed. Yaacov Bar-Siman-Tov (New York: Oxford University Press, 2004), 63.

29. Kacowicz and Bar-Siman-Tov, "Stable Peace," 24–25.

30. See Daniel Bar-Tal and Gemma H. Bennink, "The Nature of Reconciliation as an Outcome and as a Process," in *From Conflict Resolution to Reconciliation,* ed. Bar-Siman-Tov, 12–13; and Bar-Siman-Tov, "Dialectics between Stable Peace and Reconciliation."

31. Bar-Siman-Tov, "Dialectics between Stable Peace and Reconciliation," 64–75. See also the nine conditions identified in Kacowicz, *Zones of Peace.*

32. This argument builds on Solingen's in *Regional Orders at Century's Dawn.* See also Steven E. Lobell, "Threat Assessment, the State, and Foreign Policy: A Neoclassical Realist Model," in *Neoclassical Realism, the State, and Foreign Policy,* ed. Steven E. Lobell, Norrin M. Ripsman, and Jeffrey W. Taliaferro (Cambridge: Cambridge University Press, 2008); McDonald, "Peace through Trade or Free Trade?"

33. Solingen, *Regional Orders at Century's Dawn,* chap. 2; see also Etel Solingen, "Internationalization, Coalitions, and Regional Conflict and Cooperation," in *Economic Interdependence and International Conflict,* ed. Mansfield and Pollins, 63.

34. See, for example, Solingen, *Regional Orders at Century's Dawn,* 30, 54–61, on the impact of the global economy.

35. Stephen Krasner, *Defending the National Interest: Raw Materials Investment and U.S. Foreign Policy* (Princeton, NJ: Princeton University Press, 1978).

36. Mancur Olson, *The Logic of Collective Action: Public Goods and the Theory of Groups,* rev. ed. (Cambridge, MA: Harvard University Press, 1971).

37. The classic statement on domestic structures and the distinction between strong and weak states is still Peter J. Katzenstein's *Between Power and Plenty: Foreign Economic Policies of Advanced Industrial States* (Madison: University of Wisconsin Press, 1978). A focus on the institutional environment rather than state-society structures was developed by G. John Ikenberry, David A. Lake, and Michael Mastanduno in a special issue of *International Organization* 42, no. 1 (winter 1988).

38. The notion of a vested interest in peace is developed by Arad, Hirsch, and Tovias in *Economics of Peacemaking.* See also Alfred Tovias, "Economic Aspects of Stable Peace-Making," in *Stable Peace among Nations,* ed. Kacowicz et al., 150–64.

39. These characteristics, argues Davis, are the organizational and institutional characteristics of a "trading state." See Patricia A. Davis, *The Art of Economic Persuasion: Positive Incentives and German Economic Diplomacy* (Ann Arbor: University of Michigan Press, 1999), chaps. 1 and 2.

40. Bar-Tal and Bennink, "Nature of Reconciliation as an Outcome and as a Process," 25–26. For a skeptical view regarding the impact of economic incentives on real reconciliation, see Ronnie D. Lipschutz, "Beyond the Neoliberal Peace: From Conflict Resolution to Social Reconciliation," *Social Justice* 2594 (winter 1998): 5–19.

41. Adler and Barnett, "Framework for the Study of Security Communities," 44.

42. See Håvard Hegre, "Size Asymmetry, Trade, and Militarized Conflict," *Journal of Peace Research* 48, no. 3 (2004): 403–29. See also Mark J. Gasiorowski, "Economic Interdependence and International Conflict: Some Cross-national Evidence," *International Studies Quarterly* 30, no. 1 (1986): 23–38; Polachek, Robst, and Chang, "Liberalism and Interdependence"; Barbieri, *Liberal Illusion*, 27–35.

43. Hegre, "Development and the Liberal Peace."

44. Hirschman, *National Power and the Structure of Foreign Trade*. See also Peter Liberman, "Trading with the Enemy: Security and Relative Economic Gains," *International Security* 21, no. 1 (1996): 147–75.

45. Abdelal and Kirshner, "Strategy, Economic Relations, and the Definition of National Interests." See also Robert North and Nazli Choucri, "Economic and Political Factors in International Conflict and Integration," *International Studies Quarterly* 27 (1983): 443–61. North and Choucri argue that more efficient and more advanced economies enjoy more favorable terms of trade, higher rates of profit, and greater benefits and that such success can appear threatening or injurious to other states, regardless of the intentions. Ibid., 453.

46. Hegre, "Size Asymmetry, Trade, and Militarized Conflict," 406, 412; John R. Oneal and Bruce M. Russett, "The Classical Liberals Were Right: Democracy, Interdependence, and Conflict, 1950–85," *International Studies Quarterly* 41, no. 2 (1997): 267–93.

47. This observation also highlights the tension between economic and political logic. Classic liberal economists would most often argue to the contrary, that it is the weaker and less developed state that stands to gain from greater integration into global markets and from greater cooperation with more advanced economies.

48. Polachek, Robst, and Chang, "Liberalism and Interdependence," 412–13. Much of the literature on the use of positive sanctions focuses on such cases of asymmetry and the use of economic tools by the powerful state. This is especially apparent in my chapter discussing German-Polish relations (chap. 7). See Michael Mastanduno, "Economics and Security in Statecraft and Scholarship," *International Organization* 52 (1998): 825–54; Davis, *Art of Economic Persuasion;* Randall E. Newnham, "More Flies with Honey: Positive Economic Linkage in German Ostpolitik from Bismarck to Kohl," *International Studies Quarterly* 44, no. 1 (March 2000): 73–96.

49. See, for example, Shaul Mishal, Ranan Kuperman, and David Boas, *Investment in Peace: The Politics of Economic Cooperation between Israel, Jordan, and the Palestinians* (Brighton, UK: Sussex Academic Press, 2001).

50. Barbieri, *Liberal Illusion*, 53.

51. Hegre, "Size Asymmetry, Trade, and Militarized Conflict," 405.

52. Barbieri, *Liberal Illusion*, 53–55.

53. In focusing on the expectations of economic dependence, this study follows Copeland's approach that also stresses the importance of trade expectations. See Copeland, "Economic Interdependence and War."

54. I assume that, unlike states, private business is more interested in obtaining absolute gains from trade. Consequently, wide economic asymmetries will be detrimental

to the transition-to-peace process if they are such that private business in the powerful state sees little potential in trade relations or, conversely, if private business in the weaker state believes that the power disparities are so wide that it will be unable to compete with its counterparts and therefore also has little to gain.

55. Norrin M. Ripsman and Jean-Marc F. Blanchard suggest that it is important to identify empirically different types of interdependence that may emerge between states, namely sensitivity interdependence and vulnerability interdependence. They develop different tests for establishing the existence of each type of interdependence. For the purposes of my argument, the main point here is that within a specific case, one should look for greater nuances and complexity instead of discussing general levels of interdependence. See Ripsman and Blanchard, "Commercial Liberalism under Fire," esp. 9–11.

56. This observation has potentially important policy implications. It is important to make these distinctions so as to identify where actors can have a better chance of utilizing economic tools for peace building, despite problems of asymmetry.

57. Jack Levy criticizes the dyadic nature of most research on the interdependence and conflict hypothesis, which tends to ignore the systemic context in which trade and financial flows take place. See Levy, "Economic Interdependence, Opportunity Costs, and Peace," 139.

58. See David Cortright, "Incentive Strategies for Preventing Conflict," in *The Price of Peace: Incentives and International Conflict Prevention,* ed. David Cortright (Lanham, MD: Rowman and Littlefield, 1997), 269.

59. Edward D. Mansfield, Jon C. Pevehouse, and David H. Bearce, "Preferential Trading Arrangements and Military Disputes," *Security Studies* 9, no. 1–2 (1999–2000): 96–118; Edward D. Mansfield and Jon C. Pevehouse, "Trade Blocs, Trade Flows, and International Conflict," *International Organization* 54, no. 4 (2000): 775–808. A recent attempt to examine the impact of trade with third parties is Yuan-Ching Chang, "Economic Interdependence and International Interaction: Impact of Third Party Trade on Political Cooperation and Conflict," *Cooperation and Conflict* 40, no. 2 (2005): 207–32. Chang argues that if the actor increases trade with a third party who is a friend of the target, then the actor will reduce conflict with the target.

60. Bearce, "Grasping the Commercial Institutional Peace." Joint membership in institutions is also one of the three cornerstones of the Kantian peace, according to Russett and Oneal in *Triangulating Peace.*

61. Benjamin Miller argues that great powers' involvement in regional conflict management and resolution can only lead to cold peace and that the achievement of warm peace is shaped by regional and domestic factors. My argument suggests that great powers can help to warm up the peace if they are willing to invest resources and make a long-term commitment, though this is of course a much more demanding strategy. See Benjamin Miller, *The Sources of Regional War and Peace* (Cambridge: Cambridge University Press, 2007). For an elaboration of the logic driving third party economic involvement, see Galia Press-Barnathan, "The Economic Role of Third Parties in Promoting Peace: Strategies and Pitfalls; The United States and European Union in the Middle East" (working paper, 2008).

62. Alexander George, "Case Studies and Theory Development: The Method of Structured, Focused Comparison," in *Diplomacy: New Approaches in History, Theory, and Policy,* ed. Paul G. Lauren (New York: Free Press, 1979), 43–68.

63. Amitav Acharya offers a similar criticism of Deutsch's notion of security communities, which did not take serious note of the possibility of security communities in the developing world. See Amitav Acharya, "Collective Identity and Conflict Management in Southeast Asia," in *Security Communities,* ed. Adler and Barnett, 198. For a different criticism of the attempt to apply international relations theory that is rooted in the Western experience to the international relations of Asia, see David C. Kang, "Getting

Asia Wrong: The Need for New Analytical Frameworks," *International Security* 27, no. 4 (spring 2003): 57–85.

64. For the most recent work, see Peter J. Katzenstein, *A World of Regions: Asia and Europe in the American Imperium* (Ithaca, NY: Cornell University Press, 2005).

65. See Ehud Harari, "Peace and Regional Integration of Former Enemies: Japan and Israel," paper presented at the International Relations Department Seminar, Hebrew University of Jerusalem, February 1999. See also Yishai Yafeh, Ehud Harari, and Eyal Ben-Ari, eds., *Lessons from East Asia for the Development of the Middle East in the Era of Peace* (Jerusalem: Harry S. Truman Research Institute for the Advancement of Peace, 1998).

66. Etel Solingen, *Nuclear Logics: Contrasting Paths in East Asia and the Middle East* (Princeton: Princeton University Press, 2007); Solingen, "Pax Aslatica versus Bella Levantina: The Foundations of War and Peace in East Asia and the Middle East," *American Political Review* 101, no. 4 (November 2007).

67. The problem facing "area-based knowledge," according to Katzenstein, is that it is criticized on the one hand by "scientific" critics who value nomothetic approaches over contextualization and, on the other, by "cultural" critics, who work from the perspective of the humanities. See Katzenstein, *World of Regions,* x. Area specialists, however, tend to belong to the latter category.

68. In their review of recent literature on interdependence and conflict, Mansfield and Pollins stress the need to focus more on the nature of the strategic interaction. See Mansfield and Pollins, "Interdependence and Conflict," 6.

Chapter 2. Shifting Priorities

1. For an analysis of the Egyptian-Israeli accord in terms of stable peace, see Yaacov Bar-Siman-Tov, "Israel-Egypt Peace: Stable Peace?" in *Stable Peace among Nations,* ed. Kacowicz et al., 220–38. He argues that the peace is enduring but cold and cannot yet be considered stable peace.

2. See, e.g., Rivka Yadlin, "Egyptian Perceptions of the Camp David Process," *Middle East Review* (fall 1985): 45–50.

3. Data from the Israeli Ministry of Foreign Affairs and Ministry of Tourism, www .israel-mfa.gov.il, http://www.tourism.gov.il (entered July 1, 2008).

4. Ephraim Dowek, *Israeli-Egyptian Relations, 1980–2000* (London: Frank Cass, 2001), chaps. 13 and 14. Dowek, a former Israeli ambassador to Egypt, unravels the various economic schemes pursued by Israeli companies and their eventual failure in light of what he interprets as Egyptian ill will. Trade data are from the Israeli Ministry of Foreign Affairs, 2003, and http://www.businessweek.com/magazine/content/04_51/b3913087_mz015.htm.

5. Egyptian culture minister Faruq Husni, in an interview with an Israeli newspaper reporter, expressed great knowledge of Israeli cinema and even appreciation for a recent award-winning movie describing the visit of an Egyptian band in Israel. Despite these statements, he expressed clear opposition to any form of cultural normalization with Israel. See Egyptian culture minister Faruq Husni, interview by Smadar Perry, *Yediot Aharonot* [in Hebrew], June 13, 2008, 6–9.

6. The Jordanian QIZ shifted to a quarter-based system in July 2007.

7. For details on the QIZ, see United States, Office of the U.S. Trade Representative, "United States, Egypt and Israel to Launch Historic Trade Partnership; USTR Zoellick to Participate in Signing in Cairo," December 10, 2004, http://www.ustr.gov/Document_Library/Press_Releases/2004/December/United States,Egypt_Israel_to_Launch_Historic _Trade_Partnerhship (entered August 11, 2005); Israel, Ministry of Industry and Trade, "Explanations of the QIZ Agreement Israel-Egypt–United States" [in Hebrew].

8. See a report of the Federation of Israeli Chambers of Commerce, November 3, 2005, http://www.chamber.org.il/Articles/Item.asp?CategoryID=44&ArticleID=10870.

9. Federation of Israeli Chambers of Commerce, February 21, 2007, http://www .chamber.org.il/Articles/Item.asp?CategoryID=44&ArticleID=18157&SearchParam=qiz.

10. Quoted in Shimon Shamir, *Egypt under Saadat's Leadership: The Search for a New Orientation* [in Hebrew] (Tel Aviv: Dvir Publishers, 1978), 115.

11. Shamir, *Egypt under Saadat's Leadership*, 125, 211.

12. On the seriousness of the economic problems following the October War of 1973, see Michael N. Barnett, *Confronting the Costs of War: Military Power, State, and Society in Egypt and Israel* (Princeton, NJ: Princeton University Press, 1992), 128–52; Gad G. Gilbar and Onn Winckler, "The Economic Factor of the Arab-Israeli Peace Process: The Cases of Egypt, Jordan, and Syria," in *Arab-Jewish Relations: From Conflict to Reconciliation?* ed. Elie Podeh and Asher Kaufman (Brighton and Portland, UK: Sussex Academic Press, 2006), 190–209 ; Yoram Meital, "Domestic Challenges and Egypt's U.S. Policy," *Middle East Review of International Affairs* (MERIA) 2, no. 4 (December 1998): 1–9; Paul Rivlin and Shmuel Even, *Political Stability in Arab States: Economic Causes and Consequences,* memorandum no. 74, Jaffee Center for Strategic Studies, Tel Aviv, December 2004, 41–45.

13. Quoted in Meital, "Domestic Challenges and Egypt's U.S. Policy," 3.

14. By 1977, it had become clear that the amount of aid from rich Arab countries was not likely to be significant enough to make a difference, compared to the crucial size of Western aid flows. Haim Barkai, "Egypt's Economic Constraints," *Jerusalem Quarterly* (winter 1980): 140–41.

15. Gad Gilbar, *The Economic Development of the Middle East in Modern Times* [in Hebrew] (Tel Aviv: Ministry of Defense, 1990), 202–3.

16. The Sinai oil fields are not, however, the major Egyptian oil fields. Of Egypt's oil production, 70 percent comes from the area of the Gulf of Suez. See "Egypt: Sector Analysis," June 2003, www.arabdatanet.com/country/profiles/profile.asp?CtryName= Egypt&CtryAbrv=eg&NavTitle=sector%20Analysis (entered December 8, 2005).

17. Neaman Workshop, *The Consequences of Peace for the State of Israel* [in Hebrew] (Haifa: Samuel Neaman Institute for Advanced Studies in Science and Technology, 1979), 30.

18. Amnon Sella and Yael Yishai, *Israel, the Peaceful Belligerent, 1967–79* (New York: Macmillan, 1986).

19. See Barnett, *Confronting the Costs of War,* 185–209.

20. To illustrate, one of the most notable books detailing the legitimacy problems facing the Begin government during the peace process does not even mention the economic considerations involved. See Yaacov Bar-Siman-Tov, *Israel and the Peace Process, 1977–1982: In Search of Legitimacy for Peace* (Albany: State University of New York Press, 1994).

21. See Dowek, *Israeli-Egyptian Relations, 1980–2000,* chap. 13; Arad, Hirsch, and Tovias, *Economics of Peacemaking.*

22. For examples of such potentially beneficial projects, see Gideon Fishelson, "Regional Economic Cooperation in the Middle East," in *The Arab-Israeli Search for Peace,* ed. Steven L. Spiegel (Boulder, CO: Lynn Rienner, 1992), 113–19; Laura Drake, "Arab-Israeli Relations in a New Middle East Order: The Politics of Economic Cooperation," in *The Political Economy of Middle East Peace: The Impact of Competing Trade Agendas,* ed. J. W. Wright Jr. (London: Routledge, 1998), 20–21; Elisha Kally, *Egyptian-Israeli Cooperation in Agricultural Development,* ed. Meir Merhav (Tel Aviv: Armand Hammer Fund for Economic Cooperation in the Middle East, 1986), 2–25; Elisha Kally with

Gideon Fishelson, *Water and Peace: Water Resources and the Arab-Israeli Peace Process* (Westport, CT: Praeger, 1993); Alfred Tovias and Hilary Wolpert, *Cooperation between the Textiles and Clothing Industries of Egypt and Israel* (Tel Aviv: Armand Hammer Fund for Economic Cooperation in the Middle East, 1987); Abraham Tal and Elisha Kally, *A Gas Pipeline: Egypt to Israel* (Tel Aviv: Armand Hammer Fund for Economic Cooperation in the Middle East, 1987); Haim Ben-Shahar, Gideon Fishelson, and Seev Hirsch, *Economic Cooperation and Middle East Peace,* ed. Meir Merhav (London: Weidenfeld and Nicolson, 1989), chap. 2.

23. Ben-Shahar, Fishelson, and Hirsch, *Economic Cooperation and Middle East Peace,* 19; Arad, Hirsch, and Tovias, *Economics of Peacemaking.*

24. Rivlin and Even, *Political Stability in Arab States,* 46.

25. Solingen, *Regional Order at Century's Dawn.*

26. President of an Egyptian irrigation company, interview by author, Cairo, October 17, 2005.

27. On the development of the private sector since the *Infitah,* see Raymond A. Hinnebusch, "Egypt under Sadat: Elites, Power Structure, and Political Change in a Post-Populist State," *Social Problems* 28, no. 4 (April 1981): 445–59.

28. Fouad N. Ibrahim and Barbara Ibrahim, *Egypt: An Economic Geography* (London: I. B. Tauris, 2003), chap. 7.

29. On the myth that peace would bring prosperity, see Eliyahu Kanovsky, *Assessing the Mideast Peace Economic Dividend* (Ramat Gan, Israel: Begin-Sadat Center for Strategic Studies [BESA], Bar-Ilan University, 1994). On the nature and impact of these unrealistic expectations, see Heba Handoussa and Nemat Shafik, "The Economics of Peace: The Egyptian Case," in *The Economics of Middle East Peace: Views from the Region,* ed. Stanley Fischer, Dani Rodrik, and Elias Tuma (Cambridge, MA: MIT Press, 1993), 20–28.

30. Meital, "Domestic Challenges and Egypt's U.S. Policy," 4. On the cost of the Arab economic embargo, see Victor Lavi, "The Economic Embargo of Egypt by Arab States: Myth and Reality," *Middle East Journal* 38, no. 3 (summer 1984): 419–32.

31. On the opposition to the treaty and the Infitah policy, see Laura Drake, "Arab-Israeli Relations in a New Middle East order," 28–30; Hinnebusch, "Egypt under Sadat," 461–62; senior Israeli CEO working in Egypt, interview by author, Cairo, October 18, 2005. For a good review of the structure of the various societal organizations in Egypt, see Mustapha K. Al-Sayyid, "A Civil Society in Egypt?" *Middle East Journal* 47, no. 2 (spring 1993): 228–42.

32. On this interaction between identity concerns and material incentives, see Ibrahim A. Karawan, "Identity and Foreign Policy: The Case of Egypt," in *Identity and Foreign Policy in the Middle East,* ed. Shibley Telhami and Michael Barnett (Ithaca, NY: Cornell University Press, 2002), 162–65.

33. See Yasser Sobhi and Niveen Wahish, "Pop QIZ Time," *Al-Ahram Weekly* (on-line), no. 717, November 18–24, 2004, http://weekly.ahram.org.eg/print/2004/717/ec3.htm (entered December 13, 2004).

34. Interview by author, Tenth of Ramadan City, Egypt, October 19, 2005.

35. Interview by author, Cairo, October 20, 2005.

36. Report cited in Niveen Wahish, "Talking Up Trade," *Al-Ahram Weekly* (on-line), no. 721, December 16–22, 2004.

37. Ibrahim and Ibrahim, *Egypt,* 95–102.

38. Quoted in Wahish, "Talking Up Trade."

39. The reformist approach is most apparent in the ministry of foreign trade. Illustrating the business-government connection, the current senior advisor to the minister of foreign trade was previously the executive director of the Egyptian Exporters Associa-

tion. The Ministry of Foreign Affairs (MFA), on the other hand, is still dominated by Nasserists.

40. Amr Hashem and Noha El-Mikawy, "Business Parliamentarians as Locomotives of Information and Production of Knowledge," in *Institutional Reform and Economic Development in Egypt,* ed. Noha El-Mikawy and Heba Handoussa (Cairo: American University Press, 2002), 57–58.

41. Maye Kassem, "Information and Production of Knowledge or Lobbying? Businessmen's Association, Federation of Labor Unions, and the Ministry of Manpower," in *Institutional Reform and Economic Development in Egypt,* ed. El-Mikawy and Handoussa, 69–73.

42. It is interesting to note that in the initial stages of the QIZ negotiations, while Israel insisted on conducting the negotiations at the customary intergovernmental level, the Egyptians insisted on allowing the senior business leaders involved in the initiative to sit through the negotiations. Once the key points of the agreement were settled, the Israeli side compromised and allowed participation of business sector representatives in some sessions. Yair Shiran, economic minister to North America in the Government of Israel Economic Mission (who at the time was closely involved in the QIZ negotiations with Egypt), interview by author, Hod Hasharon, Israel, July 16, 2008.

43. Senior official in MFTI, interview by author, Cairo, October 19, 2005.

44. Quoted in Niveen Wahish, "FTA: Wishful Thinking?" *Al-Ahram Weekly* (online), no. 639 May 22–28, 2003.

45. Quoted in Mona El-Nahhas, "Out of the Cold," *Al-Ahram Weekly* (on-line), no. 721, December 16–22, 2004.

46. Gamal Essam El-Din, "NDP Rallies to Defend the QIZ," *Al-Ahram Weekly* (on-line), no. 722, December 23–29, 2004; Yoav Stern, "Economic Cooperation with Israel? It's Insulting," *Haaretz* [in Hebrew], December 22, 2004, 4B.

47. Interviews by author, Cairo, October 17–20, 2005.

48. Press conference with an Egyptian business delegation to Israel, hosted by the Friedrich-Ebert-Stiftung, Israel, Tel Aviv, September 28, 2005.

49. Quoted in Stern, "Economic Cooperation with Israel?"

50. When Ehud Olmert, at the time the Israeli industry and trade minister, arrived to sign the QIZ treaty in Egypt, he encountered loud demonstrations, only to discover that they were demonstrations by angry employees from areas not covered by the agreement. Gabby Bar, joint chairman of the Egypt-Israel QIZ committee and of the Jordan-Israel QIZ committee, and senior regional director, Middle East & North Africa Division, Foreign Trade Administration, Israel Ministry of Industry, Trade & Labor, interview by author, Jerusalem, June 3, 2008.

51. Quoted in Stern, "Economic Cooperation with Israel?" See also Yoav Stern, "Voters Are Not Interested in Israel, but Candidates Are Attacking It," *Haaretz* [in Hebrew], September 6, 2005, 11A. In what appears to be another interesting attempt both to reconcile economic needs with opposition to trade with Israel and to legitimize the signing of the QIZ, the mufti of Egypt, Dr. Ali Gomaa, announced that, because the QIZ agreement was promoting Egyptian interests, there was no religious opposition to it. He noted that the Muslims did not boycott trade with Europe during the Crusades. Cited in http://www.masrawy.com/News/2004/Egypt/Politics/december/24/gomaa.aspx (entered May 25, 2008).

52. For an elaboration of this argument, see Shmuel Even, "Israeli Natural Gas: The Economic and Strategic Significance," *Strategic Assessment* 4, no. 3 (November 2001), http://www.tau.ac.il/jcss/sa/v4n3p5Eve.html.

53. For a detailed description of the history of the deal and the eventual signing, see Amiram Cohen, "The Egyptians Suffered from Every Moment," *Haaretz* [in Hebrew],

July 5, 2005, http://finance.walla.co.il/?w=/114/741500/@@/item/printer. For earlier reviews of the ongoing negotiations, as reported in the Israeli newspaper *Yediot Aharonot*, see, for example: http://www.ynet.co.il/articles/1.7340,L-262528.html; http://www/ynet.co.il/articles/1,7340,L-262528,00.html, both from November 15, 2000; http://www.ynet.co.il/articles/1,7340,L-466728,00.html, January 25, 2001; http:www.ynet.co.il/articles/1,7340,L-795288,00.html, June 5, 2001.

54. Quoted in Cam McGrath, "Government Not Ready to Cut Economic Ties with Israel," Inter Press Service English news wire, April 10, 2002 (entered November 11, 2008).

55. Ehud Olmert, presentation at the conference "The Economic Relations between Israel and Egypt: On the Verge of a New Era?" Tel Aviv, June 19–20, 2005.

56. Shiran interview.

57. Bar interview.

58. Bar and Shiran interviews.

59. Oded Beit-Halachmi, chairman and CEO of Delta Egypt, interview by author, Cairo, October 19, 2005.

60. See http://devdata.worldbank.org/dataonline.

61. See http://devdata.worldbank.org/dataonline; http://ddp-ext.worldbank.org.

62. In 2008, the population of Egypt was 75,099,806, compared to 7,325,999 in Israel, according to http://www.world-gazetteer.com.

63. Quoted in Yael Tamir, "Peace Economy: The Possible Impact of Economic Ties between Israel and Egypt on the Peace Process" [in Hebrew] (master's thesis, Hebrew University of Jerusalem, 1990), 50.

64. See Laura Drake, "Arab-Israeli Relations in a New Middle East Order," 22; Henry Bruton, *The Promise of Peace : Economic Cooperation between Egypt and Israel* (Washington, DC: Brookings Institution, 1981), 19.

65. See Jaffee Center for Strategic Studies, "Progress or Breakdown in the Middle East Peace Process," May 2000, Geneva, http://www.css-jordan.org/activities/workshops/peace/#egisr.

66. On the changes in the Israeli economic orientation and economic philosophy since the mid-1980s, see Gershon Shafir and Yoav Peled, "Peace and Profits: The Globalization of Israeli Business and the Peace Process," in *The New Israel: Peacemaking and Liberalization*, ed. Gershon Shafir and Yoav Peled (Boulder, CO: Westview, 2000), 243–64. On the nature of the Egyptian economy, see Ibrahim and Ibrahim, *Egypt*, chap. 7.

67. See Ali F. Darrat and Sam R. Hakim, "Winners and Losers in the Middle East: The Economics of 'Peace Dividends'," *Middle East Policy* 9, no. 3 (September 2002). They present different data to show that over the years Israel has benefited disproportionately from the peace process. On the dangers of the "New Middle East" concept for Arab economies, see also Atif A. Kubursi, "Prospects for Arab Economic Integration after Oslo," in *Middle East Dilemma: The Politics and Economics of Arab Integration*, ed. Michael C. Hudson (New York: Columbia University Press, 1999), 299–319.

68. For details on the post-Madrid development of regional economic cooperation, see Dalia Dassa-Kaye, *Beyond the Handshake: Multilateral Cooperation in the Arab-Israeli Peace Process, 1991–1996* (New York: Columbia University Press, 2001).

69. On the Egyptian considerations regarding Egypt's regional leadership role and the issue of normalization with Israel, see Avraham Sela, "Identity and Peacemaking: The Arab Discourse on Peace with Israel in the 1990s," *Israel Studies* 10, no. 2 (2005): 15–71.

70. Ben-Shahar, Fishelson, and Hirsch, *Economic Cooperation and Middle East Peace*, 11.

71. Jeremy M. Sharp, "U.S. Foreign Aid to Israel," CRS Report to Congress (updated January 2, 2008), 15, http://www.fas.org/sgp/crs/mideast/RL33222.pdf (entered May 22, 2008).

72. Edward S. Walker, "The United States–Egyptian Relations: Strengthening Our Partnership," *SAIS Review* 17, no. 1 (1997): 149–59.

73. On the nature and magnitude of American aid to Egypt, see Robert Satloff and Patrick Clawson, "U.S. Economic Aid to Egypt: Designing a New, Pro-Growth Package," http://www.biu.ac.il/SOC/besa/meria/news/1998/98news11.html#U.S.%20Economic %20Aid; Gilbar and Winckler, "Economic Factor of the Arab-Israeli Peace Process," 21; Marvin G. Weinbaum, "Egypt's *Infitah* and the Politics of U.S. Economic Assistance," *Middle Eastern Studies* 21, no. 2 (1985): 206–22; Denis J. Sullivan, "American Aid to Egypt, 1975–96: Peace without Development," *Middle East Policy* 4, no. 4 (1996): 36–49; Duncan J. Clarke, "U.S. Security Assistance to Egypt and Israel: Politically Untouchable?" *Middle East Journal* 51, no. 2 (spring 1997): 200–14.

74. Bessma Momani, "Promoting Economic Liberalization in Egypt: From U.S. Foreign Aid to Trade and Investment," *Middle East Review of International Affairs* 7, no. 3 (September 2003): 88.

75. Dowek, *Israeli-Egyptian Relations, 1980–2000*, chap. 14.

76. U.S. Office of the USTR, "United States, Egypt and Israel to Launch Historic Trade Partnership."

77. Shiran interview.

78. U.S. State Department, "The Middle East Initiative," http://usinfo.state.gov/mena/ Archive_Index/THE_MIDDLE_EAST_INITIATIVE.html. For an Egyptian perspective, see Maghawri Shalabi Ali, "Economic and Political Implications of the MEFTA Initiative," *International Politics Journal*, October 2003, http://www.siyassa.org.eg/esiyassa/ AHRAM/2003/10/1/ECON1.HTM.

79. Vikash Yadav, "The Political Economy of the Egyptian-Israeli QIZ Trade Agreement," *Middle East Review of International Affairs* 11, no. 1 (March 2007): 74–96.

80. Irit Ben-Abba, deputy director general, Economic Affairs Division in the Israeli Ministry of Foreign Affairs, interview by author, Jerusalem, July 24, 2008.

81. Senior Israeli manager of Delta Egypt, interview by author, Cairo, October 20, 2005.

Chapter 3. The Limits of Peacemaking from Above

1. For a good review of the history of the Israeli-Jordanian-Palestinian triangular relationship, see, e.g., Asher Susser, "The Israeli-Palestinian-Jordanian Triangle," and Avraham Sela, "Israeli-Jordanian Relations: The Shadow of the Palestinian Actor," both in *Neighbors in a Maze: Israel-Jordan Relations before the Peace Treaty and After* [in Hebrew], ed. Yoseph Nevo (Tel Aviv: Yitzhak Rabin Center for the Study of Israel, 2004).

2. For details, see Yoram Meital, *Normalization and Economic Ties in the Treaties between Israel and Jordan* [in Hebrew] (Tel Aviv: Armand Hammer Fund for Economic Cooperation in the Middle East, 1998), chap. 3.

3. Boaz Hirsch, head of the Bilateral Trade Agreements Department, Foreign Trade Section, Ministry of Industry, Trade and Employment, "The Improved Trade Agreement between Israel and Jordan," http://www.moit.gov.il (entered November 7, 2005).

4. Israeli Central Bureau of Statistics, www.cbs.gov.il/statistical/trade/_39_h.pdf; and www.cbs.gov.il/www/fr_trade/td1.htm (entered June 20, 2008). See also "59% Increase in Israeli Exports to Jordan," http://www.ynet.co.il/articles/1,7340,L-3473630,00 .html (entered January 4, 2008).

5. The number of Israeli tourists to Jordan includes Arab Israelis but not Palestinians, as there is a separate category for tourists from the Palestinian Territories. See Ministry of Tourism and Antiquities of Jordan, http://www.locateme.jo/stat2007. The number of Jordanian tourists is from the Israeli Ministry of Tourism, http://www.tourism.gov.il.

6. Figure cited in Russell E. Lucas, "Jordan: The Death of Normalization with Israel," *Middle East Journal* 58, no. 1 (winter 2004): 109.

7. Irit Ben-Abba, deputy director general, Economic Affairs Division, Ministry of Foreign Affairs, interview by author, Jerusalem, July 24, 2008.

8. Based on an interview with Yitzhak Rabin by Moshe Zack, "Rabin and Hussein: From War to Peace," in *Neighbors in a Maze* [in Hebrew], ed. Nevo, 121–24.

9. On the deteriorating conditions in Jordan before the treaty, see Eliyahu Kanovsky, *The Forgotten Dimension: Economic Development in the Arab Countries and Their Possible Impact on Peace Agreements* (Ramat Gan, Israel: BESA, Bar-Ilan University, 1992).

10. Onn Winckler, "The Economic Factor of the Middle East Peace Process: The Jordanian Case," in *The Jordanian-Palestinian-Israeli Triangle: Smoothing the Path to Peace*, ed. Joseph Ginat and Onn Winckler (Brighton, UK: Sussex Academic Press, 1998), 170–73; Hani Abu-Jabara, "The Economics of Peace: Jordan," in *Economics of Middle East Peace*, ed. Fischer, Rodrik, and Tuma, 181–99.

11. World Development Indicators (WDI) Online, http:ddd-ext.worldbank.org/ext/DDPQQ/showReport?method=showReport (entered July 7, 2008).

12. Researchers have tried to assess the economic value of cooperation with Jordan. Most of them concluded that while potential existed on certain items, the levels of economic gain would not be dramatic. See, e.g., Arie Arnon, Avia Spivak, and J. Weinblatt, "The Potential for Trade between Israel, the Palestinians and Jordan," *World Economy* 19, no. 1 (1996): 113–34; Seev Hirsch and Niron Hashai, "The Trade Potential between Israel and Arab States in Distance-Sensitive Products," in *Israel at the Beginning of the Twenty-first Century: Society, Law, Economy, and Media* [in Hebrew], ed. Hillel Nossek (Tel Aviv: Cherikover Publishers, 2002), 289–325; Nadav Halevi, *Trade Links between Israel and Jordan: Prospects and Considerations* (Tel Aviv: Armand Hammer Fund for Economic Cooperation in the Middle East, 1994).

13. For numerous examples and first-hand accounts of such cooperative projects, see Shimon Shamir, ed., *Israel-Jordan Relations: Projects, Economics, Business* (Tel Aviv: Tel Aviv University Institute for Diplomacy and Regional Cooperation, 2004). See also Mishal, Kuperman, and Boas, *Investment in Peace*, chaps. 5 and 6; Simcha Bahiri et al., *Israeli-Palestinian-Jordanian Trade Relations* (Israel/Palestine Center for Research and Information [IPCRI], and Konrad-Adenauer-Stiftung, September 1997); Ben-Shahar, Fishelson, and Hirsch, *Economic Cooperation and Middle East Peace.*

14. See Laurie A. Brand, *Jordan's Inter-Arab Relations: The Political Economy of Alliance Making* (New York: Columbia University Press, 1994); Scott Greenwood, "Jordan's 'New Bargain': The Political Economy of Regime Security," *Middle East Journal* 57, no. 1 (2003): 248–68.

15. See Rivlin and Even, *Political Stability in Arab States*, 38–40.

16. Yoseph Nevo, "Neighbors in a Maze: Israel-Jordan Relations before the Peace Treaty and After; Introduction," in *Neighbors in a Maze* [in Hebrew], ed. Nevo, 18–20.

17. Lucas, "Jordan," 105–9. The dramatic increase in FDI inflows to Jordan also took time. The major jump to $815 million occurred only in 2000, then went down again, and began surging only from 2004 on. See WDI Online, http:ddd-ext.worldbank.org/ext/DDPQQ/showReport?method=showReport (entered July 7, 2008).

18. Danishai Kornbluth, "Jordan and the Anti-Normalization Campaign, 1994–2001," *Terrorism and Political Violence* 14, no. 3 (autumn 2002): 84–85; Muhna Hadad, "Israel in the Eyes of Jordan after the Peace Treaty: Hope and Illusion," in *Neighbors in a Maze* [in Hebrew, essay originally in English], ed. Nevo, 261–62.

19. Kornbluth, "Jordan and the Anti-Normalization Campaign," 91–92; Hadad, "Israel in the Eyes of Jordan," 261–62. Hasan A. Brary, of the Center for Strategic Stud-

ies in Jordan University, termed these threats and manipulations "intellectual terror." Brary, "Jordan and Israel: A Decade After the Peace Treaty," in *Neighbors in a Maze* [in Hebrew, essay originally in English], ed. Nevo, 291.

20. Mishal, Kuperman, and Boas, *Investment in Peace,* 30.

21. Markus E. Bouillon, "The Failure of Big Business: On the Socio-Economic Reality of the Middle East Peace Process," *Mediterranean Politics* 9, no. 1 (spring 2004): 8–11.

22. Hadad, "Israel in the Eyes of Jordan," 262–63.

23. Glenn E. Robinson, "Defensive Democratization in Jordan," *International Journal of Middle East Studies* 30, no. 3 (August 1998): 390.

24. Hilal Khashan, *Partner or Pariah? Attitudes toward Israel in Syria, Lebanon, and Jordan* (Washington, DC: Washington Institute for Near East Policy, 1996), 26–27.

25. Jack L. Snyder, *From Voting to Violence: Democratization and Nationalist Conflict* (New York: Norton, 2000); Edward Mansfield and Jack L Snyder, "The Dangers of Democratization," *International Security* 20, no. 1 (summer 1995): 1–33.

26. Laurie A. Brand, "The Effects of the Peace Process on Political Liberalization in Jordan," *Journal of Palestine Studies* 28, no. 2 (winter 1999): 52–67.

27. Kornbluth, "Jordan and the Anti-Normalization Campaign," 88–89.

28. This argument is made by several scholars. See Brand, "The Effects of the Peace Process on Political Liberalization"; Robinson, "Defensive Democratization in Jordan"; Kornbluth, "Jordan and the Anti-Normalization Campaign"; and Lucas, "Jordan."

29. Meital, *Normalization and Economic Ties,* 11.

30. Hadad, "Israel in the Eyes of Jordan," 260–61.

31. Dov Lautman, "Economic Ties Stabilize Peace between People," in *Neighbors in a Maze* [in Hebrew], ed. Nevo, 199–200.

32. Marc Lynch, *State Interests and Public Spheres: The International Politics of Jordan's Identity* (New York: Columbia University Press, 1999), chap. 6.

33. Ibid., 200–202 (quotation, 200). See also Marc Lynch, "Jordan's Identity and Interests," in *Identity and Foreign Policy in the Middle East,* ed. Telhami and Barnett, 53.

34. Dan Catrivas, director of the Division of Foreign Trade & International Relations, Manufacturers' Association of Israel, interview by author, Tel Aviv, July 22, 2008. Catrivas at the time was actively involved in economic interactions with Jordan and created the Middle East division in the International Trade Administration, which did not exist before.

35. See Guy Ben-Porat, "A New Middle East? Globalization, Peace, and the 'Double Movement'," *International Relations* 19, no. 1 (2005): 39–62; Shafir and Peled, "Peace and Profits." It is important to note, though, that this basic belief that regional peace and stability were essential for maintaining economic growth and prosperity was somewhat undermined following the intifada years, during which the Israeli market continued growing despite the security situation. Catrivas interview.

36. Dan Propper, "The Israeli Industry as a Factor in Shaping the Peace in the Middle East," in *Neighbors in a Maze* [in Hebrew], ed. Nevo, 194.

37. Guy Ben-Porat, "Between Power and Hegemony: Business Communities in the Peace Process," *Review of International Studies* 31, no. 2 (April 2005): 339–40.

38. Gabby Bar, in charge of the Middle East desk in the Ministry of Industry, Trade and Labor, and joint chair of the Israel-Jordan QIZ committee, in Shamir, *Israel-Jordan Relations,* 99–100.

39. Bar interview.

40. Ben-Porat, "Between Power and Hegemony"; Bouillon, "Failure of Big Business," 21.

41. Even according to official statements, the level of socioeconomic inequality in Israel in 2007 was a record high among Organisation for Economic Co-operation and Development (OECD) countries. See "Socio-Economic Agenda, Israel 2008–2010," Prime Minister's Office, http://www.pmo.gov.il/PMOEng/PM+Office/Departments/eco20082010.htm.

42. Comments of Gili Dekel, Shimon Peres, and Moti Krystal (former secretary of the committee that followed up on the application of the peace treaty with Jordan), all in Shamir, *Israel-Jordan Relations,* 72–75, 31–34, 90–93, respectively.

43. http://devdata.worldbank.org/dataonline.

44. Mishal, Kuperman, and Boas, *Investment in Peace,* 30.

45. Washington Declaration, http://www.knesset.gov.il/process/docs/washington_eng.htm.

46. Ben-Abba interview.

47. Hisham Awartani and Ephraim Kleiman, "Economic Interaction among Participants in the Middle East Peace Process," *Middle East Journal* 51, no. 2 (spring 1997): 215–29.

48. Meital, *Normalization and Economic Ties,* 17–21.

49. Propper, "Israeli Industry as a Factor in Shaping the Peace in the Middle East," 190.

50. See Israel, Ministry of Industry, Trade, and Tourism Newsletter, Foreign Trade Administration, no. 39, January 2005, http://www.moit.gov.il/NR/exeres/A50D1EE6-F11D-4EA9-AD6C31DD1FD66825.htm.

51. Khashan, *Partner or Pariah?* 31–36.

52. See, e.g., Kornbluth, "Jordan and the Anti-Normalization Campaign," 84.

53. Quoted in Bouillon, "Failure of Big Business," 7.

54. Ibid., 5.

55. Mishal, Kuperman, and Boas, *Investment in Peace,* 107–9.

56. Krystal in Shamir, *Israel-Jordan Relations.*

57. Information from the official Web site of the Israeli Ministry of Foreign Affairs, http://mashav.mfa.gov.il/mfm/web/main/document.asp?SubjectID=35242&MissionID=16210&LanguageID=0&StatusID=0&DocumentID=-1 (entered May 23, 2008).

58. Greenwood, "Jordan's 'New Bargain'," 255.

59. Gilbar and Winckler, "Economic Factor of the Arab-Israeli Peace Process," 23–24.

60. Alfred B. Prados, "Jordan: U.S. Relations and Bilateral Issues," January 28, 2005, CRS Issue Brief for Congress, Foreign Affairs, Defense and Trade Division, http://fpc.state.gov/document/organization/43389.pdf.

61. Mishal, Kuperman, and Boas, *Investment in Peace,* 111–12.

62. Bar interview.

63. "Textile Industry Exports Doing Well; Manufacturers Should Look into Diversifying Export Markets," *Jordan Times,* April 8, 2002.

64. Figure cited by Rob Portman, USTR, October 31, 2005, http://www.ustr.gov/Document_Library/Press_Releases/2005/October/USTR_Portman_Announces_Additional_Efforts_To_Support_Trade_And_Development_In_The_Middle_East.

65. Gabby Bar, in Shamir, *Israel-Jordan Relations,* 103.

66. "59% Increase in Israeli Exports to Jordan," http://www.ynet.co.il/articles/1'7340'L-3473630,00.html (entered January 4, 2008).

67. Mishal, Kuperman, and Boas, *Investment in Peace,* 104–5.

68. Bar interview.

69. Bouillon, "Failure of Big Business," 10–11; Pete W. Moore, "The Newest Jordan: Free Trade, Peace, and an Ace in the Hole," Middle East Research and Information Proj-

ect (MERIP), *Middle East Report Online,* July 26, 2003, http://www.merip.org; Benjamin Orbach, "Egyptian Officials Visit Israel to Discuss QIZs: Jordan Sets Most Successful Example of U.S.-Arab Free Trade," *Daily Star* (Beirut), March 25, 2004.

70. Quoted in Robert J. Bookmiller, "Abdullah's Jordan: America's Anxious Ally," *Alternatives: Turkish Journal of International Relations* 2, no. 2 (summer 2003): 175.

71. A congressional delegation of members of the Ways and Means Committee that visited Tunisia, Jordan, Oman, and Egypt in November 2004 concluded that the QIZ requirement for Israeli inputs makes the Jordanian products less competitive because these inputs are relatively expensive. They therefore advised that Jordan move quickly to use the FTA qualifying rule instead of the QIZ. The report appears at http://tokyo.usembassy .gov/e/p/tp-20041122-31.html.

72. Bar interview.

Chapter 4. Postwar Relations in Southeast Asia

1. On the occupation period in both countries, see Keith Lightfoot, *The Philippines* (London: Ernest Benn, 1973), 120–22; George McTurnan Kahin, *Nationalism and Revolution in Indonesia* (Ithaca, NY: Cornell University Press, 1952), 101–33; Christine Drake, *National Integration in Indonesia: Patterns and Policies* (Honolulu: University of Hawaii Press, 1989), chap. 1.

2. See Lawrence Olson, *Japan in Postwar Asia* (New York: Praeger, 1970), 25–26. Olson's book offers the most detailed account of the reparations negotiations period.

3. See Sueo Sudo, "Japan-ASEAN Relations: New Dimensions in Japanese Foreign Policy," *Asian Survey* 28, no. 5 (May 1988): 509.

4. Jusuf Wanadi, "ASEAN-Japan Relations: The Underpinning of East Asian Peace and Stability," in *ASEAN-Japan Cooperation: A Foundation for East Asian Community* (Tokyo: Japan Center for International Exchange, 2003), 8–9.

5. Data for the Philippines is from Philippines, Department of Trade and Industry, "Proposed Japan-Philippines Economic Partnership Agreement (JPEPA)," March 2005, http://tradelinephil.dti.gov.ph/downloads/jpepa_brieffiengpresentation_10march2005.pdf (entered December 4, 2005). Data for Indonesia is from Japan, Ministry of Foreign Affairs, "Japan-Indonesia Economic Partnership Agreement: A Joint Study Group Report," May 2005, http://www.mofa.go.jp/region/asia-paci/Indonesia/summito506/joint-3-2.pdf (entered December 4, 2005).

6. See "Japan, Indonesia to Sign FTA," *Japan Times,* August 11, 2007, http://search .japantimes.co.jp/cgi-bin/nb20070811a5.html (entered July 6, 2008).

7. Data from the Japanese Ministry of Foreign Affairs, http://www.mofa.go.jp/policy/ economy/apec/2002/Indonesia.html.

8. See full text of JPEPA at the Web site of the Japanese Ministry of Foreign Affairs, http://www.mofa.go.jp/region/asia-paci/asean/conference/jointo711.html (entered July 11, 2008). On the delay in the senate of the Philippines, "Senate Delays JPEPA Approval," http://www.gmanews.tv/story/92116/Philippines-Senate-delays-JPEPA-approval, April 29, 2008.

9. See, e.g., Nissim Kadosh Otmazgin, "Cultural Commodities and Regionalization in East Asia," *Contemporary Southeast Asia* 27, no. 3 (2005): 499–523; Nissim Kadosh Otmazgin, "Contesting Soft Power: Japanese Popular Culture in East and Southeast Asia," *International Relations of the Asia-Pacific* 8 (2008): 73–101; John Clammer and Eyal Ben-Ari, "Japan in Southeast Asia: An Introductory Essay," in *Japan in Singapore: Cultural Occurrences and Cultural Flows,* ed. Eyal Ben-Ari and John Clammer (Richmond, Surrey, UK: Curzon Press, 2000), 1–36; David Wurfel, "Japan-Philippine Relations:

Economic and Cultural Determinants of Mutual Images in an Unequal Cooperative Dyad," *Journal of Northeast Asian Studies* 5, no. 2 (summer 1986): 18–23; Lydia N. Yu Jose, "State and Non-State Actors in Philippines-Japan Relations" *Philippine Studies* 51, no. 2 (2003): 177–216; Saya S. Shiraishi, "Japan's Soft Power: Doraemon Goes Overseas," in *Network Power: Japan and Asia*, ed. Peter J. Katzenstein and Takashi Shiraishi (Ithaca, NY: Cornell University Press, 1997), 234–74.

10. For an insightful review of the changing perceptions of ASEAN countries toward Japan, see Bhubhindar Singh, "ASEAN's Perceptions of Japan: Change and Continuity," *Asian Survey* 42, no. 2 (2002): 276–96.

11. "Opinion Poll on Japan in Six ASEAN Countries (Summary of Results)," Ministry of Foreign Affairs of Japan, http://www.mofa.go.jp/announce/announce/2008/5/1179528_1010html (entered July 25, 2008).

12. See Warren I. Cohen, "China in Japanese-American Relations," in *The United States and Japan in the Postwar World*, ed. Akira Iriye and Warren I. Cohen (Lexington: University Press of Kentucky, 1989), 42–44. On Japan's urgent need for raw materials, see also Akira Suehiro, "The Road to Economic Re-entry: Japan's Policy toward Southeast Asian Development in the 1950s and 1960s," *Social Science Japan Journal* 2, no. 1 (1999): 88; David Arase, *Buying Power: The Political Economy of Japan's Foreign Aid* (Boulder, CO: Lynne Rienner, 1995), 16–27.

13. Quoted in Takashi Shiraishi, "Japan and Southeast Asia," in *Network Power*, ed. Katzenstein and Shiraishi, 177.

14. See Masashi Nishihara, *The Japanese and Sukarno's Indonesia: Tokyo-Jakarta Relations, 1951–1966* (Honolulu: University Press of Hawaii, 1976), chap. 1; Wijarso, "Indonesian Oil and Japan: Present Situation and Future Possibilities," *Indonesian Quarterly* 13, no. 3 (1985): 311; "Japan, Indonesia to Sign FTA," *Japan Times*, August 11, 2007, http://search.japantimes.co.jp/cgi-bin/nb20070811a5.html.

15. Iyanatul Islam and Anis Chowdhury, *Asia-Pacific Economies: A Survey* (London: Routledge, 1997), 243. For a detailed review of the economic structure of the Philippines in the 1940s and 1950s, see Frank H. Golay, *The Philippines: Public Policy and National Economic Development* (Ithaca, NY: Cornell University Press, 1961), chap. 3.

16. J. L. Vellut, "Japanese Reparations to the Philippines," *Asian Survey* 3, no. 10 (October 1963): 496.

17. Sudarsono Hardjosoekarto, "Japan's Role in Indonesia's Development," *Indonesian Quarterly* 21, no. 4 (1993): 410–33.

18. Chitoshi Yanaga, *Big Business in Japanese Politics* (New Haven: Yale University Press, 1968), 222.

19. Alan Rix, *Japan's Foreign Aid Challenge: Policy Reform and Aid Leadership* (London: Routledge, 1993), 151.

20. On this special relationship, especially during these postwar years, see Chalmers Johnson, *MITI and the Japanese Miracle* (Stanford, CA: Stanford University Press, 1982).

21. On this period, see, e.g., John W. Dower, *Empire and Aftermath: Yoshida Shigeru and the Japanese Experience, 1878–1954* (Cambridge, MA: Council on East Asian Studies, Harvard University, 1988); Theodore Cohen, *Remaking Japan: The American Occupation as New Deal* (New York: Free Press, 1987).

22. Yanaga, *Big Business in Japanese Politics*, 202–4 (quotation, 204); Arase, *Buying Power*, 30–33.

23. Olson, *Japan in Postwar Asia*, 56–60.

24. Quoted in Suehiro, "Road to Economic Re-entry," 88.

25. On the Yoshida Doctrine, see, e.g., John Welfield, *An Empire in Eclipse: Japan in the Postwar American Alliance System* (London: Athlone Press, 1988).

26. Quoted in Suehiro, "Road to Economic Re-entry," 92.

27. Suehiro, "Road to Economic Re-entry," 92–93.

28. Arase, *Buying Power,* 25–27.

29. Olson, *Japan in Postwar Asia,* 19.

30. During the 1930s, there was lively Japanese economic activity in the Philippines, with the most notable example being the large and highly successful agricultural colony established by Japanese in Davao. On this period, see Joseph Ralston Hayden, *The Philippines: A Study in National Development* (New York: Macmillan, 1942), 711–18.

31. Suehiro, "Road to Economic Re-entry," 97–102.

32. Charles E. Morrison, "Japan and the ASEAN Countries: The Evolution of Japan's Regional Role," in *The Political Economy of Japan,* vol. 2, *The Changing International Context,* ed. Takashi Inoguchi and Daniel I. Okimoto (Stanford, CA: Stanford University Press, 1988), 427.

33. William R. Liddle, "The Relative Autonomy of the Third World Politician: Soeharto and Indonesian Economic Development in Comparative Perspective," *International Studies Quarterly* 35, no. 4 (December 1991): 403–27. See also Ramlan Surbakti, "Formal Political Institutions," in *Indonesia: The Challenge of Change,* ed. Richard W. Baker et al. (Leiden, Netherlands: KITLV Press, 1999), 62, 70.

34. Nishihara, *The Japanese and Sukarno's Indonesia,* xiii–xiv.

35. Eduardo C. Tadem, "The Japanese Type of Cooperation in Southeast Asia: The Philippine Case," *East Asia* 2 (1984): 202.

36. James K. Boyce, *The Philippines: The Political Economy of Growth and Impoverishment in the Marcos Era* (Basingstoke, UK: Macmillan, 1993), chap. 1.

37. Harold Crouch, "Generals and Business in Indonesia," *Pacific Affairs* 48, no. 4 (winter 1975–1976): 519–40. On the nature of the private sector, see Richard W. Baker and M. Hadi Soesastro, "Conclusion," in *Indonesia,* ed. Baker et al., 255–71. On the emergence of liberalizing coalitions throughout Southeast Asia, especially since the late 1970s, see Etel Solingen, "ASEAN Quo Vadis? Domestic Coalitions and Regional Cooperation," *Contemporary Southeast Asia* 21, no. 1 (April 1999): 30–53; Etel Solingen, "Southeast Asia in a New Era: Domestic Coalitions from Crisis to Recovery," *Asian Survey* 44, no. 2 (2004): 189–212.

38. Donald C. Hellman, "Japan and Southeast Asia: Continuity amidst Change," *Asian Survey* 19, no. 12 (December 1979): 1198.

39. Islam and Chowdhury, *Asia-Pacific Economies,* 240.

40. Yanaga, *Big Business in Japanese Politics,* 216–21; Olson, *Japan in Postwar Asia,* 20–121.

41. Olson, *Japan in Postwar Asia,* 61.

42. Kahin, *Nationalism and Revolution in Indonesia,* 130.

43. Dewi Fortuna Anwar, "Indonesia's Relations with China and Japan: Images, Perception, and Realities," *Contemporary Southeast Asia* 12, no. 3 (December 1990): 238.

44. Olson, *Japan in Postwar Asia,* 25, 55–57. Forty-eight years later, in 2008, the Philippine Senate once again was holding back on approving the free trade agreement that was signed with Japan in 2006. It is interesting that the criticisms raised in 2008 are similar to those put forward in 1960—that the treaty was lopsided in favor of Japan, that its provisions would further reinforce the historically unequal economic relations, and that the agreement was tantamount to a second "Japanese invasion" of the Philippines. See "An Appeal to the Senate to Reject the Japan-Philippines Economic Partnership Agreement (JPEPA),"http://www.petitiononline.com/NoDeal/petition.html (entered July 10, 2008).

45. Olson, *Japan in Postwar Asia,* 184.

46. Ibid., 59–60, 189–92.

47. These were the conclusions of an important conservative Japanese leader who visited the region in spring 1952 as Prime Minister Yoshida's special envoy. See Olson, *Japan in Postwar Asia*, 31.

48. Suehiro, "Road to Economic Re-entry," 94–98; Wakamiya Yoshibumi, *The Postwar Conservative View of Asia: How the Political Right Had Delayed Japan's Coming to Terms with Its History of Aggression in Asia* (Tokyo: LTCB International Library Foundation, 1995), 223–28.

49. Raul S. Manglapus, *Japan in Southeast Asia: Collision Course* (New York: Carnegie Endowment for International Peace, 1976), 73–94.

50. Kano Hiroyoshi, "Indonesian Business Groups and Their Leaders," *East Asian Cultural Studies* 28, no. 1–4 (1989): 147; Takashi Shiraishi, "Japan and Southeast Asia," 182.

51. On the Fukuda Doctrine, see Sueo Sudo, "The Road to Becoming a Regional Leader: Japanese Attempts in Southeast Asia, 1975–1980," *Pacific Affairs* 61, no. 1 (spring 1988): 27–50; Sueo Sudo, "Japan-ASEAN Relations: New Dimensions in Japanese Foreign Policy," *Asian Survey* 28, no. 5 (May 1988): 509–25.

52. Paridah Abdul Samad and Mokhtar Muhammad, "Japan in Southeast Asia: Its Diplomatic, Economic, and Military Commitment," *Indonesian Quarterly* 22, no. 3 (1994): 263–67.

53. Sudo, "Road to Becoming a Regional Leader," 29–31.

54. See http://www.devdata.worldbank.org/dataonline.

55. Data from Morrison, "Japan and the ASEAN Countries," 416–17.

56. Olson, *Japan in Postwar Asia*, 56–57.

57. Quoted in Anwar, "Indonesia's Relations with China and Japan," 236–37.

58. Robert O. Tilman, *Southeast Asia and the Enemy Beyond: ASEAN Perceptions of External Threats* (Boulder, CO: Westview Press, 1987), 114–20.

59. Hirschman, *National Power and the Structure of Foreign Trade*. For a discussion of the dependence/interdependence nature of the relations between Japan and ASEAN, see Lim Hua Sing, *Japan's Role in Asia: Issues and Prospects* (Singapore: Times Academic Press, 1995), 120–28.

60. Anwar, "Indonesia's Relations with China and Japan," 244; Shin'ichi Ichimura, "Japan and Southeast Asia," *Asian Survey* 20, no. 7 (July 1980): 761.

61. Sudo, "Road to Becoming a Regional Leader," 37–38. See also Sudo, "Japan-ASEAN Relations," 511–14.

62. Examining the role of economic interaction between Japan and ASEAN states today and its political and strategic impact is more related to the general question posed by commercial liberalism scholars (i.e., interdependence and conflict) than to the question of this book: how economic interaction and incentives can promote the transition to peace.

63. See Roger Dingman, "The Diplomacy of Dependency: The Philippines and Peacemaking with Japan, 1945–1952," *Journal of Southeast Asian Studies* 17, no. 2 (September 1986): 307–10.

64. Galia Press-Barnathan, *Organizing the World: The United States and Regional Cooperation in Asia and Europe* (New York: Routledge, 2003), chap. 6.

65. On the various regional trade schemes of the Americans, see William Borden, *The Pacific Alliance: United States Foreign Economic Policy and Japanese Trade Recovery, 1947–1955* (Madison: University of Wisconsin Press, 1984); Michael Schaller, *The American Occupation of Japan: The Origins of the Cold War in Asia* (New York: Oxford University Press, 1985), chap. 12; Press-Barnathan, *Organizing the World*, chap. 6.

66. Yoshibumi, *Postwar Conservative View of Asia*, 223–24.

67. For more details on this ideological conflict, see David Wightman, *Toward Economic Cooperation in Asia: The United Nations Economic Commission for Asia and the Far East* (New Haven: Yale University Press, 1963).

68. For an official update, see http://www.mofa.go.jp/region/asia-paci/asean/relation/overview.html. For an interesting book surveying the current and potential contributions of this institutionalized cooperation for community building in Asia, see *ASEAN-Japan Cooperation: A Foundation for East Asian Community* (Tokyo: Japan Center for International Exchange, 2003).

69. See the joint statement on the conclusion of the negotiations at the Web site of Japan's Ministry of Foreign Affairs, November 21, 2007, http://www.mofa.go.jp/region/asia-paci/asean/conference/joint0711.html (entered July 11, 2008).

70. See Kinju Atarashi, "Japan's Economic Cooperation Policy towards the ASEAN Countries," *International Affairs* 61, no. 1 (winter 1984–1985): 109–27.

Chapter 5. Government and Big Business

1. On the history of the relations between the two states, see, e.g., James Lewis, "The Japan That Does Not Exist and the Ugly Korean: An Essay on the History of Korean-Japanese Relations and Their Contemporary Images of Each Other," in *Korea and Globalization: Politics, Economics, and Culture*, ed. James Lewis and Amadu Sesay (London: RoutledgeCurzon, 2002), 104–18. Specifically on the colonial period, see Chong-Sik Lee, *The Politics of Korean Nationalism* (Berkeley: University of California Press, 1963), chap. 14; Alexis Dudden, *Japan's Colonization of Korea: Discourse and Power* (Honolulu: University of Hawai'i Press, 2005); Jung-en Woo, *Race to the Swift: State and Finance in Korean Industrialization* (New York: Columbia University Press, 1991), chap. 2.

2. For information on the comfort women, see the interesting project of George Washington University, "Memory and Reconciliation in the Asia-Pacific," http://www.gwu.edu/~memory/issues/comfortwomen/index.html.

3. Victor D. Cha, "Hate, Power, and Identity in Japan-Korea Security: Toward a Synthetic Material-Ideational Analytical Framework," *Australian Journal of International Affairs* 54 no. 3 (2000): 313–17; Victor D. Cha, "Hypotheses on History and Hate in Asia: Japan and the Korean Peninsula," in *Reconciliation in the Asia-Pacific*, ed. Yoichi Funabashi (Washington, DC: U.S. Institute of Peace, 2003), 41–44.

4. These five problems are described in most reviews of the negotiations that took place prior to the normalization agreement of 1965. See, e.g., Shigeru Oda, "The Normalization of Relations between Japan and the Republic of Korea," *American Journal of International Law* 61, no. 1 (January 1967): 35–56; Kwan Bong Kim, *The Korea-Japan Treaty Crisis and the Instability of the Korean Political System* (New York: Praeger, 1971), chap. 2.

5. Sung-hwa Cheong, "The Politics of Antagonism: The Case of the First Conference for Normalization of Diplomatic Relationships between Japan and South Korea, 1951–1952," *Asian Perspective* 14, no. 2 (fall–winter 1990): 190.

6. Oda, "Normalization of Relations between Japan and the Republic of Korea," 41.

7. For the details surrounding the crisis, see Chung-in Moon, "International Quasi-Crisis: Theory and a Case of Japan–South Korean Bilateral Friction," *Asian Perspective* 15, no. 2 (fall–winter 1991): 99–123.

8. For a detailed account, see Seung K. Ko, "South Korean–Japanese Relations since the 1965 Normalization Pacts," *Modern Asian Studies* 6, no. 1 (1972): 51–54.

9. Bae-ho Hahn, "Korea-Japan Relations in the 1970s," *Asian Survey* 20, no. 1 (November 1980): 1089.

10. Data from Dong-kuen Jeong, "A Study of Changes in Korea's Bilateral Trade Structure with Japan and the United States," *Asian Profile* 23, no. 3 (June 1995): 215–16.

11. Brian Bridges, *Japan and Korea in the 1990s: From Antagonism to Adjustment* (Aldershot, UK: Edward Elgar, 1993), 13–17.

12. Data from the Web site of the Japanese External Trade Organization (JETRO) http://www.jetro.go.jp/jpn/stats/data/pdf/trade2005.pdf (entered July 1, 2008).

13. Victor D. Cha, *Alignment Despite Antagonism: The U.S.-Korea-Japan Security Triangle* (Stanford, CA: Stanford University Press, 1999), 124–27.

14. Bridges, *Japan and Korea in the 1990s*, 138–39.

15. A lot has been written on this issue of persistent antipathy toward the Japanese. See, e.g., Cha, "Hate, Power, and Identity in Japan-Korea Security"; O. Sonfa, "The Cultural Roots of Japanese-Korean Friction," *Japan Echo* 20 (1993): 23–28; Won-deog Lee, "A Normal State without Remorse: The Textbook Controversy and Korea-Japan Relations," *East Asia Review* 13, no. 3 (autumn 2001): 21–40; Chunghee Sarah Soh, "Politics of the Victim/Victor Complex: Interpreting South Korea's National Furor over Japanese History Textbooks," *American Asian Review* 21, no. 4 (winter 2003): 145–78; Lewis, "The Japan That Does Not Exist and the Ugly Korean"; Peng Er Lam, "The Apology Issue: Japan's Differing Approaches toward China and South Korea," *American Asian Review* 20, no. 3 (fall 2002): 31–54.

16. Seongho Sheen, "Japan–South Korea Relations: Slowly Lifting the Burden of History?" *Asia Pacific Center for Security Studies*, Occasional Papers Series, October 2003.

17. Cha, "Hypotheses on History and Hate in Asia," 48–49.

18. Figures from Japan's Ministry of Foreign Affairs Web site, http://www.mofa.go.jp/asia-paci/korea/index.html (entered July 14, 2008).

19. Jason U. Manosevitz, "Japan and South Korea: Security Relations Reach Adolescence," *Asian Survey* 43, no. 5 (September–October 2003): 801–25. In July 2008, another incident occurred following the expressed intention of the Japanese Ministry of Education to refer in a textbook to the contested islets of Takeshima/Dokto as part of Japan. This led South Korea to recall its ambassador. While the incident was unresolved by the time of the completion of this manuscript, my argument suggests that it reflects the ongoing tensions in relations but is unlikely to severely undermine them.

20. The mixed feelings toward Japan are apparent in a recent survey of undergraduate and graduate South Korean students. More than 30 percent of respondents chose Japan as the country they feel to be most distant from them. At the same time, given the historical context, it is also quite impressive that more 60 percent of respondents did not disagree with the suggestion that Japan should be allowed to rearm through a revision of its constitution (article 9) (5.5 percent strongly agreed, 35.5 percent agreed, and 22.5 percent said maybe). See the results of the survey in Tae-hyo Kim, "South Korea's Security Policy toward Japan: Balancing Perceived Costs and Tangible Benefits," in *U.S.-Korea-Japan Relations: Building Toward a "Virtual Alliance,"* ed. Ralph A. Cossa (Washington, DC: Center for Strategic and International Studies Press, 1999), 110–14.

21. See Cha, "Hate, Power, and Identity in Japan-Korea Security," 315n13.

22. Manosevitz, "Japan and South Korea," 802.

23. Ezra Vogel, *The Four Little Dragons: The Spread of Industrialization in East Asia* (Cambridge, MA: Harvard University Press, 1991), 43.

24. Peter K. Kang, "Political and Corporate Group Interests in South Korea's Political Economy," *Asian Profile* 16 no. 3 (June 1988): 210–13; Bae Ho Hahn, "Policy toward Japan," in *The Foreign Policy of the Republic of Korea*, ed. Youngnok Koo and Sung-joo Han (New York: Columbia University Press, 1985), 176–84.

25. Martin Hart-Landsberg, *The Rush to Development: Economic Change and Political Struggle in South Korea* (New York: Monthly Review Press, 1993), 145. This book is a very critical analysis of South Korea's economic and political development.

26. See, e.g., Hyun-Chin Lim, *Dependent Development in Korea, 1963–1979* (Seoul: Seoul National University Press, 1985).

27. Olson, *Japan in Postwar Asia,* 104.

28. Young-iob Chung, "Chaebol Entrepreneurs in the Early Stage of Korean Economic Development," *Journal of Modern Korean Studies* 2 (December 1985): 17.

29. Ibid., 111; Bae Ho Hahn, "Policy toward Japan," 176.

30. Hart-Landsberg, *Rush to Development,* 150–52.

31. A more critical approach suggests a deliberate Japanese plan to bring the Korean economy under Japanese influence. See for example Dal-Joong Chang, "Integration and Conflict in Japan's Corporate Expansion into South Korea," *Korea and World Affairs* 7, no. 1 (1983): 114–37. Chang compares the strategy of Japanese multinational firms after World War II to that of the Japanese imperial government before the war. See also Dal-Joong Chang, *Economic Control and Political Authoritarianism: The Role of Japanese Corporations in Korean Politics, 1965–1979* (Seoul: Sogang University Press, 1985).

32. Yun-Tae Kim, "The Origins of the Developmental State in South Korea, 1910–1979," *Asian Profile* 26, no. 6 (December 1998): 466–67; Chang-Hee Nam, "South Korea's Big Business Clientelism in Democratic Reform," *Asian Survey* 35, no. 4 (April 1995): 359–60.

33. Kwan Bong Kim, *Korea-Japan Treaty Crisis,* 85–86, 143.

34. Ibid.; Yun-Tae Kim, "Origins of the Developmental State," 469–71. One of the key books examining South Korea's industrialization process is Alice A. Amsden, *Asia's Next Giant: South Korea and Late Industrialization* (Oxford: Oxford University Press, 1989).

35. Bridges, *Japan and Korea in the 1990s,* 10–11.

36. Cha, "Hate, Power, and Identity in Japan-Korea Security," 314–15.

37. Yun-Tae Kim, "Origins of the Developmental State," 465.

38. Chung, "Chaebol Entrepreneurs in the Early Stage of Korean Economic Development," 17.

39. Yun-Tae Kim, "Origins of the Developmental State," 469–71; Peter K. Kang, "Political and Corporate Group Interests in South Korea's Political Economy," 215–17.

40. Kwan Bong Kim, *Korea-Japan Treaty Crisis,* 87–89.

41. Bridges, *Japan and Korea in the 1990s,* 34–38.

42. Yun-Tae Kim, "Origins of the Developmental State," 468–69; Peter K. Kang, "Political and Corporate Group Interests in South Korea's Political Economy," 217–18. For a more detailed analysis of these complex relations, see Mark L. Clifford, *Troubled Tiger: Businessmen, Bureaucrats, and Generals in South Korea* (Armonk, NY: M. E. Sharp, 1994).

43. For an example of this interpretation, see Dal-Joong Chang, *Economic Control and Political Authoritarianism,* 52–133.

44. Kwan Bong Kim, *Korea-Japan Treaty Crisis,* 97, 102.

45. Nam, "South Korea's Big Business Clientelism," 361–63; Bae-ho Hahn, "Korea-Japan Relations in the 1970s," 1090.

46. Cha, "Hate, Power, and Identity in Japan-Korea Security," 313–14.

47. Kwan Bong Kim, *Korea-Japan Treaty Crisis,* 102–8; Alon Levkowitz, "Legitimacy and De-Legitimacy" (master's thesis, Hebrew University, Jerusalem, 1995), 96. The Americans interpreted the antitreaty riots at the time as stemming less from anti-Japanese sentiments than from a public perception that the Korean negotiators, especially Kim

Chong-Pil, were obviously turning the negotiations to their own personal financial profit. See Robert W. Komer, National Security Council staff (Seoul), memo to the president's special assistant for national security affairs (McGeorge Bundy), March 26, 1964, *Foreign Relations of the United States (FRUS)*, 1964–1968, vol. 20, Korea, http://www.state .gov/www/about_state/history/vol_XXIX/b.hotmail.

48. Kwan Bong Kim, *Korea-Japan Treaty Crisis*, 109–16.

49. Bae Ho Hahn, "Policy toward Japan," 174.

50. Cha, *Alignment Despite Antagonism*, 27–28.

51. Bae-ho Hahn, "Korea-Japan Relations in the 1970s," 1091.

52. Kwan Bong Kim, *Korea-Japanese Treaty Crisis*, 89–90.

53. For a more detailed discussion of all the arguments in favor of and against the normalization treaty, see ibid., 96–101.

54. Hans H. Baerwald, "Tensions in Japanese Politics: Coal and Korea," *Asian Survey* 3, no. 4 (April 1963): 182–88.

55. Olson, *Japan in Postwar Asia*, 102–4.

56. On the basic question of whether individuals "liked" or "disliked" Korea, Japanese responses barely changed in opinion polls held in 1984, 1988, and 1990, with 23 percent disliking Korea in the last poll. Bridges, *Japan and Korea in the 1990s*, 23.

57. G. Cameron Hurst III, "Historical Perspectives on Contemporary Japanese-Korean Relations," Universities Field Staff International (UFSI) Reports, no. 10, 1985.

58. Bridges, *Japan-Korea Relations in the 1990s*, 23–24. By contrast, in the same polls, 21 percent of Japanese questioned did not even know that Japan had colonized Korea!

59. The democratization process, especially the changing political-economic realities in South Korea, is nicely described by John Kie-chiang Oh in *Korean Politics: The Quest for Democratization and Economic Development* (Ithaca, NY: Cornell University Press, 1999).

60. Nam, "South Korea's Big Business Clientelism," 364–65.

61. Cha, "Hypotheses on History and Hate in Asia," 48–51.

62. Won-deog Lee, "Normal State without Remorse," 38.

63. http://devdata.worldbank.org (entered December 19, 2005).

64. http://web.worldbank.org/WBSITE/EXTERNAL/DATASTATISTICS (entered November 15, 2008).

65. Data based on table A.I in Cha, *Alignment Despite Antagonism*, 235–36.

66. See Dong-kuen Jeong, "Study on Changes in Korea's Bilateral Trade Structure with Japan and the United States," 221–22, and especially table 8, 218. See also Bridges, *Japan and Korea in the 1990s*, chap. 6.

67. For a classic example, see Dal-Joong Chang, "Integration and Conflict in Japan's Corporate Expansion into South Korea," comparing the activities of Japanese multinational corporations to prewar colonial schemes.

68. Evelyn Colbert, "Japan and the Republic of Korea: Yesterday, Today, and Tomorrow," *Asian Survey* 26, no. 3 (March 1986): 286–87. On the Korean victim complex, see Soh, "Politics of the Victim/Victor Complex."

69. Sonfa, "Cultural Roots of Japanese-Korean Friction," 27–28.

70. Kwan Bong Kim, *Korea-Japan Treaty Crisis*, 103.

71. Quoted in Chong-Sik Lee, "Japanese-Korean Relations in Perspective," *Pacific Affairs* 35, no. 4 (winter 1962–1963): 322.

72. Bridges, *Japan and Korea in the 1990s*, 33.

73. Soong-Hoom Kil, "Two Aspects of Korea-Japan Relations," *Korea and World Affairs* 8, no. 3 (1984): 508.

74. Sheen, "Japan–South Korea Relations," 2.

75. Vogel, *Four Little Dragons*, 59.

76. Cha, "Hate, Power, and Identity in Japan-Korea Security," 315–17. This is what he calls the "quasi alliance argument."

77. Ki-Hoon Kim, "The Development of Contemporary U.S.-ROK Economic Relations," in *U.S.-Korean Relations 1882–1982*, ed. Tae-Hwan Kwak et al. (Seoul: Institute for Far Eastern Studies, Kyungnam University, 1982), 325–28.

78. Cha, *Alignment Despite Antagonism*, 28–30.

79. See, e.g., Herbert P. Bix, "Regional Integration: Japan and South Korea in America's Asian Policy," in *Without Parallel: The American-Korean Relationship since 1945*, ed. Frank Baldwin (New York: Pantheon Books, 1973), 179–232.

80. For a description of the presidential travails vis-à-vis Congress earlier on, see James Irving Matray, *The Reluctant Crusade: American Foreign Policy in Korea, 1941–1950* (Honolulu: University of Hawaii Press, 1985). Once Congress came to be dominated by Republicans, the administration had to deal with the "economy bloc," which constantly stressed the priority of improving the American balance of payments by reducing such external costs. On this problem, see John D. Montgomery, *The Politics of Foreign Aid* (New York: Praeger, 1962); Michael Kent O'Leary, *The Politics of American Foreign Aid* (New York: Atherton Press, 1967); Vernon W. Rutton, *United States Development Assistance Policy: The Domestic Politics of Foreign Economic Aid* (Baltimore: Johns Hopkins University Press, 1996).

81. Sung-hwa Cheong, "Politics of Antagonism," esp. 185–89.

82. Komer memo to Bundy, March 26, 1964.

83. Telegram from the U.S. Embassy in Korea to Department of State, July 6, 1964 (Berger), *Foreign Relations of the US [FRUS] 1964–1968*, vol. 22, Korea, http://www.state .gov/www/about_state/history/vol_xxix/b.html.

84. See J. Mark Mobius, "The Japan-Korea Normalization Process and Korean Anti-Americanism," *Asian Survey* 6, no. 4 (April 1966): 241–48.

85. Aide-mémoire presented by the Korean government to the visiting secretary of state, Dean Rusk, January 29, 1964, *Foreign Relations of the US [FRUS] 1964–1968*, vol. 22, Korea, http://www.state.gov/www/about_state/history/vol_xxix/b.html.

86. Kwan Bong Kim, *Korea-Japan Treaty Crisis*, 78–80; Cha, *Alignment Despite Antagonism*, 30–34.

87. Cha, "Hate, Power, and Identity in Japan-Korea Security," 316.

Chapter 6. The "Classic" Case in Perspective

1. For a good review, see Alistair Cole, *Franco-German Relations* (Harlow, UK: Pearson Education, 2001).

2. See Alan S. Milward, *The Reconstruction of Western Europe, 1945–51* (Berkeley: University of California Press, 1984), 127, 140–41.

3. On the details of the economic logic behind the Schuman Plan, see K. K. F. Zawadzki, "The Economics of the Schuman Plan," *Oxford Economic Papers*, n.s., 5, no. 2 (June 1953): 157–89. See also John A. McKesson, "The Schuman Plan," *Political Science Quarterly* 67, no. 1 (March 1952): 18–35.

4. John Gillingham, *Coal, Steel, and the Rebirth of Europe, 1945–1955: The Germans and French from Ruhr Conflict to Economic Community* (New York: Cambridge University Press, 1991), 224–29.

5. See Alice Ackermann, "Reconciliation as a Peace-Building Process in Postwar Europe: The Franco-German Case," *Peace and Change* 19, no. 3 (July 1994): 239.

6. Frank Roy Willis, *France, Germany, and the New Europe, 1945–1967*, rev. ed. (Oxford: Oxford University Press, 1968), 235–26.

7. Ibid., 262. In fact, most French politicians actually believed the opposite—that the Rome Treaty would isolate France from its natural anti-Germany ally, Britain. See Andrew Moravcsik, *The Choice for Europe: Social Purpose and State Power from Messina to Maastricht* (Ithaca, NY: Cornell University Press, 1998), 118.

8. Quoted in Alfred Grosser, *French Foreign Policy under De Gaulle*, trans. Lois Ames Pattison (Boston: Little, Brown, 1967), 68–72.

9. Julius Friend, *The Linchpin: French-German Relations, 1950–1990* (New York: Praeger, in association with the Center for Strategic and International Studies, 1991), 38–41; Grosser, *French Foreign Policy under De Gaulle*, 72–75. On the progress made, see Federal Foreign Minister Joschka Fischer, speech to the German Bundestag on January 16, 2003, to mark the fortieth anniversary of the Elysée Treaty, http://www.germany.info/relaunch/politics/speeches/011603.htm (entered March 17, 2007).

10. On these developments, see Cole, *Franco-German Relations*, 51–52, 108–13.

11. I adopt Miller's definition of cold peace in this study.

12. Benjamin Miller, *States, Nations, and the Great Powers: The Sources of Regional War and Peace* (Cambridge: Cambridge University Press, 2007), chap. 8. Miller stresses the important role of the changing state-to-nation balance in Europe, primarily with regard to Germany, in the pacification of the region.

13. Norrin M. Ripsman, "Two Stages of Transition from a Region of War to a Region of Peace: Realist Transition and Liberal Endurance," *International Studies Quarterly* 49 (2005): 669–93

14. Marc Trachtenberg, *A Constructed Peace: The Making of the European Settlement, 1945–1963* (Princeton, NJ: Princeton University Press, 1999), 108, 123.

15. Cole, *Franco-German Relations*, 49–51.

16. Willis, *France, Germany, and the New Europe*, 236–40.

17. Friend, *Linchpin*, 41.

18. Willis, *France, Germany, and the New Europe*, 241. For another description of the extent of normalization and reconciliation, see Lily Gardner-Feldman, "The Principle and Practice of 'Reconciliation' in German Foreign Policy: Relations with France, Israel, Poland, and the Czech Republic," *International Affairs* 75, no. 2 (April 1999): 333–56.

19. John E. Farquharson and Stephen C. Holt, *Europe from Below: An Assessment of Franco-German Popular Contacts* (London: Allen & Unwin, 1975), 99–104.

20. See Norrin Ripsman, *Peacemaking by Democracies: The Effect of State Autonomy on the Post–World War Settlements* (University Park: Pennsylvania State University Press, 2002), 185.

21. Data from opinion polls taken by l'Institut Français d'Opinion Publique, cited in Ripsman, "Two Stages of Transition," 685–86.

22. See Friend, *Linchpin*, 23, 37.

23. Donald J. Puchala, "Integration and Disintegration in Franco-German Relations, 1954–1965," *International Organization* 24, no. 2 (spring 1970): 188–91. It is interesting to note that Puchala also finds that, in the early 1960s, there was a gap between the growth in societal sense of community and the growth of political conflicts between the two states.

24. Quoted in Willis, *France, Germany, and the New Europe*, 326.

25. Milward, *Reconstruction of Western Europe*, 127–29. See Gillingham, *Coal, Steel, and the Rebirth of Europe*, 95–96, 137–77, on the Monnet Plan.

26. Günther Kloss, *West Germany: An Introduction*, 2nd ed. (Basingstoke, UK: Macmillan Education, 1990), 112–13.

27. On West Germany's export-led growth strategy, see Michael Kreile, "West Germany: The Dynamics of Expansion," in *Between Power and Plenty*, ed. Katzenstein, 191–224. On Germany's reliance on external markets, see Haig Simonian, *The Privileged Partnership: Franco-German Relations in the European Community, 1969–1984* (Oxford: Clarendon Press, 1985), 18–20.

28. Moravcsik, *Choice for Europe*, chap. 1.

29. Cole, *Franco-German Relations*, 23.

30. Grosser, *French Foreign Policy under De Gaulle*, 2–3.

31. Indeed, there are debates on this question in the literature. See, e.g., Moravcsik, *Choice for Europe*, on commercial interests, and Trachtenberg, *Constructed Peace;* Milward, *Reconstruction of Western Europe;* Ripsman, "Two Stages of Transition"; and Miller, *States, Nations, and the Great Powers*, all of which focus on the strategic logic, at least in the early stages of transition.

32. Willis, *France, Germany, and the New Europe*, 88.

33. Gillingham, *Coal, Steel, and the Rebirth of Europe*, chap. 1.

34. Simonian, *Privileged Partnership*, 20, 61–62.

35. Gillingham, *Coal, Steel, and the Rebirth of Europe*, 62–64.

36. Ibid., 189–204.

37. Willis, *France, Germany, and the New Europe*, 120–22.

38. Ibid., 123–24.

39. Milward, *Reconstruction of Western Europe*, 413, 419.

40. Kloss, *West Germany*, 117–18, 121–23.

41. Ibid., 132–36. For more on industrial relations in Germany, see Peter J. Katzenstein, *Policy and Politics in West Germany: The Growth of a Semisovereign State* (Philadelphia: Temple University Press, 1987), chap. 3.

42. Kreile, "West Germany," 202–3. This issue is also discussed in chapter 7, on German-Polish relations.

43. Gabriel A. Almond, "The Political Attitudes of German Business," *World Politics* 8, no. 2 (January 1956): 176–77.

44. Ripsman, *Peacemaking by Democracies*, 185–86.

45. Willis, *France, Germany, and the New Europe*, 98.

46. Craig Parsons, "Showing Ideas as Causes: The Origins of the European Union," *International Organization* 56, no. 1 (winter 2002): 47–84. For a characterization of the process as being driven by elites, see also Cole, *Franco-German Relations*, 52.

47. Willis, *France, Germany, and the New Europe*, 94–98.

48. For details, see Henry W. Ehrmann, "The French Trade Associations and the Ratification of the Schuman Plan," *World Politics* 6, no. 4 (July 1954): 453–81, esp. 461, 479.

49. Moravcsik, *Choice for Europe*, 89.

50. In fact, French farmers even preferred to strike a bilateral deal with German farmers instead of pursuing a broader European framework. Moravcsik, *Choice for Europe*, 112, 426–27.

51. For detailed descriptions of agricultural interests and the bargaining process leading to the Rome Treaty, see Moravscik, *Choice for Europe*, 98, 110–16, 143–48; Milward, *Reconstruction of Western Europe*, 427–61.

52. Cole, *Franco-German Relations*, 69–71; Moravscik, *Choice for Europe*, 116–18.

53. Milward, *Reconstruction of Europe*, 420.

54. According to an American survey, even in 1944 only 6.5 percent of German manufacturing equipment had been damaged or destroyed. See W. Abelshauser, "Probleme des Wiederaufbaus der westdeutschen Wirtschaft 1945–1953," in *Politische Weichenstellungen im Nachkriegsdeutschland*, ed. H. A. Winkler (Göttingen: Vandenhoeck und

Ruprecht, 1979), 208–54, reprinted in translation in *The Germans, 1945–1990* [in Hebrew], ed. Oded Heilbruner and Moshe Zimmerman (Jerusalem: Magnes Press, Hebrew University, 1998), 103–21.

55. Gillingham, *Coal, Steel, and the Rebirth of Europe*, 60–61, 95–96; Anthony Glees, *Reinventing Germany: German Political Development since 1945* (Oxford: Berg, 1996), 33.

56. Quoted in Friend, *Linchpin*, 18.

57. Willis, *France, Germany, and the New Europe*, 262–64.

58. Cole, *Franco-German Relations*, 86–88.

59. For a thorough analysis of the debate over German rearmament and the Paris Agreements, see Ripsman, *Peacemaking by Democracies*, 190–212.

60. For a concise description of the changing power disparities, especially with the growth of German economic power during the 1970s and 1980s and its impact on political relations with France, see Cole, *Franco-German Relations*, 13–17.

61. Gillingham, *Coal, Steel, and the Rebirth of Europe*, 233.

62. Almond, "Political Attitudes of German Business," 179.

63. Friend, *Linchpin*, 47–48.

64. Renata Fritsch-Bournazel, "German Unification: A Durability Test for the Franco-German Tandem," *German Studies Review* 14, no. 1 (February 1991): 579–80; Alistair Cole, "Looking On: France and the New Germany," *German Politics* 2, no. 3 (December 1993): 358–59.

65. Cole, *Franco-German Relations*, 45–47.

66. For a review, see Cole, "Looking On," 360–73.

67. Moravcsik, however, argues that unification did not dramatically change the pre-existing German support for integration and European activism. Moravcsik, *Choice for Europe*, 387.

68. On the importance of these new strategic circumstances, see Franz Knipping, "Que Faire de l'Alemagne? French Policy toward Germany, 1945–1947," in *France and Germany in an Age of Crisis, 1900–1960*, ed. Haim Shamir (Leiden, Netherlands: E. J. Brill, 1990), 67–84.

69. See, e.g., Melvin P. Leffler, "The United States and the Strategic Dimensions of the Marshall Plan," *Diplomatic History* 12, no. 3 (summer 1988): 277–306.

70. Much has been written on this point. For example, Ripsman argues it was the combination of Soviet military superiority on the continent and the extended U.S. security commitment that made possible the transition to peace between the two countries. Ripsman, "Two Stages of Transition," 9. Miller also argues that American hegemony played a crucial role in creating a window of opportunity to move to peace at the early stage of the transition (which he terms stage II). Miller, *States, Nations, and the Great Powers*. Trachtenberg argues that the American willingness to set up a security system for Western Europe was a key factor shaping France's policy on the German question. Trachtenberg, *Constructed Peace*, 77.

71. The Marshall Plan has been thoroughly studied. Key books describing and analyzing the events surrounding the plan are Michael J. Hogan, *The Marshall Plan: America, Britain, and the Reconstruction of Western Europe, 1947–1952* (Cambridge: Cambridge University Press, 1987); Ernst H. van der Beugel, *From Marshall Aid to Atlantic Partnership: European Integration as a Concern of American Foreign Policy* (Amsterdam: Elsevier, 1966); Pascaline Winand, *Eisenhower, Kennedy, and the United States of Europe* (New York: St. Martin's Press, 1993); Harry Bayard Price, *The Marshall Plan and Its Meaning* (Ithaca, NY: Cornell University Press, 1955); Max Beloff, *The United States and the Unity of Europe* (Washington, DC: Brookings Institution, 1963); John Gimbel,

The Origins of the Marshall Plan (Stanford, CA: Stanford University Press, 1976); and Milward, *Reconstruction of Western Europe*.

72. Milward, *Reconstruction of Western Europe*, 140–41; Gimbel, *Origins of the Marshall Plan*, chap. 1.

73. For the European debates and American position during the Paris conference and afterward, see Hogan, *Marshall Plan*, chaps. 2 and 3.

74. Hogan, *Marshall Plan*, 197–99; Beloff, *United States and the Unity of Europe*, chap. 1.

75. Milward, *Reconstruction of Western Europe*, 114–15. Interestingly, the United States also wanted to insert an MFN clause regarding Japan but met staunch British opposition and had to withdraw on the issue.

76. Press-Barnathan, *Organizing the World*, 183–86; Beloff, *United States and the Unity of Europe*, 39–40.

77. Gillingham, *Coal, Steel, and the New Europe*, 234.

78. Beugel, *From Marshall Aid to Atlantic Partnership*, 230–48.

79. Milward, *Reconstruction of Western Europe*, 363, 426–27, 474–75.

80. For a good, concise description of the evolving partnership of France and Germany within Europe see Friend, *Linchpin*.

81. Simonian, *Privileged Partnership*, 377–78.

82. Parsons, "Showing Ideas as Causes," 73.

Chapter 7. From Enemies to Partners

1. Timothy Garton Ash, *In Europe's Name: Germany and the Divided Continent* (New York: Vintage Books, 1994), 217–18. Ash also notes that the post-1945 Polish and German historiographies of the prewar period were like distorted mirror images of each other. Ibid., 220.

2. For a good review, see W. W. Kulski, *Germany and Poland: From War to Peaceful Relations* (Syracuse, NY: Syracuse University Press, 1976), chap. 1.

3. For descriptions of the Warsaw Treaty and how it was perceived in the media at the time, see S. Szechanowski, "The Polish-West German Treaty," *Poland and Germany (East & West)* [London] 14, no. 3–4 (53–54) (July–December 1970): 3–9; "Press Notes: The Polish–West Germany Treaty," in the same volume, 43–63.

4. Jeanne Lavon Jensen, "Cooperation and Conflict in the Normalization of Relations between the People's Republic of Poland and the Federal Republic of Germany" (PhD diss., University of South Carolina, 1985), 125.

5. Ash, *In Europe's Name*, 237–40.

6. For details on the evolving economic cooperation between the two states in the 1970s and 1980s, see Erhard Cziomer, "The Main Issues of Economic Cooperation between Poland and the Federal Republic in the 1970s and 1980s," *Polish Western Affairs* 30, no. 1 (1989): 51–62.

7. Poland insisted that the border issue be resolved before it recognized German reunification.

8. Randall E. Newnham, *Poland and Germany, 1989–1991: The Role of Economic Factors in Foreign Policy* (Treadgold Studies No. 26, Henry M. Jackson School of International Studies, University of Washington, 2000), 46–59, 66.

9. See Joanna M. M. Kepka, "The Nysa Euroregion: The First Ten Years," *Eurasian Geography and Economics* 45, no. 3 (2004): 162–89; Stefan Krätke, "Regional Integration or Fragmentation? The German-Polish Border Region in a New Europe," *Regional Studies* 33, no. 7 (October 1999): 631–41.

10. For a detailed description of the various cooperation initiatives, see Davis, *Art of Economic Persuasion,* chaps. 3 and 4.

11. A term coined in 1991 by the Polish foreign minister, Krzysztof Skubiszewski. See Roland Freudenstein, "Poland, Germany, and the EU," *International Affairs* 74, no. 1 (1998): 41–54.

12. On these problems, see Christoph-Benedikt Scheffel, "Problems and Conflicts of Interest in German-Polish Relations at the Turn of the Century," *Polish Foreign Affairs Digest* 3, no. 2 (7) (2003): 187–206. For a more pessimistic view of the current state of relations, see Anna Wolff-Pow?ska, "Poland-Germany: Partnership from a Distance," *Polish Foreign Affairs Digest* 5, no. 1 (14) (2005): 17–36.

13. Adrian Hyde-Price, "Stable Peace in Mitteleuropa: The German-Polish Hinge," in *Stable Peace among Nations,* ed. Kacowicz et al., 260–62. Hyde-Price uses the typology of Alexander George, according to which "precarious peace" refers to a situation when peace is little more than the temporary absence of war and depends on immediate deterrence, "conditional peace" reflects a situation in which general deterrence plays the predominant and effective role in maintaining peace, and "stable peace" reflects a situation in which both states consider it unthinkable to use military force. See Alexander George's foreword to *Stable Peace among Nations,* ed. Kacowicz et al.

14. Kulski, *Germany and Poland,* 90–92.

15. For a list of the sixty-one agreements that were signed between the two states by June 17, 1991, see Kryzysztof Bałon, "Annex 1: A list of International Agreements between the Republic of Poland and the Federal Republic of Germany, Signed by June 17 1991," in "Consequences of the Treaty between the Republic of Poland and the Federal Republic of Germany on Good Neighbourliness, Friendship, and Co-operation of June 17, 1991," ed. Włodzimierz Borodziej, *Polish Foreign Affairs Digest* 2, no.1 (2) (2002): 237–45.

16. Kulski, *Germany and Poland,* 133–36; Laszlo Görgey, *Bonn's Eastern Policy, 1964–1971: Evolution and Limitations* (Hamden, CT: Archon Books, 1972), 8–10.

17. Quoted in Görgey, *Bonn's Eastern Policy, 1964–1971,* 30–37.

18. Ash, *In Europe's Name,* 298–311.

19. For details regarding the nearly two years of negotiations leading up to the Warsaw Treaty, see Kulski, *Germany and Poland,* chaps. 10 and 11, and on normalization, 271.

20. Ann L. Phillips, *Power and Influence after the Cold War: Germany in East-Central Europe* (Lanham, MD: Rowman and Littlefield, 2000), 97.

21. Data from http://www.auswaertiges-amt.de/diplo/en/Laenderinformationen/01-Laender/Polen.html (entered July 10, 2008).

22. A telling example of the gap between government policies and public sentiments occurred when, on September 12, 2004, Poland's legislature, the Sejm, passed almost unanimously a resolution urging the Polish government to start negotiations with the German government over war reparations, a demand that both governments rejected. On normalization and its limits, see Klaus Ziemer, "Poland and Germany: What Past, What Future?" *Polish Quarterly of International Affairs,* no. 1 (2005).

23. "A History of Hostility between Poland and Germany," *Spiegel Online,* June 20, 2007, http://www.spiegel.de/international/europe/0,1518,druck-489510,00.html (entered December 24, 2007).

24. See: "EU Leaders Agree New Treaty Deal," http://newsvote.bbc.co.uk/mpapps/pagetools/print/news.bbc.co.uk/2/hi/europe/7051999.stm (entered December 25, 2007); "Reform Treaty Signed," *Warsaw Voice,* December 19, 2007, http://www.warsawvoice.pl/view/16848 (entered December 25, 2007).

25. "A Long List of Cross-Border Salvos," *Spiegel Online,* June 18, 2007, http://www.spiegel.de/international/europe/0,1518,druck-489454,00.html (entered December 24, 2007).

26. Nicholas Kulish, "Memo from the Poland-Germany Border: Once Volatile, Crossing Is Opening with a Whisper," *New York Times,* http://www.nytimes.com/2007/12/20/world/europe/20border.html?_r=1&oref=slogin&ref (entered December 21, 2007).

27. This is the central argument in Davis, *Art of Economic Persuasion,* 16–19. See also Robert Mark Spaulding, *Osthandel and Ostpolitik: German Foreign Trade Policies in Eastern Europe from Bismarck to Adenauer* (Providence, RI: Berghahn Books, 1997), 487. As I describe later, there were economic goals to be advanced as well, but overall Germany's normalization of relations with Poland and Eastern Europe more generally was driven by "high politics." For a good discussion, see Kreile, "West Germany," 204–6.

28. Ash, *In Europe's Name,* 244–45.

29. Görgey, *Bonn's Eastern Policy, 1964–1971,* 19–21.

30. Ibid., 8–10.

31. Davis, *Art of Economic Persuasion,* 71.

32. Ash, *In Europe's Name,* 246.

33. Reinhard Neebe, "German Big Business and the Return to the World Market after World War II," in *Quest for Economic Empire: European Strategies of German Big Business in the Twentieth Century,* ed. Volker R. Berghahn (Providence, RI: Berghahn Books, 1996), 107. See also Robert Mark Spaulding Jr., "'Reconquering Our Old Position': West German Osthandel Strategies of the 1950s," in ibid., 123–41.

34. Quoted in Ash, *In Europe's Name,* 246–47. On the history of German business activities in Eastern Europe, see Spaulding, *Osthandel and Ostpolitik.*

35. Neebe, "German Big Business and the Return to the World Market," 117.

36. Spaulding, "'Reconquering Our Old Position,'" 147.

37. Peter J. Katzenstein, *Mitteleuropa: Between Europe and Germany* (Providence, RI: Berghahn Books, 1997), 19; Kreile, "West Germany," 201–2.

38. Davis, *Art of Economic Persuasion,* 37.

39. Ibid., 37–39, 48–49.

40. Ibid., 74–75.

41. Spaulding, *Osthandel and Ostpolitik,* 8–9. On the development of Polish agriculture during Communist Party rule and after the transition to a market economy and its ongoing crisis, see Silvia Borzutzky and Emmanuel Kranidis, "A Struggle for Survival: The Polish Agricultural Sector from Communism to EU Accession," *East European Politics and Societies* 19, no. 4 (2005): 614–45.

42. Kulski, *Germany and Poland,* 100–102.

43. On this problem, see also Newnham, *Poland and Germany, 1989–1991,* 34; Ash, *In Europe's Name,* 227–30.

44. S. Gomulka, "The New Policy for Poland's Industrialization," *Poland and Germany (East & West)* 19, no. 1–2 (71–72) (January–June 1975): 9.

45. Jensen, "Cooperation and Conflict in the Normalization of Relations," 28–69.

46. Newnham, *Poland and Germany, 1989–1991,* 12–16.

47. See Georg Menz, "Beyond the Anwerbestopp? The German-Polish Bilateral Labor Treaty," *Journal of European Social Policy* 11 (2001): 253–69.

48. Włodek Aniot, Timothy A. Byrnes, and Elena A. Iankova, "Poland: Returning to Europe," in *Mitteleuropa,* ed. Katzenstein, 43.

49. "History of Hostility," *Spiegel Online,* June 20, 2007.

50. Berlin is considered an excellent market to test the popularity of Polish products in Germany because consumers in Berlin are more willing to buy goods from Eastern Europe. See Andrzej Ratajczyk, "Polish Firms Drawn to Germany," *Warsaw Voice*, December 13, 2006.

51. Roland Freudenstein, "The Future of Polish-German Relations," in "Consequences of the Treaty," ed. Borodziej, 176.

52. Newnham, "More Flies with Honey," 84n1.

53. Jensen, "Cooperation and Conflict in the Normalization of Relations," 115-18 (data for the years 1970-1977).

54. Kepka, "Nysa Euroregion," 168, table 2.

55. Bronislaw Sulimierski, "Issues in Financial and Investment Relations between Poland and Germany," *Russian & East European Finance and Trade* 31, no. 4 (July-August 1995): 1-2.

56. Borodziej, "Consequences of the Treaty," 151.

57. Freudenstein, "Future of Polish-German Relations," 175.

58. Newnham, *Poland and Germany, 1989-1991*, 64-65.

59. Kepka, "Nysa Euroregion," 174-75. For more on the problems of regional cooperation in the border region, see Krätke, "Regional Integration or Fragmentation?"

60. Quoted in Newnham, *Poland and Germany, 1989-1991*, 38.

61. The central works dealing with this issue are Newnham, *Poland and Germany, 1989-1991;* Davis, *Art of Economic Persuasion;* Phillips, *Power and Influence after the Cold War;* and Newnham's book on German-Russian relations, *Deutsche Mark Diplomacy: Positive Economic Sanctions in German-Russian Relations* (University Park: Pennsylvania State University Press, 2002).

62. Hirschman himself applies his pathbreaking theory to the case of Nazi Germany and how it used its foreign trade as a tool of national power vis-à-vis its neighbors. See Hirschman, *National Power and the Structure of Foreign Trade*, chap. 2.

63. Described in Newnham, *Poland and Germany, 1989-1991*, 21-41.

64. Hyde-Price also argues that the key material factor that complicated the process of transition to stable peace is the socioeconomic disparities between the two states and their asymmetric power relationship. See Hyde-Price, "Stable Peace in Mitteleuropa," 259.

65. Zdzisław Nowak, "Changes in Economic Relations between Poland and the Federal Republic of Germany," *Polish Western Affairs*, no. 2 (1984): 244-45.

66. See Gardner-Feldman, "Principle and Practice of 'Reconciliation' in German Foreign Policy," 353.

67. Douglas Selvage, "The Treaty of Warsaw: The Warsaw Pact Context," *GHI Bulletin Supplement* 1 (2003).

68. Wayne C. Thompson, "Germany and the East," *Europe-Asia Studies*, 53, no. 6 (September 2001): 929, 933.

69. Jerzy Kranz, "Germany, Quo Vadis? A View from Poland," *German Politics* 10 (April 2001): 141-54.

70. Handl Vladimir, "Comparative Czech and Polish Perspectives and Policies on the Eastern Enlargement of the EU and the Prominence of the German Factor," Research Support Scheme 2000, 28-30, http://e-lib.rss.cz (downloaded December 2007).

71. Quoted in Sarah Meiklejohn Terry, "Poland's Foreign Policy since 1989: The Challenges of Independence," *Communist and Post-Communist Studies* 33 (2000): 11.

72. See Peter J. Katzenstein, "United Germany in an Integrating Europe"; Simon J. Bulmer, "Shaping the Rules? The Constitutive Politics of the European Union and German Power"; and Jeffrey J. Anderson, "Hard Interests, Soft Power, and Germany's Changing Role in Europe," all in *Tamed Power: Germany in Europe*, ed. Peter J. Katzenstein (Ithaca, NY: Cornell University Press, 1997).

73. Hyde-Price, "Stable Peace in Mitteleuropa," 268–70.

74. Marcin Zaborowski, *Germany, Poland, and Europe: Conflict, Co-operation, and Europeanisation* (Manchester, UK: Manchester University Press, 2004), 176.

75. Tytus Jaskułowski, "Poland's Relations with Germany," *Yearbook of Polish Foreign Policy,* 2006.

76. "EU Leaders Agree New Treaty Deal," BBC News, http://newsvote.bbc.co.uk/mpapps/paagetools/print/news.bbc.co.uk/2/hi/europe/7051999.stm (entered December 25, 2007).

77. Quoted in Gardner-Feldman, "Principle and Practice of 'Reconciliation' in German Foreign Policy," 337.

78. On the German reaction to the Solidarity crisis, see Ash, *In Europe's Name,* 94.

Chapter 8. Politics, Economics, and Peace

1. See Markus E. Bouillon, *The Peace Business: Money and Power in the Palestine-Israel Conflict* (London: I. B. Tauris, 2004), 68.

2. Another classic illustration of the importance of a ruling coalition with a liberalizing orientation is the starting point of the transition to peace between Chile and Argentina. There as well, one important reason for the transition was General Augusto Pinochet's adoption of a liberalizing-economic strategy, which required the expansion of foreign trade and investment, which in turn led to greater policy moderation.

3. During the negotiations at Camp David in September 1978, Prime Minister Begin managed to upset President Sadat by arguing that "the people of Egypt could be easily manipulated by Sadat, and their beliefs and attitudes could be shaped by their leader." This view regarding public opinion in the Arab world was common in both Israel and the United States. Quoted in Shibley Telhami, *The Stakes: American in the Middle East; The Consequences of Power and the Choice for Peace* (Boulder, CO: Westview Press, 2002), 67–68.

4. Bouillon, "Failure of Big Business," 3, 15, 16. On the power of corrupt Palestinian monopolies, see also Glenn E. Robinson, "The Growing Authoritarianism of the Arafat Regime," *Survival* 39, no. 2 (summer 1997); Adel Samara, "Globalization, the Palestinian Economy, and the 'Peace Process'," *Journal of Palestine Studies* 29, no. 2 (winter 2000): 20–34; Peter Lagerquist, "Privatizing the Occupation: The Political Economy of an Oslo Development Project," *Journal of Palestine Studies* 32, no. 2 (winter 2003): 5–20; Talya Einhorn, "The Customs Union between Israel and the Palestinian Authority," *Mechkarey Mishpat* [in Hebrew], 14, no. 2 (1998): 439–75.

5. Guy Ben-Porat, "Business and Peace: The Rise and Fall of the New Middle East," *Encounters* 1, no. 1 (2005): 47.

6. Jodi Nachtwey and Mark Tessler, "The Political Economy of Attitudes toward Peace among Palestinians and Israelis," *Journal of Conflict Resolution* 46, no. 2 (April 2002): 260–85.

7. The reader may recall that, in the 1980s, the West German government apparently preferred stability in Poland to democratization because it chose to endorse the declaration of martial law following the Solidarity crisis and to continue building its economic ties with Poland under General Jaruzelski. A more nuanced examination of the difficulties of peacemaking by democracies (one that also examines the Franco-German case) is Ripsman, *Peacemaking by Democracies.* A good example of an analysis of the role of domestic economic groups in Germany is Neebe, "German Big Business and the Return to the World Market after World War II."

8. See Arie M. Kacowicz, "Stable Peace in South America: The ABC Triangle, 1979–1999," in *Stable Peace among Nations,* ed. Kacowicz et al., 200–219; David R. Mares,

"Exploring the Impact of Economic Cooperation on Political and Security Relations between Argentina and Chile," in *Economic Cooperation and Regional Security,* ed. Michael Krepon and Chris Gagne, Report 36, Henry Stimson Center, October 2000, http://www.stimson.org (entered December 5, 2007).

9. See, e.g., E. C. Murphy, "Israel and the Palestinians: The Economic Rewards of Peace?" (Centre for Middle Eastern and Islamic Studies, University of Durham, 1995); A. Arnon and S. Weinblatt, "Sovereignty and Economic Development: The Case of Israel and Palestine," *Economic Journal* 111, no. 472 (2001): 291–308; Jan Selby, "Dressing Up Domination as 'Cooperation': The Case of Israeli-Palestinian Water Relations," *Review of International Studies* 29 (2003): 121–38; Mohammad Shtayyeh, *Israel in the Region: Conflict, Hegemony, or Cooperation?* (Jerusalem: Palestinian Economic Council for Development and Reconstruction, 1998); Mohammad Shtayyeh, *The Benelux: A Paradigm for the Middle East?* (papers and proceedings of "The Benelux Model: A Paradigm for the Middle East?" conference, October 1997, Palestinian Center for Regional Studies, Al-Bireh, 1998).

10. On these problems, see Bent D. Jørgensen, "South Asia: An Anxious Journey towards Regionalization?" in *Regionalization in a Globalizing World: A Comparative Perspective on Forms, Actors, and Processes,* ed. Michael Schultz, Fredrik Söderbaum, and Joakim Öjendal (London and New York: Zed Books, 2001), 140–41; Poonam Barua, "Economic CBMs between India and Pakistan," in *Crisis Prevention, Confidence Building, and Reconciliation in South Asia,* ed. Michael Krepon and Amit Sevak (New York: St. Martin's Press, 1996), 163–65; Haris Gazdar, "The Economics of Accommodation," *Himāl Southasian,* July 2006, http://www.himalmag.com/2006/july/analysis1.htm (entered January 8, 2008).

11. On this issue, see Nissim Kadosh Otmazgin, "Contesting Soft Power: Japanese Popular Culture in East and Southeast Asia," *International Relations of the Asia Pacific* 8 (2008): 73–101; Katzenstein, *World of Regions,* chap. 5.

12. On the American logic linking the Marshall Plan and the pacification of Western Europe, see Press-Barnathan, *Organizing the World,* chap. 8.

13. Excerpt from the 9/11 Commission Report is cited in USTR press release, "United States and Oman Sign Free Trade Agreement," January 19, 2006, http://www.ustr.gov.

14. For a good overview of the MEFTA plan and achievements so far, see Catherine Novelli, assistant U.S. trade representative for Europe and the Mediterranean, "Middle East Free Trade Area (MEFTA) Two Years Later," Foreign Press Center Briefing, Washington, DC, May 6, 2005, http://fpc.state.gov/fpc/45701.htm; Alan Larson, undersecretary for economic, business, and agricultural Affairs, testimony before the Senate Finance Committee, Washington, DC, March 10, 2004, "United States Economic and Trade Policy in the Middle East," http://www.state.gov/e/rls/rm/2004/30346.htm. More information on MEFTA appears on the official Web site of the U.S. Trade Representative at http://www.ustr.gov.

BIBLIOGRAPHY

Books and Articles

Abdelal, Rawi, and Jonathan Kirshner. "Strategy, Economic Relations, and the Definition of National Interests." *Security Studies* 9, no. 1–2 (1999–2000): 119–56.

Abelshauser, W. "Probleme des Wiederaufbaus der westdeutschen Wirtschaft 1945–1953." In *Politische Weichenstellungen im Nachkriegsdeutschland,* edited by H. A. Winkler, 208–54. Göttingen: Vandenhoeck und Ruprecht, 1979. Reprinted in translation in *The Germans, 1945–1990* [in Hebrew], edited by Oded Heilbruner and Moshe Zimmerman, 103–21. Jerusalem: Magnes Press, Hebrew University, 1998.

Abu-Jabara, Hani. "The Economics of Peace: Jordan." In *The Economics of Middle East Peace: Views from the Region,* edited by Stanley Fischer, Dani Rodrik, and Elias Tuma, 181–99. Cambridge, MA: MIT Press, 1993.

Acharya, Amitav. "Collective Identity and Conflict Management in Southeast Asia." In *Security Communities,* edited by Emanuel Adler and Michael Barnett, 198–227. Cambridge: Cambridge University Press, 1998.

Ackerman, Alice. "Reconciliation as a Peace-Building Process in Postwar Europe: The Franco-German Case." *Peace and Change* 19, no. 3 (July 1994): 229–50.

Adler, Emanuel, and Michael Barnett. "A Framework for the Study of Security Communities." In *Security Communities,* edited by Emanuel Adler and Michael Barnett, 29–66. Cambridge: Cambridge University Press, 1998.

Ala'i, Padideh, Tomer Broude, and Colin Picker, eds. *Trade as Guarantor of Peace, Liberty, and Security? Critical, Historical, and Empirical Perspectives.* Washington, DC: American Society of International Law, 2006.

Almond A., Gabriel. "The Political Attitudes of German Business." *World Politics* 8, no. 2 (January 1956): 157–86.

Al-Sayyid, Mustapha K. "A Civil Society in Egypt?" *Middle East Journal* 47, no. 2 (spring 1993): 228–42.

Amsden, Alice A. *Asia's Next Giant: South Korea and Late Industrialization.* Oxford: Oxford University Press, 1989.

Aniot, Włodek, Timothy A. Byrnes, and Elena A. Iankova. "Poland: Returning to Europe." In *Mitteleuropa: Between Europe and Germany,* edited by Peter J. Katzenstein, 39–100. Providence, RI: Berghahn Books, 1997.

Anwar, Dewi Fortuna. "Indonesia's Relations with China and Japan: Images, Perception, and Realities." *Contemporary Southeast Asia* 12, no. 3 (December 1990): 225–46.

Arad, Ruth, Seev Hirsch, and Alfred Tovias. *The Economics of Peacemaking: Focus on the Egyptian-Israeli Situation.* London: Macmillan, 1983.

Arase, David. *Buying Power: The Political Economy of Japan's Foreign Aid.* Boulder, CO: Lynne Rienner, 1995.

Arnon, Arie, Avia Spivak, and J. Weinblatt. "The Potential for Trade between Israel, the Palestinians, and Jordan." *World Economy* 19, no. 1 (1996): 113–34.

Ash, Timothy Garton. *In Europe's Name: Germany and the Divided Continent.* New York: Vintage Books, 1994.

Atarashi, Kinju. "Japan's Economic Cooperation Policy towards the ASEAN Countries." *International Affairs* 61, no. 1 (winter 1984–1985): 109–27.

Awartani, Hisham, and Ephraim Kleiman. "Economic Interaction among Participants in the Middle East Peace Process." *Middle East Journal* 51, no. 2 (spring 1997): 215–29.

Baerwald, Hans H. "Tensions in Japanese Politics: Coal and Korea." *Asian Survey* 3, no. 4 (April 1963): 182–88.

Bahiri, Simcha, et al. *Israeli-Palestinian-Jordanian Trade Relations.* Israel/Palestine Center for Research and Information (IPCRI) and Konrad-Adenaur-Stiftung, September 1997.

Baker, Richard W., and M. Hadi Soesastro. "Conclusion." In *Indonesia: The Challenge of Change,* edited by Richard W. Baker, M. Hadi Soesastro, J. Kristiadi, and Douglas E. Ramage, 255–71. Leiden, Netherlands: KITLV Press, 1999.

Barbieri, Katherine. *The Liberal Illusion: Does Trade Promote Peace?* Ann Arbor: University of Michigan Press, 2002.

———, and Gerald Schneider. "Globalization and Peace: Assessing New Directions in the Study of Trade and Conflict." *Journal of Peace Research* 36, no. 4 (1999): 387–404.

Barkai, Haim. "Egypt's Economic Constraints." *Jerusalem Quarterly* 14 (winter 1980): 112–44.

Barnett, Michael N. *Confronting the Costs of War: Military Power, State, and Society in Egypt and Israel.* Princeton, NJ: Princeton University Press, 1992.

Bar-Siman-Tov, Yaacov. "Dialectics between Stable Peace and Reconciliation." In *From Conflict Resolution to Reconciliation,* edited by Yaacov Bar-Siman-Tov, 61–80. New York: Oxford University Press, 2004.

———. *Israel and the Peace Process, 1977–1982: In Search of Legitimacy for Peace.* Albany: State University of New York Press, 1994.

———. "Israel-Egypt Peace: Stable Peace?" In *Stable Peace among Nations,* ed. Arie M. Kacowicz et al., 220–38. Lanham, MD: Rowman and Littlefield, 2000.

Bar-Tal, Daniel, and Gemma H. Bennink. "The Nature of Reconciliation as an Outcome and as a Process." In *From Conflict Resolution to Reconciliation,* edited by Yaacov Bar-Siman-Tov, 11–38. New York: Oxford University Press, 2004.

Bearce, David H. "Grasping the Commercial Institutional Peace." *International Studies Quarterly* 47, no. 3 (2003): 347–70.

Ben-Porat, Guy. "Between Power and Hegemony: Business Communities in the Peace Process." *Review of International Studies* 31, no. 2 (April 2005): 325–48.

———. "A New Middle East? Globalization, Peace, and the 'Double Movement'." *International Relations* 19, no. 1 (2005): 39–62.

Ben-Shahar, Haim, Gideon Fishelson, and Seev Hirsch. *Economic Cooperation and Middle East Peace.* London: Weidenfeld and Nicolson, 1989.

Berghahn, Volker R., ed. *Quest for Economic Empire: European Strategies of German Big Business in the Twentieth Century.* Providence, RI: Berghahn Books, 1996.

Bix, Herbert P. "Regional Integration: Japan and South Korea in America's Asian Policy." In *Without Parallel: The American-Korean Relationship since 1945,* edited by Frank Baldwin, 179–232. New York: Pantheon Books, 1973.

Blainey, Geoffrey. *The Causes of War.* 3rd ed. New York: Free Press, 1988.

Blanchard, Jean-Marc, Edward D. Mansfield, and Norrin M. Ripsman, eds. *Power and the Purse: Economic Statecraft, Interdependence, and National Security.* London: Frank Cass, 2000.

Bookmiller, Robert J. "Abdullah's Jordan: America's Anxious Ally." *Alternatives: Turkish Journal of International Relations* 2, no. 2 (summer 2003). http://www.alternatives journal.net/volume2/number2/robert.htm.

Borden, William. *The Pacific Alliance: United States Foreign Economic Policy and Japanese Trade Recovery, 1947–1955.* Madison: University of Wisconsin Press, 1984.

Borodziej, Włodzimierz, ed. "Consequences of the Treaty between the Republic of Poland and the Federal Republic of Germany on Good Neighbourliness, Friendship and Co-operation of June 17, 1991." *Polish Foreign Affairs Digest* 2, no.1 (2) (2002): 144–282.

Borzutzky, Silvia, and Emmanuel Kranidis. "A Struggle for Survival: The Polish Agricultural Sector from Communism to EU Accession." *East European Politics and Societies* 19, no. 4 (2005): 614–45.

Bouillon, Markus E. "The Failure of Big Business: On the Socio-Economic Reality of the Middle East Peace Process." *Mediterranean Politics* 9, no. 1 (spring 2004): 1–28.

Boulding, Kenneth E. *Stable Peace.* Austin: University of Texas Press, 1978.

Boyce, James K. *The Philippines: The Political Economy of Growth and Impoverishment in the Marcos Era.* Basingstoke, UK: Macmillan, 1993.

Brand, Laurie A. "The Effects of the Peace Process on Political Liberalization in Jordan." *Journal of Palestine Studies* 28, no. 2 (winter 1999): 52–67.

———. *Jordan's Inter-Arab Relations: The Political Economy of Alliance Making.* New York: Columbia University Press, 1994.

Brary, Hasan A. "Jordan and Israel: A Decade after the Peace Treaty." In *Neighbors in a Maze: Israel-Jordan Relations before the Peace Treaty and After,* edited by Yoseph Nevo [in Hebrew; essay originally in English]. Tel Aviv: Yitzhak Rabin Center for the Study of Israel, 2004.

Bridges, Brian. *Japan and Korea in the 1990s: From Antagonism to Adjustment.* Aldershot, UK: Edward Elgar, 1993.

Brunk, Conrad G. "Shaping a Vision: The Nature of Peace Studies." In *Patterns of Conflict, Paths to Peace,* edited by Larry J. Fisk and John L. Schellenberg, 11–34. Toronto: Broadview Press, 2000.

Bruton, Henry. *The Promise of Peace: Economic Cooperation between Egypt and Israel.* Washington, DC: Brookings Institution, 1981.

Buzan, Barry, Ole Weaver, and Jaap de Wilde. *Security: A New Framework for Analysis.* Boulder, CO: Lynne Rienner, 1998.

Cha, Victor D. *Alignment Despite Antagonism: The U.S.-Korea-Japan Security Triangle.* Stanford, CA: Stanford University Press, 1999.

———. "Hate, Power, and Identity in Japan-Korea Security: Towards a Synthetic Material-Ideational Analytical Framework." *Australian Journal of International Affairs* 54, no. 3 (November 2000): 309–23.

———. "Hypotheses on History and Hate in Asia: Japan and the Korean Peninsula." In *Reconciliation in the Asia-Pacific,* edited by Yoichi Funabashi, 37–60. Washington, DC: U.S. Institute of Peace, 2003.

Chang, Dal-Joong. *Economic Control and Political Authoritarianism: The Role of Japanese Corporations in Korean Politics, 1965–1979.* Seoul: Sogang University Press, 1985.

———. "Integration and Conflict in Japan's Corporate Expansion into South Korea." *Korea and World Affairs* 7, no. 1 (1983):114–37.

Chang, Yuan-Ching. "Economic Interdependence and International Interaction: Impact of Third Party Trade on Political Cooperation and Conflict." *Cooperation and Conflict* 40, no. 2 (2005): 207–32.

Cheong, Sung-hwa. "The Politics of Antagonism: The Case of the First Conference for Normalization of Diplomatic Relationships between Japan and South Korea, 1951–1952." *Asian Perspective* 14, no. 2 (fall–winter 1990): 167–94.

Chung, Young-iob. "Chaebol Entrepreneurs in the Early Stage of Korean Economic Development." *Journal of Modern Korean Studies* 2 (December 1985): 15–49.

Clammer, John, and Eyal Ben-Ari. "Japan in Southeast Asia: An Introductory Essay." In *Japan in Singapore: Cultural Occurrences and Cultural Flows,* edited by Eyal Ben-Ari and John Clammer, 1–36. Richmond, Surrey, UK: Curzon Press, 2000.

Clarke, Duncan L. "U.S. Security Assistance to Egypt and Israel: Politically Untouchable?" *Middle East Journal* 51, no. 2 (spring 1997): 200–214.

Clifford, Mark L. *Troubled Tiger: Businessmen, Bureaucrats, and Generals in South Korea.* Armonk, NY: M. E. Sharp, 1994.

Cohen, Theodore. *Remaking Japan: The American Occupation as New Deal.* New York: Free Press, 1987.

Cohen, Warren I. "China in Japanese-American Relations." In *The United States and Japan in the Postwar World,* edited by Akira Iriye and Warren I. Cohen, 36–60. Lexington: University Press of Kentucky, 1989.

Colbert, Evelyn. "Japan and the Republic of Korea: Yesterday, Today, and Tomorrow." *Asian Survey* 26, no. 3 (March 1986): 273–91.

Cole, Alistair. *Franco-German Relations.* Harlow, UK: Pearson Education, 2001.

———. "Looking On: France and the New Germany." *German Politics* 2, no. 3 (December 1993): 358–76.

Copeland, Dale C. "Economic Interdependence and War: A Theory of Trade Expectations." *International Security* 20, no. 4 (spring 1996): 5–41.

———. "Trade Expectations and the Outbreak of Peace: Détente 1970–74 and the End of the Cold War, 1985–91." In *Power and the Purse: Economic Statecraft, Interdependence, and National Security,* edited by Jean-Marc Blanchard, Edward D. Mansfield, and Norrin M. Ripsman, 15–58. London: Frank Cass, 2000.

Corbey, Dorrette. "Dialectical Functionalism: Stagnation as a Booster of European Integration." *International Organization* 49 (1996): 253–84.

Cortright, David. "Incentive Strategies for Preventing Conflict." In *The Price of Peace: Incentives and International Conflict Prevention,* ed. David Cortright. Lanham, MD: Rowman and Littlefield, 1997.

Crouch, Harold. "Generals and Business in Indonesia." *Pacific Affairs* 48, no. 4 (winter 1975–1976): 519–40.

Cziomer, Erhard. "The Main Issues of Economic Cooperation between Poland and the Federal Republic in the 1970s and 1980s." *Polish Western Affairs* 30, no. 1 (1989): 51–62.

Darrat, Ali F., and Sam R. Hakim. "Winners and Losers in the Middle East: The Economics of 'Peace Dividends'." *Middle East Policy* 9, no. 3 (September 2002): 34–39.

Dassa-Kaye, Dalia. *Beyond the Handshake: Multilateral Cooperation in the Arab-Israeli Peace Process, 1991–1996.* New York: Columbia University Press, 2001.

Davis, Patricia A. *The Art of Economic Persuasion: Positive Incentives and German Economic Diplomacy.* Ann Arbor: University of Michigan Press, 1999.

Deutsch, Karl W., et al. *Political Community and the North Atlantic Area: International Organization in the Light of Historical Experience.* Princeton, NJ: Princeton University Press, 1957.

Dingman, Roger. "The Diplomacy of Dependency: The Philippines and Peacemaking with Japan, 1945–1952." *Journal of Southeast Asian Studies* 17, no. 2 (September 1986): 307–21.

Dombrowski, Peter, ed. *Guns and Butter: The Political Economy of International Security.* Boulder, CO: Lynne Rienner, 2005.

Dowek, Ephraim. *Israeli-Egyptian Relations, 1980–2000.* London: Frank Cass, 2001.

Dower, John W. *Empire and Aftermath: Yoshida Shigeru and the Japanese Experience, 1878–1954.* Cambridge, MA: Council on East Asian Studies, Harvard University, 1988.

Drake, Christine. *National Integration in Indonesia: Patterns and Policies.* Honolulu: University of Hawaii Press, 1989.

Drake, Laura. "Arab-Israeli Relations in a New Middle East Order: The Politics of Economic Cooperation." In *The Political Economy of Middle East Peace: The Impact of Competing Trade Agendas,* edited by J. W. Wright Jr., 11–39. London: Routledge, 1998.

Dudden, Alexis. *Japan's Colonization of Korea: Discourse and Power.* Honolulu: University of Hawai'i Press, 2005.

Dumas, Lloyd J. "Finding the Future: The Role of Economic Conversion in Shaping the Twenty-first Century." In *Approaches to Peace: A Reader in Peace Studies,* edited by David Barash, 100–105. New York: Oxford University Press, 2000.

"Egypt: Sector Analysis." June 2003. www.arabdatanet.com/country/profiles/profile.asp? CtryName=Egypt&CtryAbrv=eg&NavTitle=sector%20Analysis (entered December 8, 2005).

El-Din, Gamal Essam. "NDP Rallies to Defend the QIZ." *Al-Ahram Weekly* (on-line), no. 722, December 23–29, 2004.

El-Nahhas, Mona. "Out of the Cold." *Al-Ahram Weekly* (on-line), no. 721, December 16–22, 2004.

Even, Shmuel. "Israeli Natural Gas: The Economic and Strategic Significance." *Strategic Assessment* 4, no. 3 (2001). http://www.tau.ac.il/jcss/sa/v4n3p5Eve.html.

Farquharson, John E., and Stephen C. Holt. *Europe from Below: An Assessment of Franco-German Popular Contacts.* London: Allen & Unwin, 1975.

Fishelson, Gideon. "Regional Economic Cooperation in the Middle East." In *The Arab-Israeli Search for Peace,* edited by Steven L. Spiegel, 103–20. Boulder, CO: Lynn Rienner, 1992.

Freudenstein, Roland. "The Future of Polish-German Relations." In "Consequences of the Treaty between the Republic of Poland and the Federal Republic of Germany on Good Neighbourliness, Friendship, and Co-operation of June 17, 1991," edited by Włodzimierz Borodziej. *Polish Foreign Affairs Digest* 2, no.1 (2) (2002).

———. "Poland, Germany, and the EU." *International Affairs* 74, no. 1 (1998): 41–54.

Friend, Julius W. *The Linchpin: French-German Relations, 1950–1990.* New York: Praeger, in association with the Center for Strategic and International Studies, 1991.

Fritsch-Bournazel, Renata. "German Unification: A Durability Test for the Franco-German Tandem." *German Studies Review* 14, no. 1 (February 1991): 575–86.

Gardner-Feldman, Lily. "The Principle and Practice of 'Reconciliation' in German Foreign Policy: Relations with France, Israel, Poland, and the Czech Republic." *International Affairs* 75, no. 2 (April 1999): 333–56.

Gartzke, Erik, Quan Li, and Charles Boehmer. "Investing in the Peace: Economic Interdependence and International Conflict." *International Organization* 55, no. 2 (spring 2001): 391–438.

Gasiorowski, Mark J. "Economic Interdependence and International Conflict: Some Cross-national Evidence." *International Studies Quarterly* 30, no. 1 (1986): 23–38.

George, Alexander. "Case Studies and Theory Development: The Method of Structured, Focused Comparison." In *Diplomacy: New Approaches in History, Theory, and Policy,* edited by Paul G. Lauren, 43–68. New York: Free Press, 1979.

George Washington University. "Memory and Reconciliation in the Asia-Pacific." http://www.gwu.edu/~memory/issues/comfortwomen/index.html.

Gilbar, Gad. *The Economic Development of the Middle East in Modern Times* [in Hebrew]. Tel Aviv: Ministry of Defense, 1990.

———, and Onn Winckler. "The Economic Factor of the Arab-Israeli Peace Process: The Cases of Egypt, Jordan, and Syria." In *Arab-Jewish Relations: From Conflict to*

Reconciliation? edited by Elie Podeh and Asher Kaufman, 190–209. Brighton and Portland, UK: Sussex Academic Press, 2006.

Gillingham John. *Coal, Steel, and the Rebirth of Europe, 1945–1955: The Germans and French from Ruhr Conflict to Economic Community.* New York: Cambridge University Press, 1991.

Glees, Anthony. *Reinventing Germany: German Political Development since 1945.* Oxford: Berg, 1996.

Golay, Frank H. *The Philippines: Public Policy and National Economic Development.* Ithaca, NY: Cornell University Press, 1961.

Gomulka, S. "The New Policy for Poland's Industrialization." *Poland and Germany (East & West)* 19, no. 1–2 (71–72) (January–June 1975).

Görgey, Laszlo. *Bonn's Eastern Policy, 1964–1971: Evolution and Limitations.* Hamden, CT: Archon Books, 1972.

Greenwood, Scott. "Jordan's 'New Bargain': The Political Economy of Regime Security." *Middle East Journal* 57, no. 1 (2003): 248–68.

Grosser, Alfred. *French Foreign Policy under De Gaulle.* Translated by Lois Ames Pattison. Boston: Little, Brown, 1967.

Haas, Ernest. *The Uniting of Europe: Political, Social, and Economic Forces, 1950–1957.* Stanford, CA: Stanford University Press, 1958.

Hadad, Muhna. "Israel in the Eyes of Jordan after the Peace Treaty: Hope and Illusion." In *Neighbors in a Maze: Israel-Jordan Relations before the Peace Treaty and After* [in Hebrew], edited by Yoseph Nevo. Tel Aviv: Yitzhak Rabin Center for the Study of Israel, 2004.

Hahn, Bae-ho. "Korea-Japan Relations in the 1970s." *Asian Survey* 20, no. 11 (November 1980): 1087–97.

———. "Policy toward Japan." In *The Foreign Policy of the Republic of Korea*, edited by Youngnok Koo and Sung-joo Han, 167–97. New York: Columbia University Press, 1985.

Halevi, Nadav. *Trade Links between Israel and Jordan: Prospects and Considerations.* Tel Aviv: Armand Hammer Fund for Economic Cooperation in the Middle East, June 1994.

Handl, Vladimir. "Comparative Czech and Polish Perspectives and Policies on the Eastern Enlargement of the EU and the Prominence of the German Factor." Research Support Scheme 2000. http://e-lib.rss.cz (entered December 2007).

Handoussa, Heba, and Nemat Shafik. "The Economics of Peace: The Egyptian Case." In *The Economics of Middle East Peace: Views from the Region,* edited by Stanley Fischer, Dani Rodrik, and Elias Tuma, 20–28. Cambridge, MA: MIT Press, 1993.

Harari, Ehud. "Peace and Regional Integration of Former Enemies: Japan and Israel." Paper presented at the International Relations Department Seminar, Hebrew University of Jerusalem, February 1999.

Hardjosoekarto, Sudarsono. "Japan's Role in Indonesia's Development." *Indonesian Quarterly* 21, no. 4 (1993): 410–33.

Hart-Landsberg, Martin. *The Rush to Development: Economic Change and Political Struggle in South Korea.* New York: Monthly Review Press, 1993.

Hashem, Amr, and Noha El-Mikawy. "Business Parliamentarians as Locomotives of Information and Production of Knowledge." In *Institutional Reform and Economic Development in Egypt,* edited by Noha El-Mikawy and Heba Handoussa. Cairo: American University Press, 2002.

Hayden, Joseph Ralston. *The Philippines: A Study in National Development.* New York: Macmillan, 1942.

Hegre, Håvard. "Development and the Liberal Peace: What Does It Take to Be a Trading State?" *Journal of Peace Research* 37, no. 1 (2000): 5–30.

———. "Size Asymmetry, Trade, and Militarized Conflict." *Journal of Peace Research* 48, no. 3 (2004): 403–29.

Hellman, Donald C. "Japan and Southeast Asia: Continuity amidst Change." *Asian Survey* 19, no. 12 (December 1979): 1189–98.

Hinnebusch, Raymond A. "Egypt under Sadat: Elites, Power Structure, and Political Change in a Post-Populist State." *Social Problems* 28, no. 4 (April 1981): 445–59.

Hiroyoshi, Kano. "Indonesian Business Groups and Their Leaders." *East Asian Cultural Studies* 28, no. 1–4 (1989): 145–72.

Hirsch, Boaz. "The Improved Trade Agreement between Israel and Jordan." http://www.moit.gov.il (entered November 7, 2005).

Hirsch, Seev, and Niron Hashai. "The Trade Potential between Israel and Arab States in Distance-Sensitive Products." In *Israel at the Beginning of the Twenty-first Century: Society, Law, Economy, and Media* [in Hebrew], edited by Hillel Nossek, 289–325. Tel Aviv: Cherikover Publishers, 2002.

Hirschman, Albert. *National Power and the Structure of Foreign Trade.* 1945. 2nd ed. Berkeley: University of California Press, 1980.

Hurst, G. Cameron, III. "Historical Perspectives on Contemporary Japanese-Korean Relations." Universities Field Staff International (UFSI) Reports, no. 10, 1985.

Hyde-Price, Adrian. "Stable Peace in Mitteleuropa: The German-Polish Hinge." In *Stable Peace among Nations,* edited by Arie M. Kacowicz et al., 257–76. Lanham, MD: Rowman and Littlefield, 2000.

Ibrahim, Fouad N., and Barbara Ibrahim. *Egypt: An Economic Geography.* London: I. B. Tauris, 2003.

Ichimura, Shin'ichi. "Japan and Southeast Asia." *Asian Survey* 20, no. 7 (July 1980): 754–62.

Islam, Iyanatul, and Anis Chowdhury. *Asia-Pacific Economies: A Survey.* London: Routledge, 1997.

Israel. Ministry of Industry and Trade. "Explanations of the QIZ Agreement Israel-Egypt–United States" [in Hebrew].

———. Ministry of Industry, Trade, and Tourism Newsletter, Foreign Trade Administration, no. 39, January 2005. http://www.moit.gov.il/NR/exeres/A50D1EE6-F11D-4EA9-AD6C31DD1FD66825.htm.

Jaffee Center for Strategic Studies. "Progress or Breakdown in the Middle East Peace Process." May 2000, Geneva. http://www.css-jordan.org/activities/workshops/peace/#egisr.

Japan. Ministry of Foreign Affairs. "Japan-Indonesia Economic Partnership Agreement: A Joint Study Group Report." May 2005. http://www.mofa.go.jp/region/asia-paci/Indonesia/summit0506/joint-3-2.pdf (entered December 4, 2005).

Jensen, Jeanne Lavon. "Cooperation and Conflict in the Normalization of Relations between the People's Republic of Poland and the Federal Republic of Germany." PhD dissertation, University of South Carolina, 1985.

Jeong, Dong-kuen. "A Study of Changes in Korea's Bilateral Trade Structure with Japan and the United States." *Asian Profile* 23, no. 3 (June 1995): 205–22.

Johnson, Chalmers. *MITI and the Japanese Miracle.* Stanford, CA: Stanford University Press, 1982.

Jose, Lydia N. Yu. "State and Non-State Actors in Philippines-Japan Relations." *Philippine Studies* 51, no. 2 (2003): 177–216.

Kacowicz, Arie M. *Zones of Peace in the Third World: South America and West Africa in Comparative Perspective.* Albany: State University of New York Press, 1998.

————, and Yaacov Bar-Siman-Tov. "Stable Peace: A Conceptual Framework." In *Stable Peace among Nations,* edited by Arie M. Kacowicz et al., 11–35. Lanham, MD: Rowman and Littlefield, 2000.

Kahin, George McTurnan. *Nationalism and Revolution in Indonesia.* Ithaca, NY: Cornell University Press, 1952.

Kally, Elisha. *Egyptian-Israeli Cooperation in Agricultural Development,* edited by Meir Merhav. Tel Aviv: Armand Hammer Fund for Economic Cooperation in the Middle East, Tel Aviv University, April 1986.

————, with Gideon Fishelson. *Water and Peace: Water Resources and the Arab-Israeli Peace Process.* Westport, CT: Praeger, 1993.

Kang, David C. "Getting Asia Wrong: The Need for New Analytical Frameworks." *International Security* 27, no. 4 (spring 2003): 57–85.

Kang, Peter K. "Political and Corporate Group Interests in South Korea's Political Economy." *Asian Profile* 16, no. 3 (June 1988): 209–23.

Kanovsky, Eliyahu. *Assessing the Mideast Peace Economic Dividend.* Ramat Gan, Israel: Begin-Sadat Center for Strategic Studies, Bar-Ilan University, 1994.

————. *The Forgotten Dimension: Economic Development in the Arab Countries and Their Possible Impact on Peace Agreements.* Ramat Gan, Israel: Begin-Sadat Center for Strategic Studies, Bar-Ilan University, 1992.

Karawan, Ibrahim A. "Identity and Foreign Policy: The Case of Egypt." In *Identity and Foreign Policy in the Middle East,* edited by Shibley Telhami and Michael Barnett, 155–68. Ithaca, NY: Cornell University Press, 2002.

Kassem, Maye. "Information and Production of Knowledge or Lobbying? Businessmen's Association, Federation of Labor Unions and the Ministry of Manpower." In *Institutional Reform and Economic Development in Egypt,* edited by Noha El-Mikawy and Heba Handoussa, 61–78. Cairo: American Universty Press, 2002.

Katzenstein, Peter J. *Between Power and Plenty: Foreign Economic Policies of Advanced Industrial States.* Madison: University of Wisconsin Press, 1978.

————, ed. *Mitteleuropa: Between Europe and Germany.* Providence, RI: Berghahn Books, 1997.

————. *Policy and Politics in West Germany: The Growth of a Semisovereign State.* Philadelphia: Temple University Press, 1987.

————. *A World of Regions: Asia and Europe in the American Imperium.* Ithaca, NY: Cornell University Press, 2005.

Kepka, Joanna M. M. "The Nysa Euroregion: The First Ten Years." *Eurasian Geography and Economics* 45, no. 3 (2004): 162–89.

Khashan, Hilal. *Partner or Pariah? Attitudes toward Israel in Syria, Lebanon, and Jordan.* Washington, DC: Washington Institute for Near East Policy, 1996.

Kil, Soong-Hoom. "Two Aspects of Korea-Japan Relations." *Korea and World Affairs* 8, no. 3 (1984): 505–13.

Kim, Ki-Hoon. "The Development of Contemporary U.S.-ROK Economic Relations." In *U.S.-Korean Relations, 1882–1982,* edited by Tae-Hwan Kwak et al., 323–40. Seoul: Institute for Far Eastern Studies, Kyungnam University, 1982.

Kim, Kwan Bong. *The Korea-Japan Treaty Crisis and the Instability of the Korean Political System.* New York: Praeger, 1971.

Kim, Tae-hyo. "South Korea's Security Policy toward Japan: Balancing Perceived Costs and Tangible Benefits." In *U.S.-Korea-Japan Relations: Building toward a "Virtual Alliance,"* edited by Ralph A. Cossa. Washington, DC: Center for Strategic and International Studies Press, 1999.

Kim, Yun-Tae. "The Origins of the Developmental State in South Korea, 1910–1979." *Asian Profile* 26, no. 6 (December 1998): 463–76.

Klein, James P., Gary Goertz, and Paul F. Diehl. "The Peace Scale: Conceptualizing and Operationalizing Nonrivalry and Peace." *Conflict Management and Peace Science* 26 (2008): 67–80.

Kloss, Günther. *West Germany: An Introduction.* 2nd ed. Basingstoke, UK: Macmillan Education, 1990.

Knipping, Franz. "Que Faire de l'Alemagne? French Policy toward Germany, 1945–1947." In *France and Germany in an Age of Crisis, 1900–1960,* edited by Haim Shamir, 67–84. Leiden, Netherlands: E. J. Brill, 1990.

Ko, Seung K. "South Korean–Japanese Relations since the 1965 Normalization Pacts." *Modern Asian Studies* 6, no. 1 (1972): 49–61.

Komer, Robert W. Memo to McGeorge Bunday, March 26, 1964. *Foreign Relations of the United States (FRUS),* 1964–1968, vol. 20, Korea. http://www.state.gov/www/about _state/history/vol_XXIX/b.hotmail.

Kornbluth, Danishai. "Jordan and the Anti-Normalization Campaign, 1994–2001." *Terrorism and Political Violence* 14, no. 3 (autumn 2002): 80–108.

Kranz, Jerzy. "Germany, Quo Vadis? A View from Poland." *German Politics* 10 (April 2001): 141–54.

Krätke, Stefan. "Regional Integration or Fragmentation? The German-Polish Border Region in a New Europe." *Regional Studies* 33, no. 7 (October 1999): 631–41.

Kreile, Michael. "West Germany: The Dynamics of Expansion." In *Between Power and Plenty: Foreign Economic Policies of Advanced Industrial States,* edited by Peter J. Katzenstein, 191–224. Madison: University of Wisconsin Press, 1978.

Kubursi, Atif A. "Prospects for Arab Economic Integration after Oslo." In *Middle East Dilemma: The Politics and Economics of Arab Integration,* edited by Michael C. Hudson, 299–319. New York: Columbia University Press, 1999.

Kulski, W. W. *Germany and Poland: From War to Peaceful Relations.* Syracuse, NY: Syracuse University Press, 1976.

Lam, Peng Er. "The Apology Issue: Japan's Differing Approaches toward China and South Korea." *American Asian Review* 20, no. 3 (fall 2002): 31–54.

Lautman, Dov. "Economic Ties Stabilize Peace between People." In *Neighbors in a Maze: Israel-Jordan Relations before the Peace Treaty and After* [in Hebrew], edited by Yoseph Nevo, 197–202. Tel Aviv: Yitzhak Rabin Center for the Study of Israel, 2004.

Lavi, Victor. "The Economic Embargo of Egypt by Arab States: Myth and Reality." *Middle East Journal* 38, no. 3 (summer 1984): 419–32.

Lee, Chong-Sik. "Japanese-Korean Relations in Perspective." *Pacific Affairs* 35, no. 4 (winter 1962–1963): 315–26.

———. *The Politics of Korean Nationalism.* Berkeley: University of California Press, 1963.

Lee, Won-deog. "A Normal State without Remorse: The Textbook Controversy and Korea-Japan Relations." *East Asia Review* 13, no. 3 (autumn 2001): 21–40.

Levkowitz, Alon. "Legitimacy and De-Legitimacy." Master's thesis, Hebrew University, Jerusalem, 1995.

Levy, Jack. "Economic Interdependence, Opportunity Costs, and Peace." In *Economic Interdependence and International Conflict: New Perspectives on an Enduring Debate,* edited by Edward Mansfield and Brian Pollins, 127–47. Ann Arbor: University of Michigan Press, 2003.

Lewis, James. "The Japan That Does Not Exist and the Ugly Korean: An Essay on the History of Korean-Japanese Relations and Their Contemporary Images of Each Other." In *Korea and Globalization: Politics, Economics and Culture,* edited by James Lewis and Amadu Sesay, 104–18. London: RoutledgeCurzon, 2002.

Liberman, Peter. "Trading with the Enemy: Security and Relative Economic Gains." *International Security* 21, no. 1 (1996): 147–75.

Liddle, William R. "The Relative Autonomy of the Third World Politician: Soeharto and Indonesian Economic Development in Comparative Perspective." *International Studies Quarterly* 35, no. 4 (December 1991): 403–27.

Lightfoot, Keith. *The Philippines.* London: Ernest Benn, 1973.

Lim, Hyun-Chin. *Dependent Development in Korea, 1963–1979.* Seoul: Seoul National University Press, 1985.

Lipschutz, Ronnie D. "Beyond the Neoliberal Peace: From Conflict Resolution to Social Reconciliation." *Social Justice* 2594 (winter 1998): 5–19.

Lucas, Russell E. "Jordan: The Death of Normalization with Israel." *Middle East Journal* 58, no. 1 (winter 2004): 93–111.

Lynch, Marc. "Jordan's Identity and Interests." In *Identity and Foreign Policy in the Middle East,* edited by Shibley Telhami and Michael Barnett, 26–57. Ithaca, NY: Cornell University Press, 2002.

———. *State Interests and Public Spheres: The International Politics of Jordan's Identity.* New York: Columbia University Press, 1999.

Manglapus, Raul S. *Japan in Southeast Asia: Collision Course.* New York: Carnegie Endowment for International Peace, 1976.

Manosevitz, Jason U. "Japan and South Korea: Security Relations Reach Adolescence." *Asian Survey* 43, no. 5 (September–October 2003): 801–25.

Mansfield, Edward D., and Brian M. Pollins. "Interdependence and Conflict: An Introduction." In *Economic Interdependence and International Conflict: New Perspectives on an Enduring Debate,* edited by Edward Mansfield and Brian Pollins, 1–30. Ann Arbor: University of Michigan Press, 2003.

———, and Jon C. Pevehouse. "Trade Blocs, Trade Flows, and International Conflict." *International Organization* 54, no. 4 (2000): 775–808.

———, Jon C. Pevehouse, and David H. Bearce. "Preferential Trading Arrangements and Military Disputes." *Security Studies* 9, no. 1–2 (1999–2000): 96–118.

Mansfield, Edward, and Jack L. Snyder. "The Dangers of Democratization." *International Security* 20, no. 1 (summer 1995): 1–33.

Mastanduno, Michael. "Economics and Security in Statecraft and Scholarship." *International Organization* 52 (1998): 825–54.

Matray, James Irving. *The Reluctant Crusade: American Foreign Policy in Korea, 1941–1950.* Honolulu: University of Hawaii Press, 1985.

McDonald, Patrick. "Peace through Trade or Free Trade?" *Journal of Conflict Resolution* 48, no. 4 (2004): 547–72.

McGrath, Cam. "Government Not Ready to Cut Economic Ties with Israel." Inter Press Service English newswire, April 10, 2002 (entered November 11, 2008).

McKesson, John A. "The Schuman Plan." *Political Science Quarterly* 67, no. 1 (March 1952): 18–35.

Meital, Yoram. "Domestic Challenges and Egypt's U.S. Policy." *Middle East Review of International Affairs* 2, no. 4 (December 1998): 1–9.

———. *Normalization and Economic Ties in the Treaties between Israel and Jordan* [in Hebrew]. Tel Aviv: Armand Hammer Fund for Economic Cooperation in the Middle East, Tel Aviv University, 1998.

Menz, Georg. "Beyond the Anwerbestopp? The German-Polish Bilateral Labor Treaty." *Journal of European Social Policy* 11 (2001): 253–69.

Miller, Benjamin. "The Concept of Security: Should It Be Redefined?" *Journal of Strategic Studies* 24, no. 2 (2001): 13–42.

———. "Explaining Variations in Regional Peace: Three Strategies for Peace-Making." *Cooperation and Conflict* 35, no. 2 (2000): 155–92.

———. *States, Nations, and the Great Powers: The Sources of Regional War and Peace.* Cambridge: Cambridge University Press, 2007.

———. "When and How Regions Become Peaceful: Potential Theoretical Pathways to Peace." *International Studies Review* 7 (2005): 229–67.

Milward, Alan S. *The Reconstruction of Western Europe, 1945–51.* Berkeley and Los Angeles: University of California Press, 1984.

Mishal, Shaul, Ranan Kuperman, and David Boas. *Investment in Peace: The Politics of Economic Cooperation between Israel, Jordan, and the Palestinians.* Brighton, UK: Sussex Academic Press, 2001.

Mobius, J. Mark. "The Japan-Korea Normalization Process and Korean Anti-Americanism." *Asian Survey* 6, no. 4 (April 1966): 241–48.

Momani, Bessma. "Promoting Economic Liberalization in Egypt: From U.S. Foreign Aid to Trade and Investment." *Middle East Review of International Affairs* 7, no. 3 (September 2003): 88–101.

Montgomery, John D. *The Politics of Foreign Aid.* New York: Praeger, 1962.

Moon, Chung-in. "International Quasi-Crisis: Theory and a Case of Japan-South Korean Bilateral Friction." *Asian Perspective* 15, no. 2 (fall–winter 1991): 99–123.

Moore, Pete W. "The Newest Jordan: Free Trade, Peace, and an Ace in the Hole." Middle East Research and Information Project (MERIP), *Middle East Report Online,* July 26, 2003. http://www.merip.org.

Moravcsik, Andrew. *The Choice for Europe: Social Purpose and State Power from Messina to Maastricht.* Ithaca, NY: Cornell University Press, 1998.

Morrison, Charles E. "Japan and the ASEAN Countries: The Evolution of Japan's Regional Role." In *The Political Economy of Japan,* vol. 2, *The Changing International Context,* edited by Takashi Inoguchi and Daniel I. Okimoto, 414–15. Stanford, CA: Stanford University Press, 1988.

Morrow, James D. "Assessing the Role of Trade as a Source of Costly Signals." In *Economic Interdependence and International Conflict: New Perspectives on an Enduring Debate,* edited by Edward Mansfield and Brian Pollins, 89–95. Ann Arbor: University of Michigan Press, 2003.

Nachtwey, Jodi, and Mark Tessler. "The Political Economy of Attitudes toward Peace among Palestinians and Israelis." *Journal of Conflict Resolution* 46, no. 2 (April 2002): 260–85.

Nam, Chang-Hee. "South Korea's Big Business Clientelism in Democratic Reform." *Asian Survey* 35, no. 4 (April 1995): 357–66.

Neaman Workshop. *The Consequences of Peace for the State of Israel* [in Hebrew]. Haifa: Samuel Neaman Institute for Advanced Studies in Science and Technology, 1979.

Nevo, Yoseph. "Neighbors in a Maze: Israel-Jordan Relations before the Peace Treaty and After; Introduction." In *Neighbors in a Maze: Israel-Jordan Relations before the Peace Treaty and After* [in Hebrew], edited by Yoseph Nevo, 7–24. Tel Aviv: Yitzhak Rabin Center for the Study of Israel, 2004.

Newnham, Randall E. *Deutsche Mark Diplomacy: Positive Economic Sanctions in German-Russian Relations.* University Park: Pennsylvania State University Press, 2002.

———. "More Flies with Honey: Positive Economic Linkage in German Ostpolitik from Bismarck to Kohl." *International Studies Quarterly* 44, no. 1 (March 2000): 73–96.

———. *Poland and Germany, 1989–1991: The Role of Economic Factors in Foreign Policy.* Treadgold Studies No. 26, Henry M. Jackson School of International Studies, University of Washington, 2000.

Nishihara, Masashi. *The Japanese and Sukarno's Indonesia: Tokyo-Jakarta Relations, 1951–1966.* Honolulu: University of Hawaii Press, 1976.

North, Robert, and Nazli Choucri. "Economic and Political Factors in International Conflict and Integration." *International Studies Quarterly* 27 (1983): 443–61.

Nowak, Zdzisław. "Changes in Economic Relations between Poland and the Federal Republic of Germany." *Polish Western Affairs*, no. 2 (1984): 235–54.

Oda, Shigeru. "The Normalization of Relations between Japan and the Republic of Korea." *American Journal of International Law* 61, no. 1 (January 1967): 35–56.

Oh, John Kie-chiang. *Korean Politics: The Quest for Democratization and Economic Development.* Ithaca, NY: Cornell University Press, 1999.

O'Leary, Michael Kent. *The Politics of American Foreign Aid.* New York: Atherton Press, 1967.

Olson, Lawrence. *Japan in Postwar Asia.* New York: Praeger, 1970.

Olson, Mancur. *The Logic of Collective Action: Public Goods and the Theory of Groups.* Rev. ed. Cambridge, MA: Harvard University Press, 1971.

Oneal, John R., and Bruce M. Russett. "The Classical Liberals Were Right: Democracy, Interdependence, and Conflict, 1950–85." *International Studies Quarterly* 41, no. 2 (1997): 267–93.

Otmazgin, Nissim Kadosh. "Contesting Soft Power: Japanese Popular Culture in East and Southeast Asia." *International Relations of the Asia-Pacific* 8 (2008): 73–101.

———. "Cultural Commodities and Regionalization in East Asia." *Contemporary Southeast Asia* 27, no. 3 (2005): 499–523.

Papayoanou, Paul. "Interdependence, Institutions, and the Balance of Power: Britain, Germany, and World War I." *International Security* 20, no. 4 (spring 1996): 42–76.

———, and Scott L. Kastner. "Sleeping with the (Potential) Enemy: Assessing the U.S. Policy of Engagement with China." *Security Studies* 9, no. 1 (1999–2000): 157–87.

Parsons, Craig. "Domestic Interests, Ideas, and Integration: Lessons from the French Case." *Journal of Common Market Studies* 38, no. 1 (March 2000): 45–70.

———. "Showing Ideas as Causes: The Origins of the European Union." *International Organization* 56, no. 1 (winter 2002): 47–84.

Peres, Shimon, and Arye Naor. *The New Middle East.* New York: Henry Holt, 1993.

Philippines. Department of Trade and Industry. "Proposed Japan-Philippines Economic Partnership Agreement (JPEPA)." March 2005. http://tradelinephil.dti.gov.ph/downloads/jpepa_brieffiengpresentation_10march2005.pdf (entered December 4, 2005).

Phillips, Ann L. *Power and Influence after the Cold War: Germany in East-Central Europe.* Lanham, MD: Rowman and Littlefield, 2000.

Polachek, Solomon W. "Conflict and Trade." *Journal of Conflict Resolution* 24, no. 1 (1980): 55–78.

———, John Robst, and Yuan Ching Chang. "Liberalism and Interdependence: Extending the Trade-Conflict Model." *Journal of Peace Research* 36, no. 4 (1999): 405–22.

Prados, Alfred B. "Jordan: U.S. Relations and Bilateral Issues." CRS Issue Brief for Congress, Foreign Affairs, Defense, and Trade Division, January 28, 2005. http://fpc.state.gov/document/organization/43389.pdf.

Press-Barnathan, Galia. "The Neglected Dimension of Commercial Liberalism: Economic Cooperation and Transition to Peace." *Journal of Peace Research* 43, no. 3 (May 2006): 261–78.

———. *Organizing the World: The United States and Regional Cooperation in Asia and Europe.* New York: Routledge, 2003.

Propper, Dan. "The Israeli Industry as a Factor in Shaping the Peace in the Middle East." In *Neighbors in a Maze: Israel-Jordan Relations before the Peace Treaty and After* [in Hebrew], edited by Yoseph Nevo, 189–96. Tel Aviv: Yitzhak Rabin Center for the Study of Israel, 2004.

Puchala, Donald J. "Integration and Disintegration in Franco-German Relations, 1954–1965." *International Organization* 24, no. 2 (spring 1970): 183–208.

Ripsman, Norrin. *Peacemaking by Democracies: The Effect of State Autonomy on the Post–World War Settlements.* University Park: Pennsylvania State University Press, 2002.

———. "Two Stages of Transition from a Region of War to a Region of Peace: Realist Transition and Liberal Endurance." *International Studies Quarterly* 49 (2005): 669–93.

———, and Jean-Marc F. Blanchard. "Commercial Liberalism under Fire: Evidence from 1914 and 1936." *Security Studies* 6, no. 2 (winter 1996–1997): 4–50.

Rivlin, Paul, and Shmuel Even. *Political Stability in Arab States: Economic Causes and Consequences.* Memorandum no. 74, Jaffee Center for Strategic Studies, Tel Aviv, December 2004.

Rix, Alan. *Japan's Foreign Aid Challenge: Policy Reform and Aid Leadership.* London: Routledge, 1993.

Robinson, Glenn E. "Defensive Democratization in Jordan." *International Journal of Middle East Studies* 30, no. 3 (August 1998): 387–410.

Rosecrance, Richard. *The Rise of the Trading State: Commerce and Conquest in the Modern World.* New York: Basic Books, 1986.

Russett, Bruce, and John Oneal. *Triangulating Peace: Democracy, Interdependence, and International Organization.* New York: Norton, 2001.

Rutton, Vernon W. *United States Development Assistance Policy: The Domestic Politics of Foreign Economic Aid.* Baltimore: Johns Hopkins University Press, 1996.

Samad, Paridah Abdul, and Mokhtar Muhammad. "Japan in Southeast Asia: Its Diplomatic, Economic, and Military Commitment." *Indonesian Quarterly* 22, no. 3 (1994): 260–69.

Satloff, Robert, and Patrick Clawson. "U.S. Economic Aid to Egypt: Designing a New, Pro-Growth Package." http://www.biu.ac.il/SOC/besa/meria/news/1998/98news11.html#U.S.%20Economic%20Aid.

Schaller, Michael. *The American Occupation of Japan: The Origins of the Cold War in Asia.* New York: Oxford University Press, 1985.

Scheffel, Christoph-Benedikt. "Problems and Conflicts of Interest in German-Polish Relations at the Turn of the Century." *Polish Foreign Affairs Digest* 3, no. 2 (7) (2003): 187–206.

Schumpeter, Joseph A. *Capitalism, Socialism, and Democracy.* 3rd ed. New York: Harper and Row, 1950.

Sela, Avraham. "Identity and Peacemaking: The Arab Discourse on Peace with Israel in the 1990s." *Israel Studies* 10, no. 2 (2005): 15–71.

———. "Israeli-Jordanian Relations: The Shadow of the Palestinian Actor." In *Neighbors in a Maze: Israel-Jordan Relations before the Peace Treaty and After* [in Hebrew], edited by Yoseph Nevo, 37–46. Tel Aviv: Yitzhak Rabin Center for the Study of Israel, 2004.

Sella, Amnon, and Yael Yishai. *Israel, the Peaceful Belligerent, 1967–79.* New York: Macmillan, 1986.

Selvage, Douglas. "The Treaty of Warsaw: The Warsaw Pact Context." *GHI Bulletin Supplement* 1 (2003).

Shafir, Gershon, and Yoav Peled. "Peace and Profits: The Globalization of Israeli Business and the Peace Process." In *The New Israel: Peacemaking and Liberalization,* edited by Gershon Shafir and Yoav Peled, 243–64. Boulder, CO: Westview Press, 2000.

Shalabi Ali, Maghawri. "Economic and Political Implications of the MEFTA Initiative." *International Politics Journal* (Al-Siyassa Al-Dawliya) October 2003. http://www

.mafhoum.com/press6; http://www.siyassa.org.eg/esiyassa/AHRAM/2003/10/1/
ECON1.HTM.

Shamir, Shimon. *Egypt under Saadat's Leadership: The Search for a New Orientation* [in Hebrew]. Tel Aviv: Dvir Publishers, 1978.

———, ed. *Israel-Jordan Relations: Projects, Economics, Business.* University Institute for Diplomacy and Regional Cooperation, Tel Aviv University, 2004.

Sharp, Jeremy M. "U.S. Foreign Aid to Israel." CRS Report to Congress, updated January 2, 2008. http://www.fas.org/sgp/crs/mideast/RL33222.pdf (entered May 22, 2008).

Sheen, Seongho. "Japan–South Korea Relations: Slowly Lifting the Burden of History?" *Asia Pacific Center for Security Studies,* Occasional Papers Series, October 2003.

Shiraishi, Saya S. "Japan's Soft Power: Doraemon Goes Overseas." In *Network Power: Japan and Asia,* edited by Peter J. Katzenstein and Takashi Shiraishi, 234–74. Ithaca, NY: Cornell University Press, 1997.

Shiraishi, Takashi. "Japan and Southeast Asia." In *Network Power: Japan and Asia,* edited by Peter J. Katzenstein and Takashi Shiraishi, 169–96. Ithaca, NY: Cornell University Press, 1997.

Simmons, Beth. "Pax Mercatoria and the Theory of the State." In *Economic Interdependence and International Conflict: New Perspectives on an Enduring Debate,* edited by Edward Mansfield and Brian Pollins, 31–43. Ann Arbor: University of Michigan Press, 2003.

Simonian, Haig. *The Privileged Partnership: Franco-German Relations in the European Community, 1969–1984.* Oxford: Clarendon Press, 1985.

Sing, Lim Hua. *Japan's Role in Asia: Issues and Prospects.* Singapore: Times Academic Press, 1995.

Singh, Bhubhindar. "ASEAN's Perceptions of Japan: Change and Continuity." *Asian Survey* 42, no. 2 (2002): 276–96.

Snyder, Jack L. *From Voting to Violence: Democratization and Nationalist Conflict.* New York: Norton, 2000.

Sobhi, Yasser, and Niveen Wahish. "Pop QIZ Time." *Al-Ahram Weekly* (on-line), no. 717, November 18–24, 2004.

Soh, Chunghee Sarah. "Politics of the Victim/Victor Complex: Interpreting South Korea's National Furor over Japanese History Textbooks." *American Asian Review* 21, no. 4 (winter 2003): 145–78.

Solingen, Etel. "ASEAN Quo Vadis? Domestic Coalitions and Regional Cooperation." *Contemporary Southeast Asia* 21, no. 1 (April 1999): 30–53.

———. "Internationalization, Coalitions, and Regional Conflict and Cooperation." In *Economic Interdependence and International Conflict: New Perspectives on an Enduring Debate,* edited by Edward Mansfield and Brian Pollins, 60–88. Ann Arbor: University of Michigan Press, 2003.

———. *Regional Orders at Century's Dawn: Global and Domestic Influences on Grand Strategy.* Princeton, NJ: Princeton University Press, 1998.

———. "Southeast Asia in a New Era: Domestic Coalitions from Crisis to Recovery." *Asian Survey* 44, no. 2 (2004): 189–212.

Sonfa, O. "The Cultural Roots of Japanese-Korean Friction." *Japan Echo* 20 (1993): 15–28.

Spaulding Robert Mark. *Osthandel and Ostpolitik: German Foreign Trade Policies in Eastern Europe from Bismarck to Adenauer.* Providence, RI: Berghahn Books, 1997.

Stein, Arthur A. "Trade and Conflict: Uncertainty, Strategic Signaling, and Interstate Disputes." In *Economic Interdependence and International Conflict: New Perspectives on an Enduring Debate,* edited by Edward Mansfield and Brian Pollins, 111–26. Ann Arbor: University of Michigan, 2003.

Stern, Yoav. "'Economic Cooperation with Israel? It's Insulting'" [in Hebrew]. *Haaretz,* December 22, 2004, 4B.

———. "Voters Are Not Interested in Israel, but Candidates Are Attacking It" [in Hebrew]. *Haaretz,* September 6, 2005, 11A.

Sudo, Sueo. "Japan-ASEAN Relations: New Dimensions in Japanese Foreign Policy." *Asian Survey* 28, no. 5 (May 1988): 509–25.

———. "The Road to Becoming a Regional Leader: Japanese Attempts in Southeast Asia, 1975–1980." *Pacific Affairs* 61, no. 1 (spring 1988): 27–50.

Suehiro, Akira. "The Road to Economic Re-entry: Japan's Policy toward Southeast Asian Development in the 1950s and 1960s." *Social Science Japan Journal* 2, no. 1 (1999): 85–105.

Sulimierski, Bronislaw. "Issues in Financial and Investment Relations between Poland and Germany." *Russian & East European Finance and Trade* 31, no. 4 (July–August 1995): 8–21.

Sullivan, Denis J. "American Aid to Egypt, 1975–96: Peace without Development." *Middle East Policy* 4, no. 4 (1996): 36–49.

Surbakti, Ramlan. "Formal Political Institutions." In *Indonesia: The Challenge of Change,* edited by Richard W. Baker et al., 61–79. Leiden, Netherlands: KITLV Press, 1999.

Susser, Asher. "The Israeli-Palestinian-Jordanian Triangle." In *Neighbors in a Maze: Israel-Jordan Relations before the Peace Treaty and After* [in Hebrew], edited by Yoseph Nevo, 25–36. Tel Aviv: Yitzhak Rabin Center for the Study of Israel, 2004.

Szechanowski, S. "The Polish-West German Treaty." *Poland and Germany (East & West)* [London] 14, no. 3–4 (53–54) (July–December 1970): 3–9.

Tadem, Eduardo C. "The Japanese Type of Cooperation in Southeast Asia: The Philippine Case." *East Asia* 2 (1984): 184–203.

Tal, Abraham, and Elisha Kally. *A Gas Pipeline Egypt to Israel.* Tel Aviv: Armand Hammer Fund for Economic Cooperation in the Middle East, 1987.

Tamir, Yael. "Peace Economy: The Possible Impact of Economic Ties between Israel and Egypt on the Peace Process" [in Hebrew]. Master's thesis, Hebrew University of Jerusalem, 1990.

Telhami, Shibley. *The Stakes: America in the Middle East; The Consequences of Power and the Choice for Peace.* Boulder, CO: Westview Press, 2002.

———, and Michael Barnett, eds. *Identity and Foreign Policy in the Middle East.* Ithaca, NY: Cornell University Press, 2002.

Terry, Sarah Meiklejohn. "Poland's Foreign Policy since 1989: The Challenges of Independence." *Communist and Post-Communist Studies* 33, no. 1 (March 2000): 7–47.

Thompson Wayne C. "Germany and the East." *Europe-Asia Studies* 53, no. 6 (September 2001): 921–52.

Tilman, Robert O. *Southeast Asia and the Enemy Beyond: ASEAN Perceptions of External Threats.* Boulder, CO: Westview Press, 1987.

Tovias, Alfred. "Economic Aspects of Stable Peace-Making." In *Stable Peace among Nations,* edited by Arie M. Kacowicz et al., 150–64. Lanham, MD: Rowman and Littlefield, 2000.

———, and Hilary Wolpert. *Cooperation between the Textiles and Clothing Industries of Egypt and Israel.* Tel Aviv: Armand Hammer Fund for Economic Cooperation in the Middle East, 1987.

Trachtenberg, Marc. *A Constructed Peace: The Making of the European Settlement, 1945–1963.* Princeton, NJ: Princeton University Press, 1999.

United States. Department of State. "The Middle East Initiative." http://usinfo.state.gov/mena/Archive_Index/THE_MIDDLE_EAST_INITIATIVE.html.

————. Office of the U.S. Trade Representative. "United States, Egypt and Israel to Launch Historic Trade Partnership; USTR Zoellick to Participate in Signing in Cairo," December 10, 2004. http://www.ustr.gov/Document_Library/Press_Releases/2004/December/UnitedStates,Egypt_Israel_to_Launch_Historic_Trade_Partnership (entered August 11, 2005).

Vellut, J. L. "Japanese Reparations to the Philippines." *Asian Survey* 3, no. 10 (October 1963): 496–506.

Vogel, Ezra. *The Four Little Dragons: The Spread of Industrialization in East Asia.* Cambridge, MA: Harvard University Press, 1991.

Wahish, Niveen, "FTA: Wishful Thinking?" *Al-Ahram Weekly* (on-line), no. 639, May 22–28, 2003.

————. "Talking Up Trade." *Al-Ahram Weekly* (on-line), no. 721, December 16–22, 2004.

Walker, Edward S. "The United States–Egyptian Relations: Strengthening Our Partnership." *SAIS Review* 17, no. 1 (1997): 149–59.

Waltz, Kenneth. "The Myth of National Interdependence." In *The International Corporation: A Symposium,* edited by Charles P. Kindleberger, 203–23. Cambridge, MA: MIT Press, 1970.

Wanadi, Jusuf. "ASEAN-Japan Relations: The Underpinning of East Asian Peace and Stability." In *ASEAN-Japan Cooperation: A Foundation for East Asian Community.* Tokyo: Japan Center for International Exchange, 2003.

Washington Declaration. http://www.knesset.gov.il/process/docs/washington_eng.htm.

Weinbaum, Marvin G. "Egypt's *Infitah* and the Politics of U.S. Economic Assistance." *Middle Eastern Studies* 21, no. 2 (1985): 206–22.

Welfield, John. *An Empire in Eclipse: Japan in the Postwar American Alliance System.* London: Athlone Press, 1988.

Wightman, David. *Toward Economic Cooperation in Asia: The United Nations Economic Commission for Asia and the Far East.* New Haven: Yale University Press, 1963.

Wijarso. "Indonesian Oil and Japan: Present Situation and Future Possibilities." *Indonesian Quarterly* 13, no. 3 (1985): 304–14.

Willis, Frank Roy. *France, Germany, and the New Europe, 1945–1967.* Rev. ed. Oxford: Oxford University Press, 1968.

Winckler, Onn. "The Economic Factor of the Middle East Peace Process: The Jordanian Case." In *The Jordanian-Palestinian-Israeli Triangle: Smoothing the Path to Peace,* edited by Joseph Ginat and Onn Winckler, 156–77. Brighton, UK: Sussex Academic Press, 1998.

Wolff-Powęska, Anna. "Poland-Germany: Partnership from a Distance." *Polish Foreign Affairs Digest* 5, no. 1 (14) (2005): 17–36.

Woo, Jung-en. *Race to the Swift: State and Finance in Korean Industrialization.* New York: Columbia University Press, 1991.

Wurfel, David. "Japan-Philippine Relations: Economic and Cultural Determinants of Mutual Images in an Unequal Cooperative Dyad." *Journal of Northeast Asian Studies* 5, no. 2 (summer 1986): 3–29.

Yadav, Vikash. "The Political Economy of the Egyptian-Israeli QIZ Trade Agreement." *Middle East Review of International Affairs* 11, no. 1 (March 2007): 74–96.

Yadlin, Rivka. "Egyptian Perceptions of the Camp David Process." *Middle East Review* (fall 1985).

Yafeh, Yishai, Ehud Harari, and Eyal Ben-Ari, eds. *Lessons from East Asia for the Development of the Middle East in the Era of Peace.* Jerusalem: Harry S. Truman Research Institute for the Advancement of Peace, 1998.

Yanaga, Chitoshi. *Big Business in Japanese Politics.* New Haven: Yale University Press, 1968.

Yoshibumi, Wakamiya. *The Postwar Conservative View of Asia: How the Political Right Has Delayed Japan's Coming to Terms with Its History of Aggression in Asia.* Tokyo: LTCB International Library Foundation, 1995.

Zaborowski, Marcin. *Germany, Poland and Europe: Conflict, Co-operation, and Europeanisation.* Manchester, UK: Manchester University Press, 2004.

Zack, Moshe. "Rabin and Hussein: From War to Peace." In *Neighbors in a Maze: Israel-Jordan Relations before the Peace Treaty and After* [in Hebrew], edited by Yoseph Nevo. Tel Aviv: Yitzhak Rabin Center for the Study of Israel, 2004.

Zawadzki, K. K. F. "The Economics of the Schuman Plan." *Oxford Economic Papers,* n.s., 5, no. 2 (June 1953): 157–89.

Ziemer, Klaus. "Poland and Germany: What Past, What Future?" *Polish Quarterly of International Affairs,* no. 1 (2005).

Selected Web Sites

Business Week. http://www.businessweek.com/magazine/content/04_51/b3913087_mz015.htm

Israeli Central Bureau of Statistics. www.cbs.gov.il/statistical/trade/_39_h.pdf

Israel Ministry of Foreign Affairs. http://www.mfa.gov.il/MFAHEB

Manufacturers Association of Israel. http://www.industry.org.il/SubIndex.asp?CategoryID=34

Ministry of Foreign Affairs of Japan. http://www.mofa.go.jp

Ministry of Tourism and Antiquities of Jordan. http://www.mota.gov.jo

Office of the United States Trade Representative. http://www.ustr.gov

U.S. Embassy, Japan. http://tokyo.usembassy.gov/e/p/tp-20041122-31.html.

World Bank. http://devdata.worldbank.org/dataonline

World Gazetteer. http://www.world-gazetteer.com

Interviews

Five interviews with Egyptian businessmen and officials conducted in Cairo, Egypt, October 2005. [Interviewees requested anonymity.]

Bar, Gabby. Israeli chairman of the joint Jordan-Israel and Egypt-Israel QIZ Committees, and senior regional director, Middle East & North Africa Division, Foreign Trade Administration, Ministry of Industry, Trade & Labor, Jerusalem, June 3, 2008.

Beit-Halachmi, Oded. Chairman and CEO, Delta Textile Egypt, Cairo, October 19, 2005.

Ben-Abba, Irit. Deputy director general, Economic Affairs Division, Ministry of Foreign Affairs, Jerusalem, July 24, 2008.

Catrivas, Dan. Director of Division of Foreign Trade & International Relations, Manufacturers Association of Israel, Tel Aviv, July 22, 2008.

Shiran, Yair. Economic minister to North America, Government of Israeli Economic Mission, Hod Hasharon, July 16, 2008.

INDEX